ASPECTS OF *HAMLET*

ASPECTS OF
HAMLET

ARTICLES REPRINTED FROM *SHAKESPEARE SURVEY*

EDITED BY

KENNETH MUIR

EMERITUS PROFESSOR OF ENGLISH LITERATURE
UNIVERSITY OF LIVERPOOL

AND

STANLEY WELLS

GENERAL EDITOR OF THE OXFORD SHAKESPEARE
AND HEAD OF THE SHAKESPEARE DEPARTMENT
OXFORD UNIVERSITY PRESS

CAMBRIDGE UNIVERSITY PRESS

CAMBRIDGE
LONDON · NEW YORK · MELBOURNE

Published by the Syndics of the Cambridge University Press
The Pitt Building, Trumpington Street, Cambridge CB2 1RP
Bentley House, 200 Euston Road, London NW1 2DB
32 East 57th Street, New York, NY 10022, USA
296 Beaconsfield Parade, Middle Park, Melbourne 3206, Australia

This collection first published 1979

Printed in Great Britain at the
University Press, Cambridge

Library of Congress Cataloguing in Publication Data
Main entry under title:
Aspects of Hamlet.
CONTENTS: Leech, C.   Studies in Hamlet, 1901–1955.
Jenkins, H.   Hamlet then till now.
Foakes, R. A.   The art of cruelty: Hamlet and Vindice [etc.]
1. Shakespeare, William, 1564–1616.   Hamlet.
I. Muir, Kenneth.   II. Wells, Stanley.
III. Shakespeare survey.
PR2807.A957   822.3'3   78–18100
ISBN 0 521 22228 1 hardcovers
ISBN 0 521 29400 2 paperback

CONTENTS

PLATES

PREFACE

Shakespeare Survey 9 contained the retrospective account of *Hamlet* criticism (1901–55) by the late Clifford Leech. Since then books and articles on the play have shown no signs of drying up, and it may put the present collection in perspective if we give a short survey of criticism written during the period. We shall make use of the yearly reviews which are one of the most valued features of *Shakespeare Survey*.

Some of the best criticism of *Hamlet* has appeared in books which cover a wider subject. We may instance chapters in the following: *Form and Meaning in Drama* by H. D. F. Kitto (1956); *The Business of Criticism* by Helen Gardner (1959); *The Story of the Night* by John Holloway (1961); *Shakespeare and the Common Understanding* by Norman Rabkin (1967); *Shakespeare's Early Tragedies* by Nicholas Brooke (1968); *Shakespearean Design* by Mark Rose (1972); *Shakespeare's Living Art* by Rosalie Colie (1974); *Shakespeare: Seven Tragedies* by Ernst Honigmann (1976).

Other good criticism has appeared in articles and pamphlets: Harold Jenkins' British Academy Lecture (1963) on 'Hamlet and Ophelia', Fredson Bowers' series of short papers which together form a valuable study of the hero (e.g. *Shakespeare Quarterly*, xv, 1964; *PMLA*, lxx, 1955) and Stephen Booth's 'On the value of *Hamlet*' (in *Reinterpretations of Elizabethan Drama*, ed. Norman Rabkin, 1969) are among the most interesting.

The main debate during the past twenty years has been between those critics who deplore Hamlet's character and those who admire it. Rebecca West devoted a large section of *The Court and the Castle* (1957) to the play. Like Madariaga, she gives a wholly hostile account of the Prince whom she stigmatizes as egotistical, cruel, a callous murderer, in a word as a 'bad' man, while Ophelia is 'disreputable'. She does not really explain how it is that the common man, as well as most critics of the past, has taken a more favourable view of the character. L. C. Knights in *An Approach to Hamlet* (1960) has modified his earlier harsh verdict on the Prince given in *Explorations*; but he still thinks that the Ghost was tempting him to evil and he will not allow that Hamlet's reference to the fall of the sparrow means that he has submitted to the will of God. To Eleanor Prosser, in her brilliantly argued book, *Hamlet and Revenge* (1967), the Ghost is what Hamlet feared it might be, the devil in his father's shape, tempting him to commit mortal sin—even though, as she admits, Hamlet's father had been murdered by Claudius. Neither Knights nor Prosser tells us what Hamlet ought to have done.

As a contrast to these three critics we may take the contributors to *Hamlet: Stratford-upon-Avon Studies 5*, edited by J. R. Brown and B. Harris (1963), who all agree that Hamlet was heroic and, on balance, a good man. This is expressed eloquently by G. K. Hunter and Patrick Cruttwell, wittily by T. J. B. Spencer, and implicitly by R. A. Foakes and J. K. Walton. In the same year Kenneth Muir expressed similar views in *Shakespeare: Hamlet*, supporting them by demonstrating that in their context the sickness images refer not to the hero but to the corruption in the Court of Elsinore; and Stanley Wells in *Royal Shakespeare* (1976), commenting on Peter Hall's production of the play, argues too for the more favourable interpretation of Hamlet's character. Maurice Charney's *Style in Hamlet* (1969) includes a good analysis of the imagery of the play, together with some more pedestrian discussion of other aspects of style. Harold Fisch in *Hamlet and the Word* (1971) is another critic who defends the hero, stressing that his real problem is to govern instinct by moral law and that he has to act in the random circumstances of real life. One of the best and most subtle of recent books on *Hamlet* is Nigel Alexander's *Poison, Play and Duel* (1971) which, with the help of iconography and a wide knowledge of drama, illuminates many passages in the play.

A few years earlier Harry Levin in *The Question of Hamlet* (1959), under the headings of Interrogation, Doubt and Irony, had provided one of the most stimulating interpretations of the play. Finally, there is a very salutary book by Morris Weitz, *Hamlet and the Philosophy of Literary Criticism* (1964). This distinguishes between the four functions of criticism—to describe, to explain, to evaluate, and to theorize about poetics. Only the first of these processes, Weitz argues, involves answers that are true or false. Even though description in criticism of a play is not so clearly defined as this would suggest, Weitz has some useful things to say about the mistakes which arise in *Hamlet* criticism from confusing the four processes. We 'hope we have reformed that indifferently with us' in the essays included in the present collection.

It should be added that *Shakespeare Survey 30* (1977) contains several interesting articles on *Hamlet*, of which we have been able to include only one.

The present volume is illustrated with photographs of post-war productions of *Hamlet* selected from the Royal Shakespeare Company's files at the Shakespeare Centre, Stratford-upon-Avon. Thanks are due to the Theatre's librarian, Miss Eileen Robinson.

KENNETH MUIR
STANLEY WELLS

STUDIES IN *HAMLET*, 1901–1955

BY

CLIFFORD LEECH

The criticism of *Hamlet* is marked by its extent, its variety and its frequent aggressiveness. A. A. Raven's *A Hamlet Bibliography and Reference Guide 1877–1935* (Chicago, 1936) listed 2167 items: in the last twenty years the tide has not slackened. The Prince has been seen as too sensitive for the rough world, as given to metaphysical speculation, as shocked out of normality by incest and murder, as an effective stage-figure resistant to psychological probing, as a man of sanguine temperament falling into melancholy adust, as the victim of an Oedipus complex, and as an altogether vigorous and right-thinking young man who would stir no suspicion in the mind of an immigration officer. The play presents itself to some as good craftsman's work; to others it is a palimpsest, with fragments of sources and early drafts unsatisfactorily showing themselves in the final version. For most critics the Prince dominates the play and their interest, but some would have us give at least comparable importance to other figures or would remind us that a dramatic poem exists primarily as a pattern of words. And it is possible, but rare, to be modest and tentative in writing of this play: more frequently we are offered a 'solution' which is, for good and all, to pluck out the play's heart and banish its mystery. Because of the vast extent of this critical writing, it can happen that such a 'solution' is an old acquaintance innocently offered as new. The extreme divergence of critical opinion may suggest a flaw in the play, that the dramatist did not come to a full awareness, or at least a full dramatic realization, of his central idea. After all, many of the critics of *Hamlet* have been men of deep understanding and great scholarship. But the aggressiveness of the critics, fantastic though it may sometimes appear, surely hints at the play's strength. We do not feel passionately committed unless our chosen cause seems important. The play lives in our minds as it does in the theatre. It inevitably becomes a starting-point for speculation and fantasy; it is a datum which we are compelled to incorporate within our private view of the world.

In this century the criticism of the play has had to endeavour to keep pace with textual study. Although we cannot claim to have reached a general agreement on the nature and provenance of the First Quarto, the dominant view since the appearance of G. I. Duthie's *The 'Bad' Quarto of Hamlet* (1941) has been that it is a memorial reconstruction derived, via a process of stage-abridgement, from the full text that lies behind the Second Quarto. Consequently all those critical studies that use the First Quarto as evidence of Shakespeare's first intentions in the writing of the play have now a somewhat old-fashioned air. Similarly, in recent years *Der bestrafte Brudermord* has rarely been seen as a straightforward derivative of the Ur-*Hamlet*. Yet critical studies that are partially dependent on out-moded textual theories cannot be dismissed from present-day consideration: though their explanations of how the full text came into existence may be suspect, their interpretations depend primarily on the impact that that text has made. In details here and there their arguments may have little importance for us, but we cannot for that reason reject their views as wholes.

In a short survey it is clearly impossible to do more than observe some of the more interesting features of the great landscape. Some few pieces of writing—*Shakespearean Tragedy*, *Art and Artifice in Shakespeare*, the commentary in J. Q. Adams's edition of the play, *What Happens in Hamlet*, Granville-Barker's *Preface*, T. S. Eliot's essay, Ernest Jones's *Hamlet and Oedipus*, the section on the play in D. G. James's *The Dream of Learning*—need far more space than can here be given to them. And other books and articles, almost numberless, have contributed something to a fairly diligent reader's view of the play: of these only a selection can be mentioned, some for their merit, others for their perhaps significant eccentricity.

BRADLEY AND HIS SUCCESSION

Before the appearance of *Shakespearean Tragedy* (1904), the dominant influences on the English views of *Hamlet* were those of Goethe (who symbolized the Prince as a china vase in which an oak disastrously grew), of Coleridge (who found him metaphysically given and unfit for action), and of Karl Werder (for whom Hamlet was an active person charged not merely with killing Claudius but with making his guilt plain to Denmark). Werder's views were published in his *Vorlesungen über Hamlet* (1875), but this book did not appear in English translation until 1907, when it was given the unfortunate title *The Heart of Hamlet's Mystery*. Meanwhile his arguments had been ably summarized and, on the whole, gently disposed of both by Bradley and by A. H. Tolman in *The Views about Hamlet and Other Essays* (Boston and New York, 1904). Tolman's essay, which is independent of Bradley, gives an excellent account of the state of *Hamlet*-criticism at the beginning of this century, and adds a number of judicious observations: in particular, he shows that Werder's view lacks warrant in the text and clashes with the evidence of the soliloquies, he sees the mouse-trap as "hardly more than a plausible excuse for doing nothing", he illustrates anti-revenge feelings in Shakespeare's time from Belleforest's version of the story and from Bacon's essay on revenge, and he shows that disputes concerning Hamlet's 'madness' depend largely on terminology. But Tolman's essay has exerted little influence, while Werder is the progenitor of an apparently unfinished line of interpreters: he attracts doubtless through his dogmatism, his insistence on the simple vigour of the hero and on the thorough healthiness of the play's atmosphere. He denies that Hamlet delayed, he finds it natural that the Ghost's word should need confirmation, he ingeniously shows that Hamlet followed simple prudence in denying shriving-time to Rosencrantz and Guildenstern. His efforts to re-interpret some of the soliloquies exhibit a mountain in labour.

For Bradley Hamlet was not the simple person that Werder made him, but he had not the giant-stature of Shakespeare's later tragic heroes. He was not constitutionally unfitted for action, for Bradley does not quarrel with the descriptions given by Ophelia and Fortinbras. He was inhibited by nervous shock and did not himself understand his delay. He could literally forget his duty of revenge and be as eager that the player should speak his words aright as he was that Horatio should scrutinize the reaction of Claudius. His assumption of an antic disposition was perhaps in part due to a fear of real distraction, in part a means of gaining a psychologically necessary freedom. He quietened his conscience by cultivating a doubt of the Ghost's word. On his return from England there was "a slight thinning of the dark cloud of melancholy", a fatalistic acceptance of the ways of Providence, a rather greater consciousness of his own power, but there was no stronger determination in him, no evidence that he would bring himself nearer to the act of revenge. Bradley found no reason to take at their face-value all of Hamlet's words in the prayer-scene (for by that point the character's inhibition has been made plain to us), but had no doubt of Gertrude's adultery (for the Ghost's words seem explicit enough). Critics who have parted company with Bradley have accused him of giving a too preponderant attention to the character of the hero, of treating the play like a nineteenth-century novel, of neglecting its poetry, and of being insufficiently versed in Elizabethan thought and stage-conditions. There is something to be said for each of these objections, yet no other account of the play has been so inclusive as his, so dependent on a scrutiny of detail and yet directed all the time towards the emergence of a tragic idea. At times he could admit puzzlement, as in the matter of Hamlet's relations with Ophelia. His views on many points must be subject to modification, have been provocative of further enquiry, but it is a rash man who rejects them out of hand. He saw *Hamlet* as one of four plays by Shakespeare that were comparable in authority with Greek tragedy, as a product of a deep consideration of the nature of things. The play has become smaller in the hands of some of Bradley's successors, so small that we must sometimes wonder at its power to make demands on us.

The influence of Bradley was very strong on W. F. Trench's *Shakespeare's Hamlet: A New Commentary with a Chapter on First Principles* (1913), yet Trench saw his book as an attack on Bradley's views. He wished to set up a more Coleridgean Prince, and saw Ophelia's and Fortinbras's words as respectively delusional and courtly. Nevertheless, Trench frequently exhibits the kind of analysis of behaviour, the kind of conjecture about what happens off-stage and outside the play's time of action, where Bradley is at his most vulnerable. He believes that Hamlet changed his mind about adding a dozen or sixteen lines to *The Murder of Gonzago*: in "O what a rogue" he decided to write a wholly new play, and in III, ii he used the name "Gonzago" in reference to the Player-King because he thought his mention of the poisoning had come too quickly. Similarly Trench suggests that Gertrude's account of Ophelia's death was sheer fiction, invented out of fear of Laertes. He seriously challenges Bradley's "disconcerting suggestions" concerning the whereabouts of Rosencrantz and Guildenstern before they were fetched to Elsinore. Yet there are good things in the book: Trench notes that Hamlet's moralizing in the closet-scene is spoken with the dead Polonius in the audience's view, and that there is something of arrogance and complacency in Hamlet's words here; he sees the irony in Hamlet's finding the leisure to fence so soon after proclaiming "The interim is mine"; and despite his generally Coleridgean view he sees Hamlet's *hamartia* in a readiness to "let himself go"—into the violent and the grotesque and the thought of suicide. Generally Coleridgean too is Stopford Brooke's account of the play in *Ten More Plays of Shakespeare* (1913), yet he could see that Hamlet was no remarkable philosopher: his thoughts, far from being of "exceptional range or excellence", are "the ordinary thoughts of his time in a cultivated youth with a turn for philosophy". For Stopford Brooke, in fact, Hamlet was distinguished from a host of men only by the beauty and authority of his utterance. This modification of Coleridge is useful, but Brooke's view of the play is a partial one. Denying even the verge of madness to the hero, he confesses himself puzzled by the treatment of Rosencrantz and Guildernstern, which he can see only as "a blot on the play".

Bradley is the strongest influence on J. Q. Adams's commentary in his edition (Cambridge, Mass., 1929). The antic disposition, he says, supplied Hamlet with "a surrogate form of *activity*", it offered the opportunity of humour, a useful antidote to grief, and it was a safety-valve for pent-up feelings. Hamlet felt no doubt of the Ghost until he spoke the words "About, my brain!" in his soliloquy at the end of Act II. The interposition of "To be, or not to be" in III, i demonstrates that for Hamlet the play is not truly "the thing". His sparing of the King in the prayer-scene is another unconscious subterfuge, but Adams makes the illuminating comment that Hamlet's desire for Claudius's damnation is in contrast to Othello's "I would not kill thy soul". Yet with all this there is an echo of Werder when Adams says that Hamlet must kill Claudius "with safety to himself", justifying the deed to the court and Denmark and not involving his mother in the disclosure. The Ophelia scenes are rather sentimentally presented, and there is an over-emphasis on Hamlet's healthier state of mind towards the end of the play: in claiming "How all occasions" as evidence of this, Adams overlooks the final, characteristic stress on "thoughts". He sees indeed that Hamlet's attitude to the dead Polonius gives the lie to a sentimental interpretation of the character, though he is inclined to minimize Hamlet's brutality here and elsewhere as well as his obscenities in the play-scene. Some oddities of interpretation include the suggestions that, when Hamlet says "We'll teach you to drink deep ere you depart", he is enthusiastically promising his friend 'a gay time', and that Hamlet sees Claudius as a possible seducer of Ophelia. Like Trench, Adams believes that Hamlet's plans for the play-scene were considerably revised towards the end of "O what a rogue". One does not feel that Adams's view of the play is, like Bradley's, of one piece: rather, he has been sensitive in many points of detail and his account derives strength from its secure placing in the Bradley tradition.

H. B. Charlton is, of course, a militant Bradleian, as is evident in his interpretation of *Hamlet* in *Shakespearian Tragedy* (1948). He effectively dismisses the idea that Hamlet needed to test the Ghost's word, and sees the Second Quarto placing of "To be, or not to be" as "a master-dramatist's revision". He notes that, when Hamlet's feelings are excited, he is given to exaggeration and to generalizing from a single particular ("Frailty, thy name is woman"), but, when his mind dwells on generalities, he forgets his own situation ("No traveller returns"). Charlton anticipates D. G. James in suggesting that the world of *Hamlet* shows "the critical inquisitiveness and the accompanying part sceptical, part agnostic forms of the modern mind". As far as it goes, Charlton's account of the play is acceptable, but we may wonder if he—or Bradley, for that matter—has sufficiently demonstrated why Hamlet's experiences have inhibited him from performing the act that he repeatedly purposes. Charlton is content, it appears, with the simple assertion that they do: he will have no dealings with Freudian conjecture.

THE TEXT

During this century there have been two authoritative brief statements on the development of *Hamlet* textual study. These have inevitably come from E. K. Chambers in *William Shakespeare: A Study of Facts and Problems* (1930) and from W. W. Greg in *The Editorial Problem in Shakespeare* (1942). Preceding Chambers there was the work of A. W. Pollard and J. Dover Wilson on the Bad Quartos in general, which in relation to *Hamlet* assumed a peculiarly elaborate form in Wilson's *The Copy of 'Hamlet' 1603 and The 'Hamlet' Transcript 1593* (1918): here the theory of First Quarto provenance was that the actor of "Voltemar" (who also played other small parts) made some use of a transcript, made for provincial performance, of a manuscript that Shakespeare had partially revised from the Ur-*Hamlet* or from an intermediate revision: "Voltemar" also had his own written part in his possession. Among rival theories may be noted those of F. G. Hubbard in his edition of the First Quarto (Madison, Wisconsin, 1920) and B. A. P. van Dam in *The Text of Shakespeare's Hamlet* (1924). Hubbard believed that the First Quarto was a complete play, dramatically effective, and consistent within itself, although he admitted that it may not have been holding the stage at the time of publication. He did not attempt to explain the relationship between the two manuscript versions of the play that he assumed to lie behind the First and Second Quartos. Editing the First Quarto on the assumption that its corruptions were only a matter of misprinting, he produced a text that Chambers has described as "quite incredible". Van Dam held to the view that the First Quarto was produced by stenography, but his evidence of anticipations and transpositions would today be seen to accord with a theory of memorial reconstruction. He had to explain the wide variations between the First and Second Quartos, and the First Quarto's not infrequent echoes of other Shakespeare plays and *The Spanish Tragedy*, by the assumption that the players were not "part-perfect". Yet he believed that the First Quarto could not have come from a pirate-actor, because such a man would have been in a position to avoid mistakes in proper names and correct mis-writings and transpositions. The Second Quarto, he thought, was printed from Shakespeare's manuscript after it had been used as a prompt-copy: van Dam needed to assume this because he believed that the Second Quarto contained actors' interpolations, though he admitted that the text was too long for "an ordinary performance". The Folio text was based on an intermittent collation of a late quarto with a transcript of the prompt-copy. In 1930, however, Chambers had little doubt that "the Second Quarto substantially represents the original text of the play, as written once and for all by Shakespeare" and that the First Quarto, the Folio version and *Der bestrafte Brudermord* are all derivatives from that: the First Quarto he saw as a reported text, with the possibility of contamination by the Ur-*Hamlet*; the Folio version was set up from a manuscript that had been used as a prompt-copy.

Dover Wilson in *The Manuscript of Shakespeare's Hamlet and the Problems of its Transmission* (1934) was primarily concerned with the nature of the copy used for the Second Quarto and the Folio. This very full enquiry led to the conclusion that the Second Quarto was set up from Shakespeare's autograph, which suffered at the hands of an inexpert compositor and a press-corrector who emended without reference to the manuscript: omissions were either inadvertent, dishonest (the compositor being anxious to have done), or tactful (in the "little eyases" passage): sometimes the First Quarto was consulted when the author's handwriting was especially difficult (hence the appearance of 'sallied flesh', as in the First Quarto). The Folio version was based on a transcript of the prompt-copy, and was thus a text of less authority. Wilson argued that the light punctuation of the Second Quarto was Shakespeare's own, and consequently that the Second Quarto phrasing of "What a piece of work is a man" should be accepted. This deduction was strenuously combated by Peter Alexander in his British Academy lecture *Shakespeare's Punctuation* (1945), which led to controversy between Wilson and Alexander in *The Review of English Studies* (January and July, 1947). Alexander did not deny that the Second Quarto punctuation was Shakespeare's, but suggested that it needs interpretation: "What a piece of work is a man" shows "commas with inversion" together with an omission of "external punctuation" (i.e. stops at the end of a separable sense-unit) which Alexander finds not uncommon in Shakespeare texts. Wilson understandably replied that this kind of punctuation would defy a player's or prompter's power of interpretation, and suggested that the Folio-pointing was due to Burbage's perverted reading of the lines. Yet, if we assume, as Wilson and Alexander do, that the Second Quarto punctuation is Shakespeare's, someone did interpret it as meaning what Alexander claims it was intended to mean. Nevertheless, Alexander's case would be much stronger if we could assume that this prose speech was set out in verse-lining in Shakespeare's manuscript: we might then have no qualms about the possibility of "external punctuation" being omitted.

While not disputing Dover Wilson's view of the provenance of the Second Quarto, T. M. Parrott and Hardin Craig in their edition of the Second Quarto (1938) argued that the Folio text could not have been derived from the prompt-book: it was too long, they suggested, to have been acted as it stood. They suggested, therefore, that it came from a transcript of Shakespeare's manuscript which was made before the preparation of the prompt-book and was again transcribed for the Folio printers. This argument seems to depend too much on a rigid acceptance of the two-hour theory, and has probably been rendered unnecessary by more recent views of the provenance of the Folio text.

G. I. Duthie's *The 'Bad' Quarto of Hamlet* (1941) returned to the provenance of the First Quarto. As Greg justly points out, this book "contains in fifty pages an admirable survey of recent research on Shakespeare's text". It presents the First Quarto as a memorial reconstruction of the full text, made for provincial performance by the actor who played Marcellus and perhaps Lucianus (as previously suggested by H. D. Gray in 1915), the part of Voltemar being available for transcription: when the actor's memory failed, he wrote blank verse of his own made up of echoes from the full text and from other plays: occasionally he drew on the phraseology and other characteristics of the Ur-*Hamlet*, deriving from that source the names Corambis and Montano. *Der bestrafte Brudermord*, he believes, was derived from a further memorial reconstruction made for a continental tour by a company that included one or two who had acted the *Hamlet*-text used for the First Quarto: the reporters in this instance made some fresh use of the Ur-*Hamlet*. These views are, of course, speculative, but Duthie has in many instances provided plausible demonstrations of the First Quarto reporter's patch-work. In any event, his theories have yet to be seriously challenged. Greg in *The Editorial Problem* cautiously approved Duthie's views and accepted the autograph and prompt-book provenances of the Second Quarto and the Folio text, though he remarked, like Parrott and Craig, that the Folio text can hardly have been acted in its entirety.

Important new speculations concerning the text of *Hamlet* have recently been made. Miss Alice Walker in 'The Textual Problem of *Hamlet*: A Reconsideration' (*Review of English Studies*, October 1951) argues that the Second Quarto was printed from a corrected copy of the First Quarto as far as the end of Act I, and that, as suggested by H. de Groot in *Hamlet, its Textual History* (Amsterdam, 1923), the Folio text was printed from a corrected copy of the Second Quarto. The manuscripts used to correct the printed copies were respectively Shakespeare's autograph and a transcript of the prompt-book. This would explain the length of the Folio text, which would thus not be based on an acting-copy. It would explain the agreements of the First Quarto and the Second Quarto (for Act I) and of the Second Quarto and the Folio in unusual spellings and manifest errors. The obvious difficulty in this theory is that the Folio omits some two hundred lines of the Second Quarto, although it must, according to Miss Walker, have taken a good deal of material from the Second Quarto and not from the prompt-book: as appears more clearly in her book *Textual Problems of the First Folio* (1953), Miss Walker has to assume a measure of 'editing' in the Folio text, but it is difficult to see why that should have happened. This point has been taken up by Harold Jenkins in 'The Relation of the Second Quarto and the Folio Text of *Hamlet*' (*Studies in Bibliography*, 1955), who believes that only in some measure was a corrected Second Quarto the basis for the Folio text. He notes the Folio's many divergences from the Second Quarto, and suggests that the scribe who made a transcript for the printer may have had "a copy of the quarto at hand, or even open, in case of need" but that we cannot say how frequently he turned to it.

In 'A Definitive Text of Shakespeare: Problems and Methods' (*Studies in Shakespeare*, Coral Gables, Florida, 1953) Fredson Bowers attacked Dover Wilson's belief that the Second Quarto was set up by a single inexpert compositor, "an untutored dolt working beyond his normal speed": Bowers saw no evidence that only one compositor worked on the text, and argued that the number of skeleton-formes suggested composition speed was ahead of press speed and that a need for haste was therefore unlikely. Following this up, J. R. Brown in 'The Compositors of *Hamlet* Q2 and *The Merchant of Venice*' (*Studies in Bibliography*, 1955) deduces from evidence of spellings that the same two compositors worked on the Second Quarto and on *The Merchant*, which was also printed by James Roberts. Consequently the 'omissions' in the Second Quarto must have been due either to the illegibility of the manuscript or to the fact that they are really later additions to the text. Bowers in 'The Printing of *Hamlet*, Q2' (*ibid.*) accepts Brown's argument, relates it to the evidence of varying running-titles, and gives further consideration to the two compositors' stints. Miss Walker in 'Collateral Substantive Texts (with special reference to *Hamlet*)' (*ibid.*) notes that, though we are moving towards a new eclecticism in the editing of *Hamlet* and certain other plays, we still need to make up our minds which is the more authoritative text, for readings in the Second Quarto and the Folio may be evenly balanced against one another and we also need as much information as possible about transmission in order to formulate coherent principles for emendation. It is clear that an editor of *Hamlet* to-day must be equipped with a sound aesthetic judgement as well as with a full acquaintance with recent bibliographical methods.

DOVER WILSON AND GRANVILLE-BARKER

What Happens in Hamlet (1935) has probably had more influence on stage-practice than any other book by a Shakespeare scholar. It is best known for its insistence on the Ghost as constituting a problem for Hamlet and a largely Protestant audience, its suggestion that Hamlet in II, ii overheard Polonius's plan to "loose" Ophelia to him, and its ingenious reconstruction of the staging of the mouse-trap with Claudius's attention momentarily diverted. But twenty years after its publication these do not seem the strongest parts of the book. Hamlet was the first character in an Elizabethan drama to doubt a ghost's veracity: the dramatic tradition, untroubled by religious controversy, used ghosts as a convenient means of bringing news. Wilson, relating the Ghost in *Hamlet* to contemporary religious notions, is forced to see it as essentially a Catholic spirit. This has led to controversy between R. W. Battenhouse ('The Ghost in *Hamlet*: A Catholic "Linchpin"?', *Studies in Philology*, April 1951) and I. J. Semper ('The Ghost in *Hamlet*: Pagan or Christian?', *The Month*, April 1953), in which the mingled Christian and Senecan elements in the Ghost's constitution have become more evident. If Hamlet overheard Polonius's words about Ophelia, the audience would have to bear this in mind a long while. Wilson's view of the mouse-trap depends on the audience watching the dumb-show carefully, so that it will have in advance an easy grasp of the play's action, and simultaneously observing Claudius's inattention. Yet we must admit that this is more convincing than the view of Richard Flatter in *Hamlet's Father* (1949), that the dumb-show was acted on the upper-stage, out of sight of Claudius and Gertrude, who sat on their thrones on the inner-stage. The special value of Wilson's book to-day seems to consist in its wide-ranging ideas, its readiness to admit difficulty. He sees Hamlet as a man who delights in acting and in fooling his enemies, who behaves in a deranged fashion yet is ever conscious of it, who can convince himself but not us by his words in the prayer-scene, who in "How all occasions" achieves an unconsciously ironic conclusion by promising himself "bloody thoughts". T. S. Eliot's view of the play Wilson cannot bring himself to accept, finding Hamlet's awareness of Gertrude's incest cause enough for his behaviour, but, as in Bradley's case, we may wonder if this accounts for some of the peculiarities that Wilson has shrewdly observed. It is evident that this book is thoroughly in the Bradley tradition and, as such, can be an admirable guide to a producer. Nevertheless, some readers have fastened on a single point and made it, as Wilson does not, dominate the play: thus Bertram Joseph in *Conscience and the King: A Study of Hamlet* (1953) and Hugh Hunt in *Old Vic Prefaces: Shakespeare and the Producer* (1954), both manifestly indebted to Wilson, have been content to see Hamlet's delay as caused solely by his doubt of the Ghost.

Granville-Barker's *Preface* (1937) also owes much to Dover Wilson. Like J. Q. Adams's scene-by-scene commentary, this preface lacks a clear line of argument, but it is of the first excellence on many points of detail. Granville-Barker saw that Shakespeare inevitably took over the pretended madness, but fused it with something else, making an "alloy of sanity and insanity, pretence and reality": only in this way could Hamlet's character be fully developed and revealed. There was cruelty too in the character, the cruelty of a sensitive mind, "ever tempted to shirk its battle against the strong" in order to triumph over the weak. When Hamlet doubts, it is because "he has lost for a while the will to believe". The heart of the play is seen as a sceptical element in the hero's character, but Granville-Barker does not show how this keeps Hamlet from action: he does not, as D. G. James does, suggest an ethical uncertainty in Hamlet. Among the many good things here we find that "the old worldling" Polonius is epitomized in the kind of verse he speaks, that the standard five-act division spoils many effects of contrast and juxtaposition that Shakespeare must have had in mind, and that the Second Quarto and Folio sequence of scenes represents probably a revision and certainly a better version than that of the First Quarto.

If at times one regrets the way in which later commentators have fastened on a single point of Wilson's and made too much of it, one may be more astonished at a simple attempt to put him right. Thus A. J. Green in 'The Cunning of the Scene' (*Shakespeare Quarterly*, October 1953) believes that the mouse-trap and its dumb-show must have gone exactly as Hamlet intended, and the actors must all have played their parts brilliantly (despite "pox, leave thy damnable faces"), for Hamlet was a capable man of action who "cannot have planned carelessly". *What Happens in Hamlet* will survive this.

The 'Historical' School

No one could accuse Dover Wilson or J. Q. Adams or Granville-Barker of being indifferent to the circumstances in which Shakespeare wrote, but their approach to *Hamlet* and other major plays of its time has been dependent on the belief that they are exceptional works, not to be totally 'explained' by reference to dramatic fashions and methods or common trends of thought. These things, however, are given a special stress by the critics that now concern us. The best of these remain conscious of *Hamlet*'s stature, and there are many who have helped to a fuller understanding of the play. We cannot say that this movement in *Hamlet*-criticism is a mere reaction to Bradley, for its presence is felt in the nineteenth century, yet there is no doubt that Bradley's lack of concern with the Elizabethan playhouse provoked revolt and strengthened an existent tendency. John Corbin in *The Elizabethan Hamlet: A Study of the Sources, and of Shakespeare's Environment, to show that the Mad Scenes had a Comic Aspect now Ignored* (1895) indicated his approach in his title, and suggested that Hamlet's brutality was to be explained as a legacy from the Ur-*Hamlet*. But the 'historical' approach was further developed in C. M. Lewis's *The Genesis of Hamlet* (New York, 1907). Lewis's main thesis was that in the extant play we have an amalgam of Belleforest, Kyd and Shakespeare. It is not subject to æsthetic judgement because it is not an entity. If we want Shakespeare, we must subtract Belleforest and Kyd. Lewis is good on what may be called the 'growingness' of the play: he suggests that, as Shakespeare worked on it, he deepened Hamlet's philosophic inclination, his hint of moral scruple, his agnosticism. But the book as a whole is unsatisfying because Lewis disregards the sense of unity that the play in performance can give, despite the problems that may arise as we afterwards brood. And he does not relate the growing complication to the mingling of the splendid and the pathological that is a general mark of Shakespeare's work in the opening years of the seventeenth century. A. A. Jack's *Young Hamlet: A Conjectural Resolution of some of the Difficulties in the Plotting of Shakespeare's Play* (1950) was based on lectures given some fifty years before its publication. It resembles Lewis's book in its view that Shakespeare began his version as a straightforward revenge-play, which through revision came to bear the weight of philosophic thought. Jack differed from Lewis in regretting that Shakespeare had not left his first draft untouched, but he had excellent things to say on the play's emotional effect, seeing it—even in its final form—as primarily a theatre-play, not troubling the depths of our minds as the later tragedies do. J. M. Robertson's *The Problem of "Hamlet"* (1919) and *"Hamlet" Once More* (1923) similarly present the play as a palimpsest: Kyd, it is suggested, wrote a two-part *Hamlet*; Shakespeare attempted to fit Kyd's material into a single play; Kyd had already complicated things by imposing a Senecan ghost-revelation and the play-within-the-play on the old tale in which madness was assumed for safety's sake; Shakespeare added a pessimism of his own, and a hero who shows the effect of "psychic shock" despite preserving the readiness for action that he had displayed in earlier versions.

E. E. Stoll has written often on *Hamlet*, but his two major contributions are in *Hamlet: An*

2-2

Historical and Comparative Study (Minnesota, 1919) and *Art and Artifice in Shakespeare: A Study in Dramatic Contrast and Illusion* (1933). In the earlier work he was anxious to present the Prince in a heroic light, and to insist on the ready intelligibility of the play to an Elizabethan audience. He saw "To be, or not to be" as a mere generalizing soliloquy, like the Duke's words on death in *Measure for Measure*, like many speeches and choruses in Greek tragedy—having little or no relation to the context: the Greek analogue is hardly convincing, for Aristotle, rebuking irrelevance in choric passages, describes it as a quite recent development. Stoll justifiably refuses to see Hamlet as a merely pathological figure, and he gives an excellent account of the sheerly theatrical excitement of the last scene of the play. At one point he admits that Titus and Hieronimo, "like most Elizabethan revengers", both feigned madness and were mad, and adds: "Even in *Hamlet* Shakespeare has not handled the situation so carefully as to preclude some question on this head." This, of course, goes against the dominant thesis of his book, that *Hamlet* is the story of a simple hero. In *Art and Artifice* Stoll's account of the tragic effect reminds us of the worlds of opera and epic: he is often illuminating in bringing out the dramatic orchestration by means of contrast, suspense, iteration; the idea of drama he presents depends on juxtapositions rather than processes. He is surely right to differentiate between tragic and philosophic writing, to see that in *Hamlet* there is "no piercing of the veil", that we remain primarily in a world of particulars; yet it is strange that he does not see this world of particulars in more human terms, with contradictions and strife within the single dramatic figure. It is notable that he says nothing of Hamlet's bawdy and brutal talk, and he is capable of strangely misunderstanding a play close to *Hamlet* in time and theme, when he says that Chapman's Clermont delays merely for dramatic effect, "with no inner reason". From Stoll we have learned much concerning Shakespeare's artistry, but he has told us little of what the tragedies are about.

In *Character Problems in Shakespeare's Plays: A Guide to the Better Understanding of the Dramatist* (1922), L. L. Schücking presents Shakespeare as taking over the action of the Ur-*Hamlet* and adding or developing Hamlet's melancholy: there is thus, he considers, no point in talking of his delay. Hamlet's pessimism, his antic disposition, his wish for Claudius's damnation are due either to the original story or to his adherence to the fashionable melancholy type. In line with the general argument of this book, Schücking says we must believe Laertes on the nature of Hamlet's love and Gertrude, not the Clown, on the manner of Ophelia's death. Schücking's *The Meaning of Hamlet* (1937) is less challenging, and provides a useful analysis of Hamlet's behaviour. In particular it stresses the Renaissance and non-Christian element in the play. His British Academy lecture, *The Baroque Character of the Elizabethan Tragic Hero* (1938), develops the idea of Hamlet as a melancholy figure and links him with the violent exaggerations of baroque. This is a corrective to the straightforward blamelessness of Stoll's Hamlet, but Schücking in one place admits that Shakespeare differs, in general, from his contemporaries in his 'psychological realism', his following of 'Nature': this should make Schücking readier than it does to see that Hamlet's conduct has a way of hanging together, as that of a Marston hero does not. We are merely affronted when Antonio kills Julio; we are disturbed when Hamlet insults Ophelia. We look, therefore, for a special reason for Hamlet's railings, and we are not content to see them as part of a baroque presentation of a melancholy man. Here as elsewhere Schücking observantly notes what is in the play, but for explanation of its presence offers us only large descriptive terms.

10

G. F. Bradby's *The Problems of Hamlet* (1928) is an odd book, with a number of obvious errors of fact. In describing all Hamlet's unattractive features as survivals from an earlier version, Bradby overlooks the range of conduct in the later tragic heroes, the 'psychological realism' of the mingling of brutality and nobility in Hamlet, the consequent and profound truth to fact. Yet he is good on the discrepancies in the presentation of Horatio, and interestingly suggests that the extant texts of the closet-scene conflate two separate endings. A. J. A. Waldock in *Hamlet: A Study in Critical Method* (1931) offers a most useful summary of *Hamlet*-criticism from the eighteenth century and shows himself attracted to C. M. Lewis's view of the play as a palimpsest. What is missing here, perhaps, is a sense of *Hamlet*'s place in Shakespeare's development and in the general development of Elizabethan drama. Around the turn of the century plays seem to have become more inclusive, Jonson and Marston as well as Shakespeare manifesting a desire to put every available element into a single play. In Shakespeare, moreover, this seems accentuated through an up-welling of barely understood thoughts and feelings. Though we must not dismiss the effect of earlier versions on the extant *Hamlet*, we should recognize that the relative formlessness of *Hamlet* and *Troilus and Cressida*, as of *The Poetaster*, *Cynthia's Revels* and the *Antonio* plays, is symptomatic of the change from Elizabethan to Jacobean drama. Miss Lily B. Campbell in *Shakespeare's Tragic Heroes: Slaves of Passion* (1930) presents Hamlet as destroyed through the excess of his grief: the "lesson of tragedy" is that reason should balance passion, as it does in Horatio and Fortinbras: Hamlet is a sanguine person, reduced to melancholy adust. This is altogether a strange book, in which the assurance of the writing does not help it to win conviction. Miss Campbell can say: "I truly believe that if a Papist and King James and Timothy Bright had seen the play, as they all probably did, each would have gone home confirmed in his own opinions about ghosts." Yet the Ghost's early appearances are seen by several people, which would not suit Bright, and the Ghost proves a speaker of truth, which would be difficult for James. In J. W. Draper's *The Hamlet of Shakespeare's Audience* (Durham, North Carolina, 1938) we have a mingling of shrewd observation and simple devotion to a 'historical' thesis. According to Draper the background of *Hamlet* is essentially realistic, so each character must be such as an Elizabethan would expect to find in a corresponding position in actuality. Polonius is a worthy and able prime minister, Claudius and Rosencrantz and Guildenstern have much to be said for them. Hamlet's doubt about the Ghost is the sole reason for his delay: when the Ghost blamed him in the closet-scene, it was because ghosts could not see into the mind. We may feel that Draper is right in seeing *Hamlet* as based on a struggle between the one and the many, of an individual against a corrupt society, but that he glides by the disturbing element in the play—Hamlet's grossness and cruelty, his speculations about the cosmos, the element that has made E. M. W. Tillyard in *Shakespeare's Problem Plays* (1950) link it with the dark comedies. Draper has usefully insisted on the Elizabethan character of *Hamlet*'s background, though exaggerating the degree of normality of setting required in a tragedy, but his concept of the Elizabethan age seems a selective one. He is free, however, from the perversity of Salvador de Madariaga, who in *On Hamlet* (1948) was so determined to see Hamlet as a typical Renaissance prince that the character became for him a monster of egoism. Contrariwise, J. V. Cunningham in *Woe or Wonder: The Emotional Effect of Shakespearean Tragedy* (Denver, Colorado, 1951) saw Hamlet as dominated by reason and guided to a point of decision by Thomistic notions. And we are in a kind of Stoll-underworld with R. P. Janaro, who in

11

'Dramatic Significance in *Hamlet*' (*Studies in Shakespeare*, Coral Gables, Florida, 1953) urges on us the belief that Hamlet is not one man but five, each used in appropriate dramatic situations.

A different kind of 'historical' study appears in the attempt to see *Hamlet* as a tract for Shakespeare's time, incorporating detailed references to political events. Miss Lilian Winstanley in *Hamlet and the Scottish Succession* (1921) would equate the play's characters with leading figures of the time, but complicates and diminishes her argument in suggesting that Hamlet was simultaneously Essex and Darnley and James (also represented by Fortinbras), Polonius was both Burleigh and Rizzio, Claudius both the Elder and the Younger Bothwell. This would surely require leisure for an Elizabethan spectator to work out. Abel Lefranc in *A la Découverte de Shakespeare* (Paris, 1945) accepted Miss Winstanley's theories and in particular stressed points of connexion between *Hamlet* and Darnley's murder. Dover Wilson in *The Essential Shakespeare* (1935) saw a close connexion between the play and the Essex revolt, as did E. S. Le Comte in a cautious and sensible article, 'The Ending of *Hamlet* as a Farewell to Essex' (*ELH*, June 1950). That Shakespeare wrote so courtly a play as *Hamlet* with certain contemporary happenings in mind is not unlikely, but this contributes little to the tragedy's total significance: the allusions, in any event, could not be too blatant and may well be beyond our determination.

THE FREUDIANS

An account of the Freudian views of the play is given in Kenneth Muir's 'Some Freudian Interpretations of Shakespeare' (*Proceedings of the Leeds Philosophical Society* (*Literary and Historical Section*), July 1952). Freud himself in 1900 saw the Oedipus complex as the unconscious motive for Hamlet's delay, and this has been developed with assiduity and fine intelligence by Ernest Jones, most satisfactorily in *Hamlet and Oedipus* (1949). Jones considers the objection that his interpretation depends on viewing Hamlet as a real person, not as a figure in a play, and retorts that critics and spectators have always done this. We might add that the dramatist, though necessarily presenting a simplification, has imagined a whole character and implied it: we may have a sense of this 'whole' and investigate it, though we are of course dependent on a personal impression and assume that it is also the author's. In giving a full account of previous interpretations, Jones makes us aware that the play has appeared to mean something important, though not something easily definable, to a wide variety of men. He suggests that Shakespeare himself did not fully comprehend the reason for Hamlet's delay, that the writing of *Hamlet* was bound up with the execution of Essex (a father-figure), the death of John Shakespeare, and the conjectural infidelity of Mary Fitton. He gives an excellent picture of Hamlet occupying himself with any other matter than the task of revenge—"just as on a lesser plane a person faced with a distasteful task, e.g. writing a difficult letter, will whittle away his time in arranging, tidying, and fidgeting with any little occupation that may serve as a pretext for procrastination". Hamlet, he points out, gives a variety of motives for his delay (cowardice, doubt of the Ghost, desire for Claudius's damnation): indeed the latter two are not mentioned until circumstances (the arrival of the players, the sight of Claudius at prayer) have made them appropriate. The main criticism that can be legitimately made of the book's argument is that it presents *Hamlet* as too exclusively a personal tragedy. Though the play is less 'cosmic' than the other major tragedies—its references to heaven, though frequent, are a little perfunctory—it does suggest a cosmic framework for

the action, it is more than a presentation of an individual's (or even Everyman's) neuroti
condition. Jones is too ready to see Shakespeare, "the first modern", as equating "Character"
and "Fate". Moreover, all the Hamlet-stories and related myths are seen here as enshrining the
Oedipus complex, yet it is only in Shakespeare that the irresolution of the hero appears. Is this
because Shakespeare was more nearly aware of the basic implications of the story? We need
not, however, see the whole play in terms of the Oedipus complex in order to feel that Jones
has made one of its components more graspable.

The Freudian influence is clearly strong on T. S. Eliot's essay (1919). He sees Hamlet's emotion
as "inexpressible, because it is in *excess* of the facts as they appear": though Dover Wilson
retorted that the idea of incest was a powerful enough cause, that may not explain the wide-
ranging character of Hamlet's aggressiveness and speculation or provide the link between
"psychic shock" and inability to carry out one particular task. Eliot also sees Shakespeare as
not fully aware of the nature of his problem in writing the play, as at times "manifesting the
buffoonery of an emotion which he cannot express in art". Linked with the Freudian inter-
preters, too, is Gilbert Murray's British Academy lecture, *Hamlet and Orestes: A Study of Tradi-
tional Types* (1914), where it is suggested that the Greek dramatists and Shakespeare were drawing
on primitive myth, the hero representing a Winter-figure. Murray does not account for the
fact that the hero's enemies (Aegisthus and Clytemnestra; Claudius) have done wrong, but
perhaps this may be seen as a sophistication inevitable on the development of myth into poetry.
In an account of a case-history, *Dark Legend: A Study in Murder* (1947), Frederic Wertham has
related to *Hamlet* the story of a young Italian immigrant in America: he suggests a strong
impulse to matricide in Hamlet, far stronger than his desire for revenge on his uncle: this
impulse, which Hamlet manages to control, is bound up with an Orestes complex seen in an
excessive attachment to the mother-image, a general hatred of women, homosexual poten-
tialities, ideas of suicide, and guilt-feelings. This has the advantage that we do not have to
assume, as with Freud and Jones, a hostility of Hamlet to his father. Because, in fact, Wertham
does not attempt too full a probing of Hamlet's character, it is easier to see his account as
presenting a motive available for Shakespeare. It should be observed that Wertham sees the
Orestes and Oedipus complexes as "not mutually exclusive", but in his references to the play,
as in the case-history he presents, he stresses only the first. Freudian views also underlie Wulf
Sachs's *Black Hamlet: The Mind of an African Negro revealed by Psychoanalysis* (1937), which
presents a real-life echo of the situation-pattern in the play, although the most difficult elements
in the situation described seem to come from black-white tension in Africa rather than from
anything that Shakespeare consciously or unconsciously employed. Michael Innes in *The Hawk
and the Handsaw* (in *Three Tales of Hamlet*, 1950) wears all these things lightly: he engagingly
suggests that Hamlet's delay was the direct result of his encounter with a Freudian doctor who
had previously attempted to minister to Lady Macbeth.

SOME INDEPENDENTS

It is convenient to divide *Hamlet*-critics into groups, but a good deal of cross-fertilization has
taken place and a number of critics will not fit easily into any of the groups so far named. In
this last section, therefore, some mention must be made of a large body of work, ranging from

...dies of *Hamlet*-imagery in Caroline Spurgeon's *Shakespeare's Imagery and what*
... and W. H. Clemen's *The Development of Shakespeare's Imagery* (1951) to A. S.
...ntasy that the complete text of *Hamlet* was written in 1588–9 (*The Problem of*
...*lution*, 1936), William Empson's small suggestion that "How all occasions" was
... of an encore to be given when a performance was going especially well ('*Hamlet*
... ', *The Sewanee Review*, Winter and Spring 1953), D. S. Savage's whimsy that the
references to pirates in *Hamlet* should be taken as references to the printing of the First Quarto
(*Hamlet and the Pirates: An Exercise in Literary Detection*, 1950), and Jean Paris's laborious analysis
of the play as a presentation of three sons, each reacting differently to the task of vengeance
(*Hamlet, ou les Personnages du Fils*, Paris, 1953).

A. Clutton-Brock's *Shakespeare's 'Hamlet'* (1922), though at times sentimental and over-
written, brings out the richness and complexity of the Prince, and suggests, vaguely, that the
play presents a notion of the dramatist's values. Hamlet "has too rich a nature to be narrowed
into a vendetta", and this richness is at odds with the attempted concentration on revenge: he
has a "double consciousness", is subject to a "conflict between the permanent attitude and the
practical task", and strives in vain to harmonize them. Clutton-Brock becomes slightly
Freudian when, quoting Eliot, he suggests that a dramatist needs not so much knowledge of
motives as sensibility and an awareness of people as people. Very different is the picture of
Hamlet and his setting given by G. Wilson Knight in *The Wheel of Fire* (1930) and *The Imperial
Theme* (1931). Knight sees Hamlet as a man who has unanswerable views about the vanity of
living, who is impelled to destroy but not to achieve, who can be cruel. His world, on the other
hand, is normal, with Claudius a good enough fellow who has sinned and whom Hamlet drives
to further sinning. But the Ghost gives a "devilish command", the priest is "churlish", the
account of Purgatory is harsh: we must accept Hamlet's views as right, and regret that we must.
Knight makes us remember that we feel at home in Elsinore, as Hamlet does not; the Prince is
a hero, and the company of heroes can be difficult to bear. For Granville-Barker in his British
Academy lecture, *From 'Henry V' to 'Hamlet'* (1925), the play showed the first clear emergence
of the "daemonic" Shakespeare, as distinct from the popular playwright: hence its moralising
and its formlessness. In another British Academy lecture, *Hamlet: The Prince or the Poem?*
(1942), C. S. Lewis saw Hamlet as mortal man "with his mind on the frontier of two worlds"
and found the details of action and motive of small significance: yet he admitted, only to brush
aside, the thought that Shakespeare made an effort to "psychologize" Hamlet. Roy Walker's
The Time is Out of Joint: A Study of Hamlet (1948) presents Hamlet as a man inclined to pacifism.
G. R. Elliott in *Scourge and Minister: A Study of Hamlet as a Tragedy of Revengefulness and Justice*
(Durham, North Carolina, 1951) sees him as suffering from pride, unable to scrutinize his task
or to realize that his nature shrinks from killing a sovereign ruler, but ultimately coming to a
correct frame of mind for the killing, in which he was truly heaven's "scourge and minister":
so the delay was right. Despite the brooding evangelism of his commentary, and his unusual
view that the Folio text represents a Shakespearian revision of the Second Quarto, there is much
in Elliott's book that sharpens the apprehension of the separate moments of the play.

Two recent books have contributed powerfully to our understanding. D. G. James's *The
Dream of Learning: An Essay on The Advancement of Learning, Hamlet and King Lear* (1951) stresses
Hamlet's scepticism and the link that this makes between him and us. Remembering the debate

on "value" in *Troilus and Cressida*, James sees in Hamlet an uncertainty concerning the nature of things and the principles of conduct. As for the delay:

Is there anything mysterious about a man who has come to no clear and practised sense of life, and who in the face of a shocking situation which quite peculiarly involves him, shuffles, deceives himself, procrastinates, and in his exasperation cruelly persecutes the person he loves best in the world?

James sees something a little callow in Hamlet at times, in his excusing himself to Laertes and his claim to have loved Ophelia more than forty thousand brothers: the play is less than *Lear*, because it is concerned, not with life itself, but with "a mind arrested in dubiety before the awful problem of life". Perhaps in this book there is too easy an assumption of a clear purpose in Shakespeare's mind, but it makes remarkably evident one reason for the play's wide appeal: Hamlet, the neurotic, the death-willer, the hero, is primarily (for us surely, for Shakespeare perhaps) the sceptic with a Christian inheritance. Peter Alexander in *Hamlet Father and Son* (1955) would reinstate Hamlet too simply as the hero. He attacks the notion of *hamartia*, understandably enough, but disregards Hamlet's brutality and bawdy. He sees the antic disposition as intended to make Claudius aware of Hamlet's enmity, for he "will not come on his enemy silently and suddenly from behind". The book would be more convincing if Alexander did not vaguely accept the notion of *catharsis*, talking of "reconciliation" and "redemption" without a clear indication of how they are brought about. The hero's imperfections do not justify his destruction, but they link him with us and they give us the notion of a human involvement in the tragic chain of events: Cordelia does not deserve her hanging, but she contributes to the sequence that includes it; Gloucester's begetting of Edmund was surely a venial affair, but the blinding lay at the end of the course; Hamlet (we have it on his authority) deserved a whipping, but instead he killed and died.

Hamlet, written by more than one, perhaps written by Shakespeare more than once, has a smack of each of us in it: Stoll gives us its theatrical excitement, Bradley and Ernest Jones the working of the protagonist's mind, D. G. James its twentieth-century appeal, Dover Wilson and Schücking its special reverberations for its first audience, Granville-Barker its available meaning for a producer. Simplification must be recognized for what it is.

'HAMLET' THEN TILL NOW

BY

HAROLD JENKINS

Many men have seen themselves in the hero of this play; and it is especially easy for me to do so at the moment, when I have a task assigned to me which I know myself unequal to performing. I do not expect to escape censure for my weakness, though I hope it will not be put down to a defect of will and that something may be allowed to me for the magnitude of the task itself. For well over a century almost every writer upon *Hamlet* has begun by remarking that more has been written on it than on any other work of literature, before adding his own ink to the ever-swelling flood. In 1877 the Furness *Variorum*, in order to keep up with the tide, needed two volumes instead of the one that still suffices for other Shakespeare plays; and beginning where Furness left off, A. A. Raven listed in his *'Hamlet' Bibliography and Reference Guide* (1936) over 2000 items between 1877 and 1935, while the *Classified Shakespeare Bibliography* of Gordon Ross Smith (1963), continuing the count down to 1958, added over 900 more items, ranging from Dover Wilson's *The Manuscript of Shakespeare's 'Hamlet'* (1934), which I suppose deals with *Hamlet then*, to 'Hamlet as Existentialist' (*Shakespeare Newsletter*, VII, 1957), which may conceivably be *Hamlet now*. As I approach this enormous task of tracing the critical fortunes of this play, my mind, like Hamlet's own in Hazlitt's phrase, sinks within me. Yet I am in one respect more favoured than my prototype; I am not isolated from the help of others. I acknowledge the assistance I have received from Paul S. Conklin's *History of 'Hamlet' Criticism* (1957) down to 1821, from the critical collections given by Furness, and, when I come to the present century, from the reviews of Clifford Leech in *Shakespeare Survey 9* (1956) and G. K. Hunter in *Critical Quarterly*, 1 (1959). When I think of this last part of my task, however, my resolution becomes still more sicklied o'er. The writers upon *Hamlet now* include most of my present audience. To all those whom time or bestial oblivion will compel me to neglect, whom necessity will cause me to over-simplify, or whom incapacity will lead me to misconstrue, I offer my apologies.

The principal difference between *Hamlet then* and *Hamlet now* will already be apparent. *They* saw *Hamlet* direct, fresh on Shakespeare's stage beneath a clear Elizabethan sky, *we* staled with custom and through a cloud of commentary. Yet if by some miracle in nature this cloud suddenly disappeared, I still could show you little of the Elizabethan *Hamlet*. I confess to a craven scruple about speaking with any confidence of what the play meant to its contemporary public. It is true that scholars *now* write books about *The 'Hamlet' of Shakespeare's Audience* (J. W. Draper, 1938), surmise how it was acted at the Globe, and assure us how the Elizabethans would have taken it. But this construct of scholarship belongs, I suggest, in what may or may not be madness, rather to *Hamlet now*. A scholarly argument about how the Elizabethans must have regarded the play is not quite the same as a record of how they did. Yet there are at least enough contemporary allusions to *Hamlet* to tell us that it was immediately liked and even famous. The way had of course been opened for it by an earlier play on the same subject, which Lodge remembered for the Ghost that cried 'Hamlet, revenge' (*Wit's Misery*, 1596). The immediate appeal of Shakespeare's play certainly owed much to the spectacular incidents it derived from its predecessor. When after 1600 the Elizabethans refer to *Hamlet*, we cannot always be sure which play they had in mind, and perhaps they could not either. It would be all the same to the spectators at *Westward Ho* in 1604 when they heard injured husbands advised to 'play mad Hamlet, and cry revenge'. But Anthony Scoloker in the same year specifically names Shakespeare when acknowledging that Prince Hamlet 'pleases all', and then slily adds that he declines to run mad himself in order to do the same (*Daiphantus*, 1604). The madness was already a legend, and, as Patrick Cruttwell has recently observed ('The Morality of Hamlet …', *Stratford-upon-Avon Studies 5*, 1963), it was evidently *then* a much more violent affair than the stage usually shows *now*. The lover in Scoloker's poem, when he goes mad, tears a passion and undresses to his shirt 'much like mad Hamlet'. The hero could not be thought of without his madness, nor could he without his encounter with the Ghost. Shakespeare's tremendous dialogue in this scene so impressed itself upon the mind that it was often echoed in plays of other dramatists. To take but one example, in Beaumont's *The Woman-Hater* (1607) a gourmet pursuing a delectable fish-head says 'Speak, I am bound to hear' and is told 'So art thou to revenge, when thou shalt hear the fish head is gone'. The jest seems to assume in the audience a knowledge of the original; and such travesties, as Dyce remarked, are the surest form of tribute. Nor were the echoes of *Hamlet* confined to the Ghost and mad scenes. D. G. McGinn (*Shakespeare's Influence on the Drama of his Age*, 1938) has counted almost five hundred echoes in plays before 1642; and even if we dismiss many of these as part of the general verbal currency, there is still evidence to suggest that this play lived in people's minds perhaps more than any other. And it did so, I suppose, not merely for its theatrical excitement but also, *then* as it has done ever since, for its wisdom unsurpassedly expressed in Shakespeare's memorable language.

This was surely the quality that Gabriel Harvey recognized in *Hamlet* from the first. In saying that it had it in it 'to please the wiser sort' (*Marginalia*) he may have meant no more by his epithet than to signalize that tragedy was grave. But what we have to notice is that Harvey joins this one stage-play with Shakespeare's already celebrated poems and lists it among the best literary works in English, along with the *Arcadia* and *The Faerie Queene* and the big historical poems of Warner and Daniel. Whether or not scholars are right to suppose Harvey made his comment before *Hamlet* was in print, he seems to have envisaged it as having a reading public.

It was on the stage, however, that *Hamlet then* made its greatest impact. Its leading role at once became a famous one. As early as 1605 the anonymous author of *Ratsey's Ghost* made his hero commend an actor by saying he would back him to play Hamlet. An elegy on Burbage in 1619 names Hamlet first among his celebrated parts; and before the end of the century this part was established in that theatrical pre-eminence it has never since lost. As Betterton performed it—to directions descending from Shakespeare, if Downes is to be credited (*Roscius Anglicanus*, 1708)—it was, to the impressionable Pepys, 'the best part, I believe, that ever man acted' (*Diary*, 31 August 1668). In estimating *Hamlet's* renown at this time, no doubt we should distinguish between the theatrical part and the character, and both of them from the play. As Shakespeare's most celebrated character Hamlet as yet yielded to Falstaff; and when Rymer chose to examine the one among all English tragedies which was 'said to bear the bell away'

(*A Short View of Tragedy*, 1693), it was of course *Othello* that he went for, which at least spares us from knowing what he would have said about *Hamlet*. G. E. Bentley tells us that in critical opinion both were outdone by Jonson's *Catiline* (*Shakespeare and Jonson*, 1945). Yet by the time we reach the centenary of Shakespeare's death his supremacy is assured and *Hamlet* has clearly emerged as his most famous play. That is why Theobald chose it for his editorial demonstration (*Shakespeare Restored*, 1726), and Shaftesbury believed it was, of all plays on the English stage, the one which had not only 'been oftenest acted' but 'most affected English hearts' (*Soliloquy, or Advice to an Author*, 1710; reprinted in *Characteristics*, 1711). Shaftesbury already thought of it as having 'but one character', and it is from accounts of how Betterton had acted this character that we get our chief impression of what *Hamlet* was to the early eighteenth century. For clearly Betterton gave it them as they thought it ought to be. Steele was impressed by his 'ardour' (*Tatler*, 71, 20 September 1709). Cibber said that in the meeting with the Ghost you felt Hamlet's terror with him (*Apology*, 1740). Betterton, in fact, helped them to realize the power which Dryden had praised in Shakespeare: 'When he describes anything, you more than see it, you feel it too.' Betterton's Hamlet, we are told, had the 'vivacity and enterprize' of 'youth', while he was at the same time 'manly'. Prince Hamlet at this date was vigorous, bold, heroic. There was no hint yet of brooding introspection, nor of a man who could not make up his mind. Nor was it yet discovered that his passion exceeded its object. What was valued in the play was its power to stir the ordinary human emotions by showing them raised to their highest pitch by *extra*ordinary circumstance.

This is the *Hamlet* described in 1736 in the first formal criticism of the play we have, *Some Remarks on the Tragedy of Hamlet*, once but not now believed to be by Hanmer. The author shows of course the limitations as well as the virtues of his age. He does not believe in mixing comedy with your tragedy: the grave-digger scene, though 'much applauded', 'is very unbecoming such a piece as this'. He is aghast at Hamlet's reasons for not killing the praying king. It did not occur to plain eighteenth-century sense that Hamlet could not have meant what he said. But in spite of reservations, the author has no doubt that this play shows unsurpassed Shakespeare's characteristic excellences; and these are truth to nature, sublimity of sentiment, and exalted diction. The scene with the Ghost, still the most momentous one, creates 'awe' beyond any other the author knows, yet the handling of it is 'entirely conformable to nature'. This is the note which is struck over and over again. The scene between Hamlet and his mother could not 'have been managed...more conformably to reason and nature'. 'The Prince's reflections on his mother's hasty marriage' it is interesting, in view of later perturbations, to find described as 'very natural'. Hamlet's delay, however, is another matter: 'there appears no reason at all in nature' for it. But it as yet presents no problem. 'Had Hamlet gone naturally to work..., there would have been an end of our play. The poet therefore was obliged to delay his hero's revenge; but then he should have contrived some good reason for it.'

Yet Hamlet's delay, at first seen as a necessary feature of the plot, gradually came to be considered in relation to his character. This is part of the remarkable shift in dramatic criticism when the priority which Aristotle gave to plot began to be disputed and the chief virtue looked for in a dramatist was the power to depict character. The admiration for Shakespeare's lifelike characterization had much to do with this; but paradoxically it led to a demand for a consistency in characterization which he was found not always to supply. In 1770 Francis Gentleman, while appreciating the 'great variety' in the character of Hamlet, lamented that he 'should be such an apparent heap of inconsistency' (*The Dramatic Censor*). Provided this could be blamed on Shakespeare, there were no very serious consequences; but once it was assumed that this inconsistent creature was what Shakespeare meant Hamlet to be, Hamlet himself became an object of puzzled study. The question was no longer why Shakespeare failed to account for Hamlet's not killing the king at once but why Hamlet failed to do it. In 1763 the actor Thomas Sheridan won the approval of Boswell (*Journal*, 6 April) for an account of 'the character of Hamlet' which described him as 'irresolute', wanting 'strength of mind', striving towards 'manly boldness' but 'in vain'. Here the heroic Hamlet disappears. Yet what redeems him for us in this new avatar is that his very irresoluteness belongs with a delicacy which springs from his 'fine feelings'. This was of course the age of sensibility. In Sterne's *Sentimental Journey* (1768) the marquis who reclaims his sword while letting fall a tear evokes the exclamation 'O how I envied him his feelings'; and the public which enjoyed this could envy Hamlet his. It was Henry Mackenzie, famed as the author of *The Man of Feeling* (1771), who was presently to explain the secret of Hamlet's appeal. In two notable essays in *The Mirror* in 1780 Mackenzie addresses himself to the task of discovering the basic principle which gives unity to Hamlet's 'variable and uncertain' character, and he finds it in 'an extreme sensibility of mind'. It is a sensibility 'so delicate as to border on weakness'; and Shakespeare has skilfully placed Hamlet in a situation where this 'amiable' quality can only 'perplex his conduct', so that his 'principles of action' become 'unhinged'. Hamlet's difficulties arise therefore 'from the doubts and hesitations of his own mind'; but it is precisely this that invests the 'sweet prince' with pathos and gives him his 'indescribable charm'.

The change in critical attitude is well illustrated by William Richardson. Inheriting an earlier eighteenth-century taste for moral disquisition, he presented Hamlet as an exemplar of virtue, and when he first wrote on him in 1774 (*A Philosophical Analysis and Illustration of Some of Shakespeare's Remarkable Characters*), he hardly perceived a fault. But ten years later, in answer to critical objections, Richardson made 'Additional Observations on Hamlet' (*Essays on Shakespeare's Dramatic Characters*, 1784) in order to excuse his virtuous hero for the 'frailties' he now had to concede. Thomas Sheridan had already supposed that Hamlet's wish to send the king's soul to damnation was really 'an excuse to himself for his delay', and this is what Richardson takes it on himself to assert: 'I will venture to affirm that these are not his real sentiments.' Hamlet is thus liberated from Shakespeare's text, and the door is open for the nineteenth century to supply him with all the motives about which the play is silent. For his part Richardson can continue to insist on Hamlet's 'exquisite sense of moral conduct', but in his later editions he combines it with those 'amiable weaknesses' which belong with 'extreme sensibility'.

The man of the exquisite feelings and the man of the exquisite moral sense appear together in the Hamlet made famous by Goethe, with rather more of the weakness but certainly no less charm. When Goethe gave this portrait to the world (*Wilhelm Meisters Lehrjahre*, 1795), it may not have represented his own conception so much as Wilhelm Meister's, but the distinction is not one which its admirers were apt to make. To Wilhelm at any rate it was 'clear that Shakespeare meant . . . to represent the effects of a great action laid upon a soul unfit for the performance of it. . . . A lovely, pure, noble, and most moral nature, without the strength of nerve which forms a hero, sinks beneath a burden which it cannot bear, and must not cast away' (Carlyle's translation).

Here then is the romantic Hamlet on the threshold of the nineteenth century—a virtuous prince with a sensitive soul in a situation of great distress, which is aggravated by the very fineness of his feelings, which undermine his resolution and so bring him to a failure which is nevertheless a sign of his superiority. Once he is *in* the nineteenth century, he undergoes modification early on at the hands of Coleridge, whose analysis of Hamlet's character (preserved in reports of his Lectures from 1811, supplemented by his own notes) has been described by T. M. Raysor as 'probably the most influential piece of Shakespearean criticism which has ever been produced'. Coleridge was not the first to be attracted to the philosophic side of *Hamlet*. The 'To be or not to be' soliloquy had been echoed by Shakespeare's contemporaries, it had been got by heart by Pepys, and the author of *Some Remarks on the Tragedy of Hamlet* in 1736 had thought it too well known to need comment. But now that its meditations on life and death had to be referred to Hamlet's character, it was necessary to attribute them to his own speculative turn of mind. It was this that fascinated Coleridge, who was only too well aware that speculative thought is wont not to issue in action. He finds in Hamlet 'an overbalance in the contemplative faculty' and an 'overpowering activity of intellect', which produces 'vacillating delays' and wastes 'in the energy of resolving the energy of acting'. Already Schlegel in Germany (*Vorlesungen über dramatische Kunst und Literatur*, II, 2, 1811; translated Black, 1815) was insisting that what defeated Hamlet's purpose was the propensity towards thinking which crippled his power of acting. What these two did, and Coleridge especially, was to transfer the interest in Hamlet's character from the sensibility to the intellect. Yet while Coleridge delighted to watch the intricate processes of Hamlet's thought, he noted as a 'most important characteristic' Hamlet's tendency to escape from his own 'individual concerns' to 'generalizations and general reasonings'. For Schlegel it was the unique power of this drama of thought that it inspired its readers and spectators to meditate with Hamlet on the enigma of human destiny and the dark perplexity of the events of this world. Hazlitt, a little more down to earth, remarks that the play abounds 'in striking reflections on human life' (*Characters of Shakespear's Plays*, 1817). Yet it would not have taken possession of the popular imagination as it did if one had not been able to enter into the experience of an individual human being and identify him with oneself. Hamlet, again in Hazlitt's words, transfers his own distresses 'to the general account of humanity. Whatever happens to him we apply to ourselves.' 'It is *we* who are Hamlet', says Hazlitt.

Through the nineteenth century Hamlet the prince became many things to many men. He was each man and every man; he was a modern born out of his time; he was a mystery; he was a genius; he was Shakespeare; and, a little more unexpectedly, at least to Shakespeare's countrymen, he was Germany, and especially the mind of nineteenth-century Germany in the plight of nineteenth-century Germany, which Shakespeare had prophetically divined. But whatever he was, always at the heart of the tragedy was the problem of Hamlet's character and with it the problem of why he left his task undone. The way to an explanation had been opened up, as we have seen, by Goethe and Coleridge, with whose views discussion would almost inevitably begin. It was possible to debate between them, whether Hamlet was frustrated by the refinement of his feelings or by his habit of thinking too precisely; but the two were not necessarily incompatible, and many interpretations sought to include both. An early synthesis was provided by Nathan Drake (*Shakespeare and his Times*) in 1817: Hamlet's 'powers of action', he says, 'are paralysed in the first instance, by the unconquerable tendency of his mind to explore . . . all the bearings and contingencies of the meditated deed; and in the second, by that tenderness of his nature which leads him to shrink from the means which are necessary to carry it into execution'. How little orthodox opinion, notwithstanding many fluctuations, was to change in the course of the century we may see by a leap ahead which, after a glance at, say, Dowden (*Shakspere: his Mind and Art*, 1875) and Boas (*Shakspere and His Predecessors*, 1896), brings us to rest in the introduction to Verity's edition in 1904. Verity has absolutely no doubt that the greatness of the play is 'the characterization of Hamlet'; and after quoting of course Goethe and Coleridge he concludes, 'I hold, then, that at bottom the cause of Hamlet's failure to execute the duty laid upon him . . . is the overbalance of the reflective faculty, the effect of which is further intensified by his great imagination and excess of the emotional temperament'.

Sometimes, however, voices would be raised on another side altogether and declare that Hamlet did not procrastinate at all. They said that what prevented Hamlet from acting was not a paralysis of will but the circumstances that opposed him, the difficulty of the task itself. The loudest of these voices was Werder's (*Vorlesungen über Shakespeare's Hamlet*, 1875), proclaiming that Hamlet's difficulty was not to kill the king but to justify to men his doing so, which, in the absence of proof, meant bringing the king to confession. That this is not in the text Werder himself conceded. Hamlet never says this, he admits, but the state of the case says it for him. What else the state of the case might have said, and sometimes did, was that to fall on a defence-less man was dishonourable, to kill a king impracticable and possibly sacrilegious, and even that Claudius's death would widow Hamlet's mother. When in 1898 A. H. Tolman reviewed the whole controversy about Hamlet's delay, he was able to list, at the cost of a little hair-splitting, eighteen different reasons which had been put forward to account for it ('A View of the Views about *Hamlet*', *PMLA*, XIII; reprinted 1906).

We cannot forget that the play of *Hamlet* in the nineteenth century was first and foremost the character of its hero. We *must* not forget that it also was a play about the universal mysteries. But another of the things it also was, was a vast congeries of problems. Second only to the delay was the problem of the madness, on which there is a whole literature—by alienists and others. The psychiatrist, Isaac Ray, pronounced that Hamlet's case showed Shakespeare's profound understanding of the symptoms of insanity ('Shakespeare's Delineations of Insanity', *American Journal of Insanity*, III, 1847; reprinted in *Contributions to Mental Pathology*, 1873); to which a distinguished man of letters retorted, no less confusing fact and fiction, that if Shakespeare could create those symptoms without himself going mad, why could not Hamlet do the same? (Lowell, *Among My Books*, 1870). Feigned or real madness became a topic of debate; usually there was both, but just occasionally neither.

Other notorious questions arose in the nineteenth century to perplex criticism ever since. Why did Claudius wait for the second enactment of his crime and not blench during the dumb-show? What exactly had Ophelia done to provoke Hamlet's cruelty? Did Hamlet know she was a decoy and that her father was behind the arras? When could she have received that letter from Hamlet that she handed to her father? On all these matters the play tiresomely says nothing and the critics fill in its gaps.

Here we see, in one of its aspects, the nineteenth-century mind: consulting my copy of Sprague (*Shakespeare and the Actors*, 1944), I am not surprised to learn that it was in the 1820's that the stage began that naughty piece of business which makes Hamlet spot the eavesdroppers. But this mind is one we all inherit—it still strongly colours *Hamlet now*—and I am afraid it is a rather prosaic one. Its habits are encouraged by the novel, which its forebears had produced. The novel has of course more room to tell us what an Elizabethan play leaves out; but it also wants to tell it us, because it thrives on verisimilitude and has a strong psychological bias. The nineteenth-century critic adds to Shakespeare's dialogue the sort of commentary with which George Eliot intersperses hers. He supplies the emotional developments between scenes: observing that Gertrude's behaviour to Claudius is unchanged after her interview with Hamlet, he shows us how she only half repented and subsequently gave up the struggle (Horn in *Shakespeares Schauspiele*, II, 1825). And the critic is not satisfied with this. He likes to regard a fiction as if it were a fragment of history, to suppose that the characters have complete lives, and that the parts we are not told of can be recovered by logical deduction and skilled reading between the lines. To avoid extreme examples, I find it being argued that Polonius could not have stood well with the dead king: if he had, Hamlet would have known and would not then have insulted him (Von Friesen, *Briefe über Shaksperes Hamlet*, 1864). And did not Bradley argue the whereabouts of Hamlet at the time of his father's death?

This is an unworthy route by which to arrive at Bradley (*Shakespearean Tragedy*, 1904). If the attitude I have spoken of is particularly associated with his name, it is surely because he is more read than his Victorian predecessors and because no one can excel him in the careful summing up of evidence which bears on both character and story. But there is always a part of his mind which remembers that *Hamlet* is a drama shaping in Shakespeare's imagination. Bradley is the bridge which joins the nineteenth century with ours. The greatest of the character critics, he concentrates—how he concentrates—on Hamlet's delay, but he refines on the psychological analysis of his predecessors, attributing Hamlet's inactivity not to his native constitution but to an abnormal state of melancholy arising from shock. The importance he attaches to Hamlet's distress at his mother's marriage gives a new critical emphasis, the effect of which will be seen in a period familiar with Freud. But while apparently absorbed in the analysis of Hamlet's character, Bradley shares the philosophical interests of the nineteenth-century Germans. He is careful to note that 'the psychological point of view is not equivalent to the tragic'. For him of course tragedy is not simply a literary genre; it is a way of interpreting the universe. For all his concern with the matter-of-fact details, the play of *Hamlet* suggests to him, especially but not only through the Ghost, how 'the limited world of ordinary experience' is but a part of some 'vaster life'; and though he does not much develop this, he perceives in the action of the play a meaning greater than itself.

The first characteristic of twentieth-century criticism, however, is its reaction against the whole school of character criticism that Bradley is taken to represent. It was after reading Bradley on *Hamlet* that a dramatic critic, A. B. Walkley, said, 'If we want to understand the play of *Hamlet* we shall not do so by assuming that it is a piece of real life, lived by people who have independent lives outside it' (*Drama and Life*, 1907). On this point, if few others, there would seem to be agreement between such diverse critics as Stoll, Wilson Knight and Dover Wilson. The one thing that unites the extremely various twentieth-century studies of *Hamlet*, always excepting the psycho-analytical, is the wish to put the prince back into the play. An early group of scholars discussed how the play grew out of its Elizabethan sources. Robertson, chief of disintegrators, found in *Hamlet* relics of the old revenge play upon which he supposed Shakespeare had grafted the motive of the son's distress at his mother's guilt, inevitably leaving incompatibilities which are the cause of all our difficulties (*The Problem of 'Hamlet'*, 1919). But Robertson is important only because T. S. Eliot, in one of his less happy moments, seems to have swallowed him whole and hence pronounced this most famous of all plays 'most certainly an artistic failure' (*The Sacred Wood*, 1920). But the key word here is 'artistic', for if I understand him rightly, Eliot thought Shakespeare had convincingly presented a psychopathological case. It being the nature of the case that the sufferer's emotions have no 'objective correlative', the play was excluded from providing one, and Shakespeare had set himself an insoluble dramatic problem. The prince would not go into the play. He was, however, being firmly shut up in it by Stoll, who kept insisting that Hamlet's delay was a necessary part of the revenge plot and had nothing to do with his character (*Hamlet: an Historical and Comparative Study*, 1919; *Art and Artifice in Shakespeare*, 1933; *Shakespeare and Other Masters*, 1940). Stoll's insistence on Elizabethan dramatic conventions was a useful corrective; and he could show that Hamlet's horrible sentiments towards the praying king, which the romantic critics had explained away, had their contemporary parallels. Many other scholars have sought to restore the play to its Elizabethan context. We have learnt a great deal about melancholy, ghosts, Montaigne, conscience and much else. And it has all helped us to interpret the play—except when the play has been distorted to fit it. When Schücking tells us that Hamlet himself typifies the Elizabethan 'melancholic' (*Die Charakter-probleme bei Shakespeare*, 1919; translated, 1922), and Lily Campbell that the play gives a demonstration of 'excessive grief leading to destruction' (*Shakespeare's Tragic Heroes*, 1930), we wonder if these views of the play are possibly as lopsided as the ones they propose to displace. The political analogies which Dover Wilson draws between Hamlet's Denmark and Elizabeth's England are unsound, as E. A. J. Honigmann has persuaded me ('The Politics in *Hamlet* . . .', *Stratford-upon-Avon Studies 5*, 1963). Yet Dover Wilson's scholarship has illuminated many dark corners of the play, not least in the notes to his edition (1934). And although we may easily disagree with his account of *What Happens in 'Hamlet'* (1935), his brilliant book has, I think, more than any other, renewed one's sense of the play's sheer excitement. He and Granville-Barker (*Prefaces to Shakespeare: 'Hamlet'*, 1936) in the thirties re-introduced to a wide public a *Hamlet* that was a piece of superb theatrical art; and they had of course a considerable influence on stage practice. They did not, I take it, change the fundamental conception of the play, nor wish to. Though their notions of Hamlet the man were very different, they both regarded *Hamlet* the play as his personal tragedy.

By now, however, a critical re-orientation had begun. In 1931 A. J. A. Waldock, after a masterly review of previous critical approaches, came to the conclusion that Hamlet's 'doubts and hesitations', though 'they are in the design', 'are not the design' (*Hamlet: a Study in Critical Method*). Henceforth, I think, it is the larger design that is looked for. Delay recedes into the background. We hear far far less of the hero's character. What we do hear of are themes. Wilson Knight, writing on *Hamlet* in *The Wheel of Fire* (1930), tried, as he afterwards explained, to see the hero 'not merely as an isolated "character"' but in relation to his 'dramatic environment'. Presently C. S. Lewis invites us to attend less to the prince than to the poem (*Hamlet:*

The Prince or the Poem?, 1942). Maynard Mack speaks of 'the imaginative environment that the play asks us to enter', and goes on to an excellent description of 'The World of *Hamlet*' (*Yale Review*, XLI, 1952; reprinted in *Shakespeare: Modern Essays in Criticism*, ed. Dean, 1957). In Shakespeare's creation of this imaginative 'world', though the characters may contribute, much is ascribed to the imagery, which will also give a clue to the themes. In her investigation of *Shakespeare's Imagery* (1935) Caroline Spurgeon found the predominant metaphors in *Hamlet* to be those of sickness and disease, and she concluded that the play was not focused on a mind 'unfitted to act' but on the rottenness in Denmark, which reflects an inner corruption destroying the whole of life. Wilson Knight saw Hamlet himself as having a 'sickness in his soul'—of which his failure to revenge was merely a 'symptom'. He saw him by his very presence spreading a poison through the kingdom. So, from the thirties onwards, although we continue to read of the Bradleian 'shock' that Hamlet suffers, we read much more of disease, corruption, and infection. D. A. Traversi, for example, describes the action of the play as 'the progressive revelation of a state of disease' (*An Approach to Shakespeare*, revised 1957). Instead of the 'native hue of resolution' being 'sicklied o'er with the pale cast of thought', the image which never fails to be quoted is the one about the 'imposthume', the tumour, which 'inward breaks, and shows no cause without Why the man dies'. But the interpretation of imagery can be a tricky business. Something seems to have gone wrong for Wilson Knight to make Hamlet himself the source of corruption amid a 'healthy' court and to contrast him in his 'death-activity' with such 'creatures of "life"' as Claudius and Laertes (*The Wheel of Fire*; *The Imperial Theme*, 1931). Others suggest that the rottenness is really in the state of Denmark and see Hamlet struggling against it or being infected by it or both. With all the disease in the play and uncertainty in the critics, perhaps it is not surprising that *Hamlet* comes to be grouped among Shakespeare's problem plays, with *Troilus* and *Measure for Measure*. Traversi, Tillyard, D. G. James all, though for different reasons, dissociate *Hamlet* from what they call the 'mature tragedies', the 'undoubted tragedies', or the 'tragedies proper'.

What all these critics would seem to agree on is that the 'problem' in *Hamlet* is not to be found in the hero's character, but rather in the nature of the universe in which he has his being. Tillyard comments on Hamlet's awareness of 'the baffling human predicament between the angels and the beasts' (*Shakespeare's Problem Plays*, 1950). And this predicament of man crawling between earth and heaven is part of that mysteriousness which Maynard Mack sees as the first attribute of the 'world' of *Hamlet*. Its other attributes are 'mortality' and 'the problematic nature of reality'. The views of the various critics do not always coincide, but it is clear that by the middle of this century critical interest in the play has moved away from the theatrical towards the poetic and still more from the psychological towards the metaphysical. C. S. Lewis suggests that many of Hamlet's own speeches give us less an impression of the speaker than of the things he speaks of. Tillyard thinks it a mistake to regard 'the turnings of Hamlet's mind as the substance of the play rather than as the means of expressing another substance'. The prince has got so much inside the play that what he says is more important than he who says it. For Lewis the 'true hero' of the play is man—man, 'incapable of achievement because of his inability to understand either himself or . . . the real quality of the universe which has produced him'. For some others Hamlet's inability to understand becomes the centre of the play. It is not a play about being but about knowing, or rather not knowing. This, I think, is how it appears

24

to D. G. James (*The Dream of Learning*, 1951), L. C. Knights (*An Approach to 'Hamlet'*, 1960), and Harry Levin (*The Question of 'Hamlet'*, 1959), though their interpretations are, again, very different. James ascribes to Shakespeare the 'momentous and profound intention' of exploring 'a mind arrested in dubiety before the awful problem of life'; the play is concerned with the inevitable plight of modern man in face of great moral and metaphysical issues. Knights, on the other hand, regards Hamlet's inability to make any affirmation about his world as a sign and consequence of his own spiritual malady. Hamlet's 'inability to affirm', we notice, has taken the place of his old inability to act.

In some respects, at any rate as I see it, this is unfortunate. For as Hamlet's action or inaction leaves the centre of the stage, it seems to take with it the dramatic action too. Levin certainly makes a design out of the play, and a very interesting one, but it is composed of questions, doubts, and ironies. Though James is careful to guard against this, in much mid-twentieth-century criticism one cannot but observe a tendency to abstraction. We have seen *Hamlet* become a play about a 'condition', about life and death themes, about 'the Hamlet consciousness'. It sometimes seems a nexus of images; to Levin it is 'primarily and finally a verbal structure'. The prince has retired so far into the play that he is almost out of sight; and a *Hamlet* without the Prince of Denmark is no longer inconceivable.

The prevailing tendency, however, I think, is to bring him back into view. He is not often *now* the noble hero with a tragic flaw. To Knights he is all flaw, a man who fails in both being and knowing. To Peter Alexander he is all nobility, combining in Shakespeare's 'complete man' the active virtues of the heroic age with the wisdom of a civilized later day (*Hamlet, Father and Son*, 1955). In neither event is he quite that complex, enigmatic person, with feelings and intellect and self-defeated will, who so fascinated our forefathers and kept escaping from the play. His character is viewed, as Alexander puts it, 'as a function of the idea that gives its form to the play'. This idea is what most critics *now* look for; but the idea, or the theme, they are coming to believe, finds expression not *in* yet *through* the hero. Mack insists that Hamlet does not merely discuss the human predicament, he 'exemplifies' it; so that the play acquires an 'almost mythic status'. The words 'myth' and 'archetype' have become common. And the mythic or archetypal quality that has been discerned in the prince, while extending his interest in one way, inevitably limits it in another. For the dramatic action in which he figures is taken to exhibit not so much his personal fortunes as his enactment of a significant role. Thus John Holloway in his recent book, *The Story of the Night* (1961), maintains that Hamlet's role is more important than his character. There seems, however, no general agreement as to what exactly the role is. We must be prepared for symbolical interpretations; and some of them are very symbolical indeed. When Christ appears in the offing, my mind tends to withdraw. Francis Fergusson (*The Idea of a Theater*, 1949) sees Hamlet as a hero who is transformed into a scapegoat, a view which Holloway develops and would extend to other plays.

Whatever we may think of this, and I confess to thinking it unsatisfactory, it is part of the attempt which is being made to reveal in *Hamlet now* that large design, which we all believe to be present, which will give coherence to its structure and will also express its meaning. It does not seem unreasonable to approach this design by way of the play's action, rather than through the imagery, though the imagery and style will help us to interpret the action. Hence Francis

Fergusson examined the interweaving of the play's various but analogous plots in order to find the 'underlying theme, to which they all point'. But misled, as I think, by the recent emphasis on the disease imagery, he centred the play in the imposthume poisoning Denmark, which he saw all the characters as trying to locate and destroy. Like Alexander and H. D. F. Kitto, he compares *Hamlet* with the tragedies of the Greeks. Kitto, though he too may be thought to have the disease imagery out of focus, gives one of the most comprehensive and deeply perceptive interpretations of the play we have (*Form and Meaning in Drama*, 1956). He especially emphasizes how in Greek tragedy a human action is played out against a divine background. In *Hamlet*, too, he views the protagonist not merely as representative man but as a man in relation to some supreme world-ordering power. This is why, if I do not oversimplify him, he would call *Hamlet* a 'religious' drama, as Bradley himself, though he thought the term inapplicable in its stricter sense, was tempted to do. Several other critics in recent years have emphasized this aspect of the play. Roy Walker (*The Time is out of Joint*, 1948) saw the hero, after he had received the revelation of the Ghost, becoming the instrument of unseen powers. More specifically his role is often seen now as that of Heaven's 'scourge and minister'. These words, which Hamlet uses of himself after the slaying of Polonius, have been made the title of one study of the play (by G. R. Elliott, 1951), form the subject of an article by Fredson Bowers (*PMLA*, LXX, 1955), and are central in the interpretation of *Hamlet* in C. J. Sisson's *Shakespeare's Tragic Justice* (1962). The words do not always mean the same thing; Bowers holds that a scourge, as distinct from a minister, is one who has committed crime himself, while Sisson shows us a Hamlet who is God's righteous 'justiciar'. The nineteenth century, beguiled by Hamlet's character and his reasons for delaying his deed, rarely went on to consider how he eventually accomplished it, and paid but scant attention to those references to Heaven and Providence towards the end of the play which we hear much more of *now*. But on the significance of Providence in the play, again opinions differ.

To bring into harmony all these critical interpretations of the tragic action of Hamlet is impossible; and you will hardly wish to add to my task that of synthesizing such of them as are not actually incompatible. But perhaps, in conclusion, I may very tentatively suggest what seem to me to be some of the essential features of this action, with acknowledgments to all those, dead and living, who have helped me to perceive them. I have to agree with Goethe that Hamlet has a great deed laid on him. And whatever the truth about delay, I observe, with the nineteenth-century critics, that for a long time he does not do it. I cannot deny that the deed is one of revenge. I accept from C. S. Lewis the importance of its being commanded by a ghost, with all that this implies. But I hope I may also add that the ghost is that of Hamlet's father, who is not less important than his mother, and whom he sees in his mind's eye as his ideal man with the seal of the god upon him. I believe, with Levin, that fundamental to the structure is the opposition between this Hyperion figure and the satyr figure who has killed him and rules the kingdom in his stead. In company with Kenneth Muir (*Shakespeare: Hamlet*, 1963) I allow myself to connect *this* with all the imagery of disease. I note that the god-man and the beast-man are brothers, sprung from the same human stock, which has also produced Hamlet. I take it from Mack that Hamlet is not only aware of the dual nature of man but exemplifies it in himself. And whatever may be said about his character, I seem to see this duality in his role. For while charged with a deed of revenge, he also incurs vengeance. One of the things that puzzles me is that Hamlet's dual role, as punisher and punished, has received so little critical stress. Yet it is only when he has come to accept it that he achieves his deed—finally killing the king at the moment when he is himself killed, and forgiven, by Laertes, whom he also kills and forgives. And in accepting this dual role, he submits himself to what is called Heaven or Providence; so that with it he also accepts, though he does not comprehend, himself and his own part, so mysteriously composed of good and evil, in that universal design which 'shapes our ends'.

THE ART OF CRUELTY:
HAMLET AND VINDICE

R. A. FOAKES

Hamlet admits to cruelty only when he is about to encounter his mother in the Closet scene, and then he seeks to qualify the term

> O heart, lose not thy nature, let not ever
> The soul of Nero enter this firm bosom,
> Let me be cruel not unnatural. (III, ii, 396–8)

The cruelty he seeks to permit himself is to be kept under a restraint, not let loose with the tyrannical savagery of which Nero served as a type. So again, at the end of the interview, Hamlet cries, 'I must be cruel only to be kind', claiming that his cruelty serves its opposite, kindness. What Hamlet seems anxious to do here is to prevent himself from inflicting cruelty for its own sake; and the fact that he alone articulates this idea in the play suggests both the measure of success he has in controlling himself, and also his awareness, so to speak, of possibilities for cruelty within himself.

If Hamlet is not at this point recalling the Ghost's speeches to him in act I, his concern about his mother, and the re-appearance of the Ghost in the Closet scene, make the link for spectator and reader. Then the Ghost had ended his account of the murder by exhorting Hamlet to revenge, but warning him too:

> Howsomever thou pursues this act,
> Taint not thy mind, nor let thy soul contrive
> Against thy mother aught... (I, v, 84–6)

It might be said that Hamlet's mind is already tainted, as the first soliloquy, 'O that this too too sullied flesh would melt', has already shown him brooding on suicide and disgusted by the speed of his mother's remarriage with a man he despises; but the Ghost himself may be seen as tainting Hamlet's mind in another way. For the Ghost, like Hamlet in his soliloquy, dwells imaginatively on what has happened in such a way as to emphasise by elaboration what is most gross and nasty. In this the Ghost and Hamlet are alike: what the Ghost speaks may be seen as articulating what is already there in Hamlet. So, like Hamlet, the Ghost dwells on remarriage in language that is itself revolting,

> So lust, though to a radiant angel linked,
> Will sate itself in a celestial bed
> And prey on garbage (I, v, 54–6)

There is a kind of self-indulgence in this, a relish of nastiness which does not relate to the Claudius and Gertrude we have seen in action. The Ghost continues with his account of the murder:

> Upon my secure hour thy uncle stole
> With juice of cursed hebenon in a vial,
> And in the porches of my ears did pour
> The leperous distillment, whose effect
> Holds such an enmity with blood of man
> That swift as quicksilver it courses through
> The natural gates and alleys of the body,
> And with a sudden vigor it doth posset,
> And curd, like eager droppings into milk,
> The thin and wholesome blood. So did it mine,
> And a most instant tetter barked about,
> Most lazarlike, with vile and loathsome crust,
> All my smooth body. (I, v, 61–73)

The Ghost seems fascinated by the details of what happened, and dwells especially on the effects of the poison, producing that 'tetter' or eruption which covers his skin with a 'loathsome crust'; it is this above all that the speech renders with the force of particularity, and which informs that great cry.[1]

> O, horrible! O, horrible! most horrible!
>
> (I, v, 80)

In other words, the Ghost does not just tell us *what* happened, but recreates imaginatively *how* it happened, the horrible atrocity of a murder which could, presumably, have been relatively quick and simple, a stab with a dagger, or smothering with a pillow. A passage from Dostoevsky's *The Brothers Karamazov* may be helpful at this point, for this is a novel much concerned with the nature of cruelty; at one point in it Ivan tries to explain to Alyosha why he cannot love his neighbours, and this passes into an extraordinary account of human cruelty, in which he tells Alyosha a story:

'By the way, not so long ago a Bulgarian in Moscow told me', Ivan went on, as though not bothering to listen to his brother, 'of the terrible atrocities committed all over Bulgaria by the Turks and Circassians who were afraid of a general uprising of the Slav population. They burn, kill, violate women and children, nail their prisoners' ears to fences and leave them like that till next morning when they hang them, and so on – it's impossible to imagine it all. And, indeed people sometimes speak of man's 'bestial' cruelty, but this is very unfair and insulting to the beasts: a beast can never be so cruel as a man, so ingeniously, so artistically cruel. A tiger merely gnaws and tears to pieces, that's all he knows. It would never occur to him to nail men's ears to a fence and leave them like that overnight, even if he were able to do it. These Turks, incidentally, seemed to derive a voluptuous pleasure from torturing children, cutting a child out of its mother's womb with a dagger and tossing babies up in the air and catching them on a bayonet before the eyes of their mothers. It was doing it before the eyes of their mothers that made it so enjoyable. But one incident I found particularly interesting. Imagine a baby in the arms of a trembling mother, surrounded by Turks who had just entered her house. They are having great fun: they fondle the baby, they laugh to make it laugh and they are successful: the baby laughs. At that moment the Turk points a pistol four inches from the baby's face. The boy laughs happily, stretches out his little hands to grab the pistol, when suddenly the artist pulls the trigger in the baby's face and blows his brains out...Artistic, isn't it? Incidentally, I'm told the Turks are very fond of sweets.'[2]

Ivan observes that man is distinguished from beasts by his artistry: we speak casually of 'bestial' cruelty, but no animal is as cruel as men can be, who do it for enjoyment and to display their skill as artists, while others, looking on as spectators, take pleasure in watching, and in this case, enjoy the anguish the murder of the baby causes to its mother.

Something of this artistry in cruelty seems to be shown in the murder of old King Hamlet, as the Ghost describes it; the poison chosen by his brother was one that visibly corrupts and makes horrible the body of the dying man. Even the Ghost, who speaks of it as if he had been an onlooker at his own murder, is fascinated by the details of the process of dying, horrible as they are. He says he was sleeping at the time, and so not conscious, but he narrates what happened as if Claudius, in the manner of Dostoevsky's artists in cruelty, had staged it so that old Hamlet would at once suffer and be a spectator at his own death.

The Ghost calls on Hamlet to revenge,

> Revenge his foul and most unnatural murder,
>
> (I, v, 25)

and to pursue it by any means so long as he leaves his mother to Heaven. Although the Ghost does not explicitly command him to kill Claudius, this is what, in effect, 'revenge' means, since it is the only way Hamlet can

---

[1] This line functions too in relation to the idea immediately preceding it, of dying, 'With all my imperfections on my head', and that following in the reference to 'luxury and damned incest', but it seems to me to carry most weight as a rhetorical climax to the account of the murder as a whole.

[2] The quotation is from the translation by David Magarshack (Harmondsworth, 1958), I, 278–9.

obtain satisfaction and repay the injuries received by his father. So Hamlet is required to contrive another killing, a deed ironically condemned in the very next words of the Ghost,

> Murder most foul, as in the best it is.
>
> (I, v, 27)

In her study of revenge,[1] Eleanor Prosser 'found no evidence to indicate that Elizabethans believed the law required blood revenge. The Law was absolute: murder, as such, was never justified.' The play shows Hamlet to be an artist, an actor–dramatist, ingenious contriver, and player of many parts; the Ghost, even as he condemns murder, demands that he put that artistry into the service of a cruelty Hamlet sees, at any rate in the Closet scene, as potentially there in himself.

This may seem a strange perspective when it is set against that view of Hamlet, which many hold, as a character imbued with a moral idealism or governed by a sense of moral scruple. It has been said, for example, very recently by Ivor Morris, in a careful account of Hamlet, that

Goodness and simple humanity are Hamlet's ideal. More truly than the heroic, it is the moral that confers nobility on man...Human excellence for Hamlet does not imply a self-aggrandizement, but rather the forsaking of an instinctive self-will, and the disciplining of the aspiring consciousness according to values which, though humble and familiar, are yet of a power to transcend. The chief passion of Hamlet's soul, therefore, is the precise antithesis of the heroic.[2]

Well, yes – but isn't this much too simple and clear-cut? For Hamlet sees his father in an heroic image, and finds a model for himself in Horatio, more an antique Roman than a Dane. It is true that Hamlet disparages himself in saying that Claudius 'is no more like my father than I to Hercules'; yet much of his idealism is bound up with the warrior-figures of the Ghost at the beginning and Fortinbras

at the end, so that it is important to notice how these figures are presented in the play.

Some think of the military imagery in the play as being there to 'emphasise that Claudius and Hamlet are engaged in a duel to the death',[3] or that it exists to call attention 'to the issues of public life, to the state of the nation'.[4] It may serve these purposes, but when the Ghost appears in armour from head to foot, and accompanied by indications of past triumphs, as when he smote the sledded Polacks on the ice, other connotations are at work too; for war here does not, of course, have its unpleasant modern associations, but rather a ring of chivalric heroism in the thought of personal encounters, personal courage and skill. Old Hamlet appears in a 'fair and warlike form', as 'valiant Hamlet', who, challenged to combat,

> Did slay this Fortinbras, who by a sealed compact,
> Well ratified by law and heraldry,
> Did forfeit (with his life) all those his lands
> Which he stood seized of, to the conqueror.
>
> (I, i, 86–9)

The word 'heraldry', referring vaguely to heraldic practice, suggests an almost medieval ceremony, an ancient practice, no longer meaningful in the new Denmark of Claudius, the modern politician, negotiating through ambassadors. Later on Hamlet sees another image of chivalric heroism in that 'delicate and tender prince', young Fortinbras, passing through on his way, like old Hamlet, to fight the Poles, merely for honour, and driven by a 'divine ambition'. It is enough to make him give Fortinbras his dying vote for the succession to the Danish throne.

[1] *Hamlet and Revenge* (Stanford, 1967), p. 18.
[2] *Shakespeare's God. The Role of Religion in the Tragedies* (London, 1972), p. 371.
[3] Nigel Alexander, *Poison, Play and Duel* (London, 1971), p. 25. This stimulating book in some measure provoked the present essay.
[4] Maurice Charney, *Style in Hamlet* (Princeton, 1969), p. 30.

Hamlet in this combines a nostalgia for a past that seems better than the present with the idea of a great soldier as simple, good and truthful. An audience sees also that Fortinbras is wasting his country's youth on a trivial and useless campaign; and if the Ghost really represents Old Hamlet, then he was also vindictive and morally perverse, condemning all murder, yet urging Hamlet to commit one. Hamlet's image is a partial one; Fortinbras and his father take on in his mind's eye grander proportions and finer qualities than are evidenced in the play, and Claudius appears worse to him than he does in the action:

> So excellent a King, that was to this
> Hyperion to a satyr,   (I, ii, 140–1)

the sun-god compared with one who is half-beast. The heroic ideal Hamlet thinks he sees in his father merges into those classical figures that spring to his lips for a comparison, Hyperion, Mars, Mercury, Caesar, Hercules, Aeneas, and others, and all help to suggest imagined models for Hamlet himself, and to exemplify to him that possibility of the godlike in man embodied in 'What a piece of work is a man!' Hamlet tends to disclaim comparison between himself and his heroes, yet there is much of the heroic in him too,[1] complicated by other qualities, as he is more fully of the Renaissance, a man of all talents and so much less the mere warrior-hero. Trained at a university, he retains the habit of sifting evidence, even the habit of taking lecture-notes ('My tables, meet it is I set it down'). He writes more than other Shakespearian protagonists; King Lear could have been illiterate, but Hamlet is clearly an intellectual, au fait with classical literature, able to turn off a few lines for Ophelia, however much he is 'ill at these numbers', and to pen a speech for the players, a dozen or so lines of verse. Hamlet the writer reflects Hamlet the thinker and scholar, but he is also an accomplished swordsman, who

throughout conveys a sense of absolute fearlessness, so that at the end it seems entirely appropriate when he is accorded martial honours, as four captains bear his body, 'like a soldier' to the stage.

Hamlet is a very complex character, and it won't do to say that 'goodness and simple humanity are Hamlet's ideal'. Insofar as he locates his ideal in his father and Fortinbras, it seems to be partly a longing for a simpler world, in which problems could be honourably settled in combat; and it is based on an uncritical association of these figures with a chivalric heroism. Hamlet's idealism is confused, and this confusion prevents him from seeing at once the contradiction in the Ghost's exhortations to him to do the very thing for which the Ghost condemns Claudius. Hamlet shows at times a moral delicacy and scrupulousness that mark him off from the world of Claudius, and this is brought out by the comparison with Laertes sweeping unhesitatingly to his revenge; but he is confused in his moral stances too, and fails to discipline his consciousness, or to remain, as Ivor Morris claims, 'morally consistent'.[2] He does not directly question the Ghost's command, although he avoids pursuing it, and has recourse to play-acting, to an antic disposition, and to the play within the play. Some see this as a substitute for real action, for killing Claudius, and put emphasis on Hamlet's delay, but it is as much a device to penetrate the mask of Claudius in order to discover his true nature and to expose his guilt. Beyond this it is also, more importantly, a means to accommodate himself to what he feels he has to do; the Ghost has emphasised in detail the horror of the murder of his father, and in order to accomplish his revenge, he

---

[1] See G. K. Hunter's analysis of 'The Heroic in Hamlet', in *Hamlet*, edited J. R. Brown and Bernard Harris (*Stratford-upon-Avon Studies 5*, London, 1963), especially pp. 103–4.
[2] *Shakespeare's God*, p. 383.

needs to act like Claudius, and face a similar horror.

In the course of the play he makes a series of moral adjustments, notably after he stabs Polonius through the arras, and so marks himself with a blood-guilt. He assigns the responsibility for this to 'heaven', as if he has been appointed a divine agent:

> For this same lord
> I do repent; but heaven hath pleas'd it so
> To punish me with this, and this with me,
> That I must be their scourge and minister.
>
> (III, iv, 172–5)

The terms 'scourge' and 'minister', it seems, 'are so contradictory that they are irreconcilable', for 'God elects as his scourge only a sinner who already deserves damnation', while a 'minister' would be a true agent and servant of God.[1] Hamlet could not be both at the same time, and the moral confusion present here is brought out further in his recognition in the same speech that, 'This bad begins, and worse remains behind.' This confusion is marked too in the way he seems to convince himself after his return from the sea-voyage in act V that it would be 'perfect conscience' to kill Claudius:

> Does it not, think thee, stand me now upon –
> He that hath kill'd my king and whor'd my
>   mother,
> Popp'd in between th' election and my hopes,
> Thrown out his angle for my proper life,
> And with such cozenage – is't not perfect
>   conscience
> To quit him with this arm? And is't not to be
>   damned
> To let this canker of our nature come
> In further evil?   (v, ii, 63–70)

Though Claudius has done these things, including the attempt to have Hamlet done to death by sending him to England bearing a commission for his own execution, Hamlet is not thereby given moral freedom to kill Claudius, to practise murder most foul, 'as in the best it is'.

In fact his claims that heaven has appointed him as its agent, and that he would be damned for not killing Claudius, do not issue in any determined action. Hamlet might be interpreted here as cheering himself up; whatever he says, he still does nothing, and rather at the end resigns himself to providence. However much he may justify murder to himself, there is no sign that he can bring himself in action to face the horror of doing it. After the encounter with the Ghost in act I, Hamlet cries out that the commandment to revenge shall alone live in his mind, but what he does is to adopt that 'antic disposition', which allows him to play any part, notably those of fool and madman. The Ghost's commandment brings out the artist in Hamlet, his concern with play-action, which is stimulated too by the entry of the players, and Shakespeare focuses our attention on these through much of acts II and III. When Hamlet first meets the players, he asks for a speech, recalling the opening of it himself: ''twas Aeneas' tale to Dido, and thereabout of it especially where he speaks of Priam's slaughter'. It is appropriate for him to have remembered this speech from a play that was 'caviare to the general', a play for the educated, based on Virgil's *Aeneid*, and so associated with that heroic world with which Hamlet likes to link himself, and which emerges especially in references to and images drawn from classical history, literature and myth. As has been skilfully shown by Nigel Alexander,[2] the player's speech also provides subtle analogies for Hamlet, as it acts out the successful vengeance of Pyrrhus upon Priam, and the destruction of a kingdom brought about by lust.

But the speech has another kind of significance which I want to emphasise; it describes

[1] The quotations are from Eleanor Prosser's analysis of this passage in *Hamlet and Revenge*, pp. 199–201.
[2] *Poison, Play and Duel*, p. 97.

Pyrrhus raging through the streets of Troy to revenge the death of his father, until eventually he finds and hacks to pieces the aged and defenceless Priam:

> 'Head to foot
> Now is he total gules, horridly trick'd
> With blood of fathers, mothers, daughters, sons,
> Bak'd and impasted with the parching streets,
> That lend a tyrannous and a damned light
> To their lord's murder. Roasted in wrath and fire,
> And thus o'er-sized with coagulate gore,
> With eyes like carbuncles, the hellish Pyrrhus
> Old grandsire Priam seeks.'   (II, ii, 460–8)

The language of this is inflated, but not too much so for its content and occasion, and the overall impression it makes is powerful. Of its kind, it is a good speech, vigorously presenting an image of Pyrrhus as literally covered in blood that is dried and baked on to him, so that he is 'impasted' or encrusted with it, through the heat generated by his anger ('roasted in wrath'), and slaughters fathers, mothers and sons at random. In other words, Pyrrhus images an ultimate in cruelty, beyond all control, and exemplifies the kind of pleasure in atrocity which Dostoevsky observes, as he goes on to make 'malicious sport' in mincing Priam before the eyes of Hecuba. If it is a reminder to Hamlet of what he feels he must do, it recalls also the Ghost's account of his murder, when the poison Claudius administered caused his skin to become covered with a 'vile and loathsome crust'. Like the Ghost's speech, this one dwells on the particularities of the event, recreating imaginatively the horror of it, and like that, it wins for a moment Hamlet's wholehearted involvement. In each case, however, the horror of the deed is made bearable to Hamlet through its presentation in art, in a kind of play within the play, where it is aesthetically distanced.[1] The point I would make about these scenes, is that they show how Hamlet can involve himself imaginatively in play-acting or dramatising the act of cruelty, but

cannot do it. Briefly now he whips himself into a heat of passion:

> Is it not monstrous that this player here,
> But in a fiction, in a dream of passion,
> Could force his soul so to his own conceit,
> That from her working all his visage wanned,
> Tears in his eyes, distraction in his aspect,
> A broken voice, and his whole function suiting
> With forms to his conceit; and all for nothing?
>   (II, ii, 554–60)

In fact, it is the fiction or art that makes it possible for Hamlet to face this image of cruel murder, and it provokes him not into acting like Pyrrhus, but into arranging a performance of another play, the murder of Gonzago.

It is not 'monstrous' to 'force the soul' to display the imagined passion; it would be monstrous rather to put that passion to work in earnest. Again Hamlet's moral confusion emerges, as he forces his own soul into a rage and unpacks his heart with words in this soliloquy. For Hamlet's moral idealism emerges not in what he tries to will himself to do, which is to abandon scruple and drive to his revenge (consciously, so to speak, this is what he thinks he is doing, as is evidenced in his confusions or rejections of morality); it is revealed rather in the energy with which he can respond to or recreate the horror imaginatively. In this the aesthetic passes into the moral; he confronts the image of what, on one level, he would like to make himself, at such a pitch of imaginative intensity, that it disables him from practising cruelty himself. His full imaginative involvement brings home to him and us the horror of what Claudius did, and of the carnage wrought by the 'hellish Pyrrhus'; so, even when he has a perfect opportunity, finding Claudius at prayer, Hamlet cannot do it, and

[1] In *Shakespeare the Craftsman* (London, 1969), p. 129, M. C. Bradbrook has argued that the First Player here was made up to look like Burbage playing Hamlet, so that during the Pyrrhus speech Hamlet was watching, as it were, a reflection of himself.

neglects the chance to kill him. The reasons he gives have some plausibility, but behind them we sense his radical inability to become 'monstrous' or 'hellish' in deed, and carry out a willed murder.

When he does kill, it is in a fit of excitement, and an unpremeditated act, stabbing blindly through the arras, not a planned murder. The death of Polonius fastens a guilt on him, and makes it easier for him to send Rosencrantz and Guildenstern to their deaths by forging a new commission to the King of England. Even this, though ingenious, is not a direct deed of cruelty, and on his return to Denmark, it is in a condition of resignation: 'If it be now, 'tis not to come; if it be not to come, it will be now; if it be not now, yet it will come – the readiness is all.' He appears to be talking about his *own* death – but he is talking also about the death of *Claudius* – for he abandons plotting, the thought of acting as revenger, of being a Pyrrhus; and the death of Claudius happens in a muddle at the end, and only after Hamlet has his own death-wound. Horatio speaks with reason here

> Of accidental judgments, casual slaughters,
> Of deaths put on by cunning and forced cause,
> And, in this upshot, purposes mistook,
> Fallen on the inventors' heads.
>
> (v, ii, 380–3)

It is all clumsy, casual and, on the part of Hamlet, unplanned and unprepared – he never does become a revenger, unless he might be thought one in that moment when, having given Claudius his death-wound with a venomed sword, he then forces him to drink the poisoned wine. Its effect, however, is to despatch Claudius at once, not to protract his death, or make it more horrible, and Laertes guides our response:

> He is justly served;
> It is a poison tempered by himself. (v, ii, 325–6)

Hamlet shows a kind of cruelty twice in the play, once when he turns on Ophelia, recognising that she is a decoy, and later when he speaks savagely to his mother. He lashes verbally the two women he loves, and his behaviour here is not, as is sometimes argued, merely a reflection of his revulsion against sex, or of his hatred of the corruption he sees around him; it relates also, and more deeply, to his imaginative engagement with, and recoil from, the horror within himself. The cruelty expressed in words is also a substitute for action, an outlet for what he knows is in him, and might perhaps be seen too as vicariously satisfying the conscious urge to drive himself to a deed of cruelty, to revenge. His attack on Ophelia springs from an inquisition into himself, beginning in the soliloquy 'To be or not to be', in which, amongst other things, a dejected Hamlet attempts to reckon with the need for action, the task of taking arms against Claudius, in the recognition that 'the pale cast of thought' is inimical to action; the self-inspection deepens into the hyperbole of his words to Ophelia:

> I am very proud, revengeful, ambitious, with more offences at my beck than I have thoughts to put them in, imagination to give them shape, or time to act them in. (III, i, 125)

He has a sense of a potential in himself for unimagined, or unimaginable offences, but those we are aware of in him exist mostly in his mind or imagination. So when he confronts his mother in the Closet scene, it is to recreate in imagination, and with a nastiness belonging to his conception, to him more than to the deed itself, the activity of sexual relations between Claudius and his mother:

> Nay, but to live
> In the rank sweat of an enseamed bed,
> Stewed in corruption, honeying, and making love
> Over the nasty sty... (III, iv, 91–4)

34

The obscenity is inside Hamlet, and bursts out in a savagery of words; if these help to bring Ophelia to suicide, and afflict Gertrude so that she cries

> These words like daggers enter in mine ears,
>   (III, iv, 95)

nevertheless, these attacks are essentially different from the deed this line recalls, Claudius pouring poison into the ears of Old Hamlet. Ophelia cannot comprehend what Hamlet says, and both she and, initially at any rate, Gertrude, are inclined to think his outbursts are expressions of madness. I think rather that Hamlet gives rein to his tongue as an alternative to the action he cannot face; and his ability to give bitterness vent in words to them, and yet refrain from a willed or planned killing, is exactly what we might expect.

The presentation of Hamlet in this way is worth comparing to that of Vindice in *The Revenger's Tragedy*, who is also something of an artist, and likes to see himself as dramaturge, even as writer of his own play. Even in the opening speech over the skull, he already uses it as a stage-property in his own dramatisation of the court, and when he is not playing the disguised roles of Piato and a malcontent, adopted to deceive Lussurioso, he is to be found stage-managing playlets of his own, most notably in the famous scene in which the skull is again introduced, now dressed in 'tires', fitted with a head-dress as if alive. As he brings it on, Vindice uses it consciously again as a property, saying to Hippolito;

> Now to my tragic business, look you, brother,
> I have not fashioned this only for show,
> And useless property; no it shall bear a part
> E'en in its own revenge...   (III, v, 103–6)

The skull itself is a reminder of Hamlet in the graveyard, but though Hamlet plays many parts, and fancies himself as an actor with the visiting company in Elsinore, there is a radical difference, namely that Hamlet is wholly involved in the decision whether to revenge, in those questions to do or not to do ('Now might I do it pat...'), and to be or not to be, that reverberate in the play; but Vindice has made his decision already before his opening speech; his attention is engaged by the question, 'How can I effect my revenge in the cleverest way?' not, 'How can I do it at all?' Because his attention is on the means rather than the end, he becomes pleased with his own cleverness, designing the little play within the play in which he murders the Duke.

While Hamlet is concerned with the nature of revenge and the horror of the act of cruelty, we see in Vindice a growing detachment from the nature of what he is doing, a detachment which is made to take effect fully as part of the play's serious action. At the beginning, his moral indignation at the corruptions of the court invites our sympathy and assent. In the opening scene, his independence from the court is imaged in the visual separation of Vindice from the procession he watches and describes, but by act III, when he contrives the murder of the Duke, he has taken his place among the courtiers, and joins those he so despised at first, crying

> 'Tis state in music for a Duke to bleed.
> The dukedom wants a head, tho' yet unknown.
> As fast as they peep up, let's cut 'em down.
>   (III, v, 224–6)

Vindice's anger at the beginning is justified insofar as he is in a position similar to that of Hamlet, unable to obtain justice for a murder in a court which seems corrupt; but when Vindice uses the skull to poison the Duke in act III, Hippolito applauds him not for a moral achievement, but more appropriately for his cleverness:

> I do applaud thy constant vengeance,
> The quaintness of thy malice.   (III, v, 108–9)

It is an ingenuity ('quaintness'), an artistry, put into the service of 'malice', of cruelty, as

Vindice enjoys poisoning the Duke in a kiss even while he watches his own wife and bastard son making love.

It is their self-satisfaction in their skill which leads Vindice and Hippolito to boast at the end of their 'wit' in murdering the Duke, and so brings on their arrest and execution. By act V, their enjoyment in plotting has reached the point where they congratulate each other on watching an innocent nobleman carried off to execution suspected of a murder they have carried out:

Hippolito.
    Brother, how happy is our vengeance!
Vindice.   Why, it hits
    Past th' apprehension of indifferent wits.

                    (V, ii, 133–4)

In relation to this delight in cruelty, it is important to notice how much of the play is funny; its general cleverness emerges in a kind of grisly humour, as in the joking of the Duchess's youngest son as he expects release from the scaffold, a release which never comes, or in the hiring of Vindice by Lussurioso to kill his *alter ego*, Piato; or in the double masque of revengers at the end. In spite of the burning moral indignation of some of Vindice's speeches, the world of the play offers an image of human existence which excludes the possibility of the heroic and moral idealism present in *Hamlet*; it is a world in which money, power, and sex dominate, and for Vindice, intelligence and artistry replace morality. The humour is necessary to make such a vision of human cruelty through ingenuity bearable. At the same time, the play shows in Vindice an 'artist', the stage-manager and writer of his own playlets, becoming so absorbed in his skill that he treats life merely as an exercise for his art, and so loses all moral sense. When he confronts his mother in act IV, it is not to threaten her with words like daggers (compare Hamlet's, 'I will speak daggers to her, but use none'), but to hold a real dagger to her breast, so that when she echoes Gertrude's 'Thou wilt *not* murder me', it is with a difference: Gratiana asks, 'What, *will* you murder me?' and there seems every reason to suppose Vindice and Hippolito may do so.

To return then to *Hamlet*: there is one moment in the play when Hamlet, like Vindice, yields to a sense of pleasure in the skill of plotting:

    'tis the sport to have the engineer
  Hoist with his own petar, and't shall go hard
  But I will delve one yard below their mines,
  And blow them at the moon: O, 'tis most sweet
  When in one line two crafts directly meet.

                (III, iv, 206–10)

This occurs after the death of Polonius, and when he learns he must go to England; but in fact, Hamlet practises craft in this way only once. All his artistry in the first part of the play is aimed at understanding himself and making apparent the guilt of Claudius; he stabs Polonius in a fit of passion, and not knowing what or who is behind the arrras; and at the end he declines to plot against Claudius, putting his trust in providence. Only once, in the boat to England, is he prompted to try his craft, when he alters the message Rosencrantz and Guildenstern are carrying to avoid his own death. There is no instance at all of Hamlet initiating a plot to kill anyone.

Although he is as much of an artist as Vindice, Hamlet does not confuse art and life; indeed, he has his theory of the art of playing, and his famous formulation is worth noting: 'whose end both at the first, and now, was and is, to hold as 'twere the mirror up to nature, to show virtue her own feature, scorn her own image, and the very age and body of the time his form and pressure' (III, ii, 20). The 'end' or aim of art is to reflect what is there, and presumably by reflecting, to reveal to him what the spectator may not otherwise see; but its success in doing this depends on the apprehension of the spectator, as Vindice knew, on his sensitivity and understanding, and Hamlet's theory says nothing of his. It does not work too well for Claudius; the play within the play shows twice, first in dumb-show and then in action, something closely resembling the murder of old Hamlet, and Claudius is not much troubled by this mirror held up to nature; what does seem to stir him is Hamlet's identification of the murderer as 'one Lucianus, nephew to the King', and a few lines later, Claudius walks out, calling for lights, and 'marvellous distempered'. What he saw acted before him was not the murder of Old Hamlet so much as an image of a secret fear, the killing of himself by his nephew, Young Hamlet.

The theory works better for Hamlet himself: the play within the play seems to him to mirror Claudius's deed, and to cause him to reveal his guilt; in addition, it provides yet one more artistic expression of the nature of that murder, which is also reflected in the Ghost's speech, and in the First Player's speech on the 'hellish Pyrrhus'. Hamlet's playing dwells on the image of a murder which reflects the cruelty of the deed and the horror of revenge; and so reveals to us what is not apparent to Hamlet himself, his moral revulsion from the task he feels the Ghost has imposed on him. This fascinated loathing of the horror in its imagined recreation finds one more outlet in the Graveyard scene, when he broods on the skull of Yorick, and after drawing out the commonplaces appropriate to that *memento mori*, passes on to Alexander, another classical hero:

Hamlet. Now get you to my lady's chamber, and tell her, let her paint an inch thick, to this favour she must come, make her laugh at that...Prithee Horatio, tell me one thing.
Horatio. What's that, my lord?
Hamlet. Dost thou think Alexander looked o'this fashion i'th' earth?
Horatio. E'en so.
Hamlet. And smelt so? pah!
Horatio. E'en so, my lord.

Hamlet. To what base uses we may return, Horatio! Why may not imagination trace the noble dust of Alexander till'a find it stopping a bung-hole?
Horatio. 'Twere to consider too curiously, to consider so.
(v, i, 187–200)

Why may not imagination trace the dust of Alexander in this way? Horatio's answer carries weight – because it is to speculate too nicely, to go too far, to become, he might have added, self-indulgent; but there are more things in heaven and earth than Horatio sees, and his response is a limited one; Hamlet's effort to trace in imagination the full consequences of physical decay in death parallels his ability to face imaginatively the full horror of revenge; the element of indulgence in both is less significant than the power they have to work as vehicles of Hamlet's deepest moral awareness; he is right to reply here to Horatio's ''Twere to consider too curiously' with the phrase 'No, faith, not a jot!'

The greatness of *Hamlet* may be measured against the more limited, if splendid, achievement of *The Revenger's Tragedy*, in which Vindice so falls in love with his art as to commit himself entirely to it. Unable then to see its moral implications for himself, he uses it, most notably in his device with the skull, as a means to effect his revenge; so, becoming like Dostoevsky's Turks, he enjoys the display of cruelty as he makes the dying Duke watch the incestuous adultery of his own wife. By contrast, it is the strength of Hamlet, not his weakness, or only superficially his weakness, that he cannot kill, that he fails to carry out his revenge. The role of Hamlet may be seen as ironically expanding from his opening lines, when he enters acting like a mourner in his customary suits of solemn black, and saying,

These indeed seem,
For they are actions that a man might play,
But I have that within which passeth show
(i, ii, 83–5)

In the action Hamlet does, in fact, reveal what is most deep within him, not, so to speak, consciously, not even in the soliloquies, but in projecting imaginatively, into art, into shows, into plays within the play, or the rhetoric of his encounters with Ophelia and Gertrude, a sense of the potential for cruelty and viciousness in himself. Shakespeare makes this art the vehicle of the moral restraint Hamlet exercises upon what is within. The combination of his full imaginative grasp of the horror of a cruelty he recognises as potentially in himself, with a moral revulsion from it of which he is unconscious, or at best obscurely aware, perhaps helps to explain why Hamlet remains both an enigma and Shakespeare's best-loved hero.

© R. A. FOAKES 1973

'FORM AND CAUSE CONJOIN'D': 'HAMLET' AND SHAKESPEARE'S WORKSHOP

KEITH BROWN

That certain analogies exist between the opening and closing scenes of *Hamlet* is a commonplace of criticism. Everyone sees that the figure of Old Hamlet – in his Polack-defeating armour – at the start of the tragedy is balanced by the armed figure of Fortinbras at the play's end, fresh from his own Polack wars, restoring the *status quo*. And similar parallels have been pointed out, for instance, between the *platform* of I, i, on which the ghost of the murdered king makes his silently-eloquent appearance, and the *stage* on which the silently-eloquent body of his son (again with Horatio present as messenger and interpreter) is to make its last appearance after v, ii.

But what does not seem to have been generally recognised, whether in the study or in the theatre, is quite how far such apparent symmetries can be traced on further into the play; certainly far enough, at all events, to make it unlikely that in doing so one is doing nothing but finding pictures in the fire.

It is convenient to plot this underlying parallelism scene by scene; indeed, the very extent to which that is possible seems in itself to say something about 'Shakespeare's workshop'.

Since the opening and closing scenes have already been referred to, let us begin by juxtaposing the second and the penultimate scenes:

I, ii – V, i
(*An uneasy wedding ceremony
An uneasy funeral ceremony.*)

...both cases where the royal will has over-ruled conventional ecclesiastical decorum. Moreover, thanks to Gertrude's 'I thought thy bride-bed to have deck'd, sweet maid, / and not have strew'd thy grave' (v, i, 239–40), the wedding–funeral association of ideas is also present on both occasions. (Seen in this light, of course, Hamlet's leap into Ophelia's grave makes rather better sense than is allowed by those who would dismiss it as merely a crude piece of vulgarisation, likely to derive rather from Burbage than Shakespeare. Essentially, it continues, however brutally, the parallel wedding–funeral entanglements.)

It is interesting, too, to see how the *sequence* of I, ii – formal court occasion / departure of King, Queen and Lords / glum ruminations by Hamlet / bitter humour, tinged with social satire, from Hamlet / conversation – is in fact repeated, in *inverse* order, in v, i. Compare II, i and IV, v in this respect, or the way the beginning of I, iii seems to pair up with the end of IV, vii.

(*third scene*) *I, iii –
IV, vii* (*third from last*)

The first of these scenes presents Ophelia to us: the latter, the story of her death. I, iii *begins* with Laertes warning Ophelia of the dangers of involvement with Hamlet; while IV, vii *ends* with Laertes learning of the end to which the Prince has indirectly brought her.

In both scenes the triangle of affection within the Polonius family is the dominating factor. In I, iii, their concern for each other is expressed through well-meant but somewhat sadly heavy-handed advice. IV, vii, is given over to the blundering determination of the survivor to do his useless best for the other two by at least avenging them.

(*fourth scene*) I, *iv and* 'v'[1]

IV, *vi* (*fourth from last*)

It might at first sight seem absurd to 'pair' a scene of 281 lines with one of 32 lines. Yet the parallel between their places in the map of the action is perfectly clear. Claudius despatches both Hamlets: Old Hamlet to Purgatory, Young Hamlet to an intended death in England – naturally not expecting either to be able later to tell the story of their journeys. But first Old Hamlet does so (four scenes from the beginning of the play): then his son does the same (four scenes from the end.)

(*fifth scene*) II, i ———

Begins with Polonius seeking information about his son.

Ends with Ophelia's vivid description of a Hamlet clearly as near mad as makes no difference: 'mad for thy love?' . . .no, but distracted by a grief and horror certainly complicated by his feelings for Ophelia.

——— IV, v (*fifth from last*)

Ends with Laertes' furious search for information about the death of his father.

Begins with the presentation of an Ophelia driven mad: by a grief and horror certainly complicated by love/amorous feeling for Hamlet. (Cf. the mildly bawdy note of the St Valentine's Day song.)

It is likely, too, that Ophelia in IV, v is wearing some sort of female equivalent to the kind of dress that Hamlet is wearing (in her story) in II, i. For this was an accepted sign of madness, and Laertes grasps that she is mad before a word has been spoken.

(It is perhaps also worth noting that while the *presented* happenings of I, iv-v were matched by *reported* adventures in IV, vi, the converse happens in this immediately adjacent pair of scenes. There are other examples of this in the play.)

(*sixth scene*) II, ii ———

Is the last time we hear of Fortinbras and his Polack campaign until IV, iv.

Rosencrantz and Guildenstern *arrive*, at the King's behest, from Wittenberg, to keep an eye on Hamlet. (Are surprised to find the latter thinks Denmark a prison.)

———IV, iv (*sixth from last*)

Fortinbras and his Polack campaign are heard of again.

Rosencrantz and Guildenstern *depart*, at the King's behest, for England (with Hamlet as virtually their prisoner.)

***

We have now carried this pairing of material, scene by scene, right through the two first acts. (It is interesting to find, therefore, that in the judgements – *inter alios* – of the editors both of the Arden and of the old Harvard editions of

---

[1] The First Folio is surely correct, whether accidentally or not, in omitting any scene-division between I, iv and I, v. For in their movement, and anxious open-air encounters, they are obviously analogous to those sequences of separate exchanges with which Elizabethan playwrights tended to represent battles; and it appears originally to have been quite normal to

the play, we have also carried it right through the tragedy's last two acts as well. The old Harvard edition actually changes the standard act-divisions, delaying the start of act IV so that the normal 'IV, iv' becomes IV, i. The Arden editor states that only the inconvenience of upsetting a traditional scheme of textual reference stops him following suit. 'Harvard' act-divisions will be assumed throughout this present discussion, except when identifying specific scenes or making detailed textual references.) Even the apparent major 'loose end' represented by the various passages in II, ii about actors and acting (often felt by critics to be slightly digressive) seems to fall into place if one is willing to pursue the pattern apparently being traced here on into the central act.

The central act. It is not, of course, strictly necessary to pursue the 'pattern' on into act III at all. Instead, it might be argued, perhaps, that all we have really been analysing so far is just Shakespeare's rough tidying of the four outer acts of *Hamlet* into a kind of more-or-less regular frame for act III as a whole. But obviously the kind of ABC/CBA symmetry that we have been tracing does tempt one to think in terms of a progression onwards – and inwards – to some specific centre.

This is interesting for several reasons. Take, first, our general notions of the structure of Shakespearian tragedy. To a quite remarkable extent, these still derive from Bradley, the near-definitiveness of whose superb opening lectures can be measured by the degree to which we continue to reproduce his basic ideas today, even when attempting to challenge them. Characteristic in this respect, for instance, is Professor Marco Mincoff's 'The Structural Pattern of Shakespeare's Tragedies'[1] – a re-thinking of the issue that chances to afford an especially convenient starting-point for the line of thought to be followed here.

Bradley himself, constantly using metaphors of *rising* and *falling*, saw the essential form of Shakespearian tragedy as a sort of stepped pyramid. Within a broad three-part division of the action, he finds 'the usual scheme' to be 'an ascending and descending movement of one side in the conflict'. This 'rise' reaches a 'zenith' in a 'crisis' (e.g., the Mouse-trap in *Hamlet*) soon followed by a 'counter-stroke' beginning a 'descent'. The stepped profile of this broad rise and descent comes partly, he suggests, from a regular minor oscillation of fortune between the opposing parties in the conflict, and partly from 'a constant alternation of rises and falls...in the emotional pitch of the work'. The 'centre' of the action – it is curious how completely Bradley takes for granted the natural-ness of looking for this in a Shakespeare play, and the possibility of finding it – can lie either in the 'crisis' or in the 'counter-stroke': or in both jointly, since sometimes the latter follows on without any pause.[2]

At first sight, Professor Mincoff's own analysis looks very different, for he rejects the notion of tripartite structural division, and differs from Bradley, too, in finding that one specific play – *Hamlet* – manifests the 'true' Shakespearian structural pattern. Yet he again is dominated by the metaphor of rise-and-fall, writing interestingly of Shakespeare's tendency to give scenes a 'pyramidal' structure, forming

regard such sequences as constituting a single scene. (See W. W. Greg, *The Shakespeare First Folio* (Oxford, 1955), pp. 142–3.) In any case, momentum and sheer continuity plainly make I, iv and 'v' into a single unit even irrespective of such formal criteria.

(The other conventionally accepted scene-number-ings in the text, despite their late date, correspond much better to the facts of the play, and to Elizabethan practice.)

[1] *Shakespeare Survey 3* (Cambridge, 1950), pp. 58–65.

[2] A. C. Bradley, *Shakespearean Tragedy* (London, 1904), Lecture II, 'Construction in Shakespeare's Tragedies'.

separate units, carefully contrasted. Admittedly, some 'Shakespearian' structural patterning can often equally well be found in Shakespeare's contemporaries; but distinctively Shakespearian Professor Mincoff too agrees, is the achievement of a kind of rhythmic pulsation of emotional tension; and also – this begins to go beyond Bradley – a marked 'centring and emotional stressing of the turn of the action'. Unlike his predecessors ('who on the whole left the pattern of the play to take care of itself, or at least paid small attention to a centring climax or definite turn of the action... and still less to making such a turn coincide with the maximum of emotional tension') Shakespeare establishes 'a definite apex', with the play's tensions 'so graduated as to lead up to and down again from that peak'. Here is an interesting flowering of Bradley's casual allusions to the 'centre' of the Shakespearian tragic structure; and one made all the more persuasive by the context in which Professor Mincoff presents it:

It would seem... correct to ascribe this effect [*viz*: the centring of the turn of the action] to that completeness of structure... exemplified in so much sixteenth century art, in the closed, symmetrical composition of the Renaissance painters, and – a much nearer parallel – in so many of the more complex lyrics of the sixteenth century, such as Wyatt's *To his Lute*, Surrey's *Complaint of the absence of her Lover*, Spenser's *Prothalamion*, *Epithalamion* and *Ditty in Praise of Eliza*, which work up to the height of lyrical emotion in the exact middle and then fall slowly to the end, often in such a way that the first and last, second and penultimate verses or groups of verses are parallel.

(p. 65)

Yet how valid, really, is this use of the metaphor of rise-and-fall, when applied to *Hamlet*?

Certainly Hamlet's fortunes do in some senses 'rise' until about the middle of the play, declining thereafter. And naturally various parts of various scenes are pitched at varying emotional levels. But that is very different from claiming to find a sequence of recurrent tensions 'so *graduated* as to lead *up to*' an '*apex*' and then *down* again. Is not this, perhaps, rather something that one can persuade oneself that one has felt, after the event, on the basis of an abstract theory, than something actually experienced in the theatre? – parts of I, v, for instance, to take only one of many possible examples, can surely reach a pitch of intensity, on stage, that nothing later outdoes.

In any case, as the reference above to painting underlines, centric effects in sixteenth-century art were achieved by many means. Emotional 'apex-ing' (surely the least practicable of all for dramatists, interested in holding their audience's attention throughout every act, to imitate) was only one such device, itself commonly built, as Professor Mincoff notes, over a formal pattern of ABC/CBA symmetries – i.e., very much the type of patterning that we seem to have been tracing through four acts of *Hamlet*. On the other hand, such formal patternings do not necessarily carry any very strong emotional correlate. It seems not impossible, therefore, that Professor Mincoff may have made the right link between *Hamlet* and Elizabethan non-dramatic poetry, but chanced to stress the wrong aspect of that link.

That possibility is not diminished by some of the studies of formal, mannerist patternings in Elizabethan art and literature that have appeared since Professor Mincoff's own article was printed. Take, for instance, Alastair Fowler's recently-published *Triumphal Forms*.[1] Although Professor Fowler has raised a number of hackles, not least by some perhaps too-rapid theorising about the Sonnets, his book remains for all that an admirable exploration of the interplay of three aspects of Elizabethan aesthetics: (i) the liking for closed symmetrical constructions noted by Professor Mincoff; (ii) the pervasively spatial character of Renaissance thought – the sort of thing which could lead Drayton to feel that he had justified the

[1] Cambridge, 1970.

use of a particular stanza form by showing that it possessed the same proportions as 'the pillar which in architecture is called the Tuscan', or that could lead Jonson to define 'action' in drama as answering to 'place' in a building, with its own 'largeness, compass and pro- portion'; (iii) the preoccupation, so general and persistent as to amount almost to a nervous tic in the culture of the age, with the idea of the sovereign mid-point. These three elements Professor Fowler interestingly shows to be integrated in the iconography of the Roman triumph (stylised into a procession tending to be symmetrically arranged about a central triumphator) – an image which exerted a pervasive influence on art and ceremonial in the period. For, to quote Professor Fowler himself:

the spatial tendency of renaissance thought facilitated direct control of ideas by formal organisation; and conventions of centralised symmetry naturally carried over from political protocol into poetry, as they did into architecture. Poets developed the habit of distri- buting matter through the metrical structure with careful regard to the centre's sovereignty. Almost as a regular practice, they would devote the central place to some principal figure or event, or make it coincide with a structural division. (p. 62)

'Almost as a regular practice': it is not too strong a claim. It is astonishing how often one does find poets of the period marking the centre of their poems – most often by some image of, or allusion to, the ideas of sovereignty or triumph, even when these can have only the most perfunctory relationship to the general tenor of the poem in question. This remains true even when one has made full allowance for the ease with which wishful thinking can 'manufacture' centres. The habit seems quite marked enough to leave little doubt that the more sophisticated Elizabethan reader would himself tend to be on the look-out for such indications of the mid-point: which further strengthens the likelihood (for which anyway there is plenty of other evidence) that he would

also notice, and savour, even quite complex formal patternings – especially when these were in fact symmetrically disposed around the central point. Nor is there any reason to suppose, either, that such a reader could not also have enjoyed the various kinds of finesse between *double* centres which Professor Fowler further analyses in sixteenth-century poetry (meeting doubts that he is being over-subtle by pointing to parallel examples of the same practice in Renaissance architecture).

Even the most sceptical will see the tempta- tion to relate all this, however tentatively, to *Hamlet*. For – quite apart from any question of 'pairings' or symmetries – the whole weight of our critical tradition clearly tends towards seeing that play, too, as a double-centred structure. Nearly every traditional-style critic seems to feel that the tragedy *has* a centre or central turning-point: though disagreeing in locating it sometimes in the Mouse-trap and sometimes in the Bedchamber scene (though seldom anywhere else).

Yet 'why not both'? Both *are*, quite literally, formal mid-points, both identifiable by means current in the mannerist patternings of the period: the play's half-way mark[1] is reached

[1] Since *Hamlet* contains many prose passages and broken lines, it would be absurd to imagine Shake- speare ever attempting to locate the *precise* metrical centre (i.e., the line exactly at the half-way point) of either the play as a whole or of individual scenes. But it is not unreasonable to consider the possibility of his having located the play's half-way mark in some looser fashion: perhaps by making some rough computation of running-time, or (more likely) by counting MS. pages – much as many readers of this essay may well have done themselves when preparing a talk or lecture. It is in this looser sense that the business of the *Murder of Gonzago* will be found to lie across 'the play's half-way mark' – as a page-count of any facsi- mile Q2 will show – even though one cannot precisely locate that notional point itself. (The episode is long enough for its physically central position not to be significantly brought in doubt by any of the various uncertainties that plague textual studies of *Hamlet*.) [*note continued overleaf*

during the central episode of III, ii; while the Bedchamber scene is numerically central (tenth of nineteen scenes).[1] An accident? Perhaps. But at least a singularly happy one: especially in view of the persistent Elizabethan association of centrality with sovereignty. For a while the tragedy abounds in actual or potential royalty (even Laertes has the popular vote for the job); it is clear, nevertheless, that it contains only one truly sovereign figure: Old Hamlet. Speech after speech enhances our sense of his majesty. Not only does he rule the drama through a call for revenge which makes him the *primum mobile* setting in action all the wheels of the plot; but he is also the last 'true' King of Denmark in the quite simple sense that his successor unjustly owes his throne to poison. As we watch him trying to protect his wife, admonishing his son, and determined still to settle scores with his brother, there is no doubt who is still the effective head of the royal family of Elsinore.

How striking, then, that this royal figure (present nowhere else in act III) should chance to be associated – and in such clearly-differentiated ways – with *both* the play's customarily-identified 'centres'. For what routs King Claudius in III, ii? An image (as he sees it) of his murdered brother, the rightful sovereign. Yet this image was 'counterfeit': he yields the stage to a mere player-king – at what many critics see as the 'strategic centre' (the phrase is Anne Righter's) of a tragedy whose fundamental metaphor is itself a pun upon two different senses of the verb *to act*. But is there not something illusory, even so, about the 'Mouse-trap's' seemingly focal role? It does not, after all, enable *Hamlet* to sweep to his revenge; and Claudius was already planning to ship his nephew off to England anyway. Even Mrs Righter, convinced of the scene's 'strategic' centrality, and showing fascinatingly just *how* fully the whole idea of that scene may be regarded as the 'natural, almost inevitable

consequence' of the conversations about theatre-matters in II, ii, still feels obliged to allow that those same conversations (partly omitted, of course, in Q2) were nevertheless 'perhaps a trifle intrusive' in a play 'concerned with fate and character in mediaeval Denmark'.[2]

And so they are. Not just in immediate

There are other Shakespeare plays, too, whose underlying structure might be thought to become clearer when one has made this sort of loose identification of their half-way mark. *Love's Labour's Lost* – which also seems to exhibit symmetrical 'pairings' – is one case in point.

[1] Many people seem to find the idea of Shakespeare counting scenes, or otherwise consciously planning in scene-units, as absurd as the notion of him totalling up individual lines. There is an apparent tendency to be hypnotised by the undeniable fact that no edition of any Shakespeare play published during the poet's lifetime ever carried a full apparatus of numbered scene-divisions. Yet really that proves very little: after all, numbering is not counting. Even early texts of Renaissance works with an acknowledged number-symbolism content are not always equipped with any numbering or other typographical aid to the detection of that symbolism. More significant, surely, is the fact that surviving Elizabethan/Jacobean theatrical 'plots' do mark scene-divisions – and all the evidence suggests that authorial plots commonly did the same. Hamlet's own praise of a play for being 'well-digested in the scenes' seems extremely suggestive in this context, too.

As W. W. Greg points out, scene-division on the Elizabethan stage was structural, and followed directly from the action. So long, therefore, as the directions were clear, there was the less need to mark or number scene-divisions in the actual manuscript. (See Greg, *The Shakespeare First Folio*, pp. 142–5).

It may be added that *Hamlet* is not the only play in which there is evidence of Shakespeare's willingness to think and plan in scene-units. However one reacts to Prof. Battenhouse's numerological theories, for instance, it is hard not to share his feeling that it is unlikely to be entirely a coincidence that twenty-one scenes lead up to, and twenty-one follow, the turning-point of the Battle of Actium in *Antony and Cleopatra*. (See Roy Battenhouse, *Shakespearean Tragedy: its Art and its Christian Premises* (Bloomington, 1969), pp. 180–1.)

[2] Anne Righter, *Shakespeare and the Idea of the Play* (London, 1962), p. 159.

subject-matter, but also – *inter alia* – in disrupting our sequence of 'pairings', which after this point cease to be bracketings of scenes, although in other respects they seem to continue to narrow down, tidily enough, on to the (numerically central) Bedchamber scene.

The Bedchamber scene has of course been endlessly discussed: even those who find the tragedy's turning-point in the play-within-the-play still note the crucial importance of the hold which the murder of Polonius gives Claudius over Hamlet. Both Freudian interpretations and readings of the play in terms of the 'minister' / scourge-of-God distinction equally point to it as the drama's heart (while it might be argued that Freudian analyses only really put more dramatically something that in more general terms has always been grasped anyway). View the play as the presentation of a *world*, rather than an *action*, and the result is the same. A recent study of the 'shape' of the Elizabethan play has shown very well how regularly dramatists employed ('on a stage well matched to the purpose') a structure which places

the individual and private person and private or personal action at the center, surrounds that action with the action belonging to a city or state, and that public action with an international action, and finally that whole earthly action (not always, but often) with an unearthly action or area for action...Whereas in later drama we are usually made aware of only one or two of these spheres, in the Elizabethan we are usually made sharply aware of all...the scheme suggests, as it appropriately should, the concentric spheres of the Ptolemaic system.[1]

Hamlet itself strongly enforces precisely this schematisation upon us. Not only is the enclosure of a private, family tragedy within a separate nationally-relevant crisis there especially well-marked, but the country which is the scene of this troubled story is also set within a particularly well-defined ring of other kingdoms, to each of which some manifestation of the power centred at Elsinore reaches out. This

effect must have been further reinforced for Shakespeare's original audience by the precision with which it dovetailed with their own image of Denmark, as the (still somewhat menacing) power at the centre of 'the Northern Regions' – to them a more-or-less distinct division of the globe. Elsinore itself, too, was well-known as the cross-roads of this whole northern world: that famous place to which, in Mercator's phrase, the ships of all nations were compelled to come 'as to one common centre'. And at the centre of this centre was the fortress/palace of Kronborg, with the private royal apartments at its heart: in reality as in the play.

To that 'heart', in the play and at the play's own heart, comes Hamlet. (Not, it should be noted, to a 'bedchamber', despite the traditional label of III, iv, but to his mother's '*closet*'. Just how elegantly apt this choice of setting was for the tragedy's focal scene, even a glance at the *OED* will show.) And at the metrical centre of the scene itself, inevitably, appears the sovereign figure of Old Hamlet – not dimly intimated by a play-king, this time, but in his proper person, still advising and commanding: the true King at the play's true centre, setting both his son and the action of the drama back on the rails again.

Or is that too glib? Claudius at least *acts* the King most convincingly: so would not something more immediate than abstract retrospective plot analysis be needed, therefore, clearly to mark the Ghost's appearance in III, iv as the more *truly* 'sovereign' role?

Of course it would: were it not that this 'something more' seems in fact already firmly provided by the preceding scene. For, apart from duplicate information,[2] what does III,

[1] T. B. Stroup, *Microcosmus: the shape of the Elizabethan play* (Lexington), 1965, p. 41.

[2] We already knew that Claudius was having trouble with his conscience (III, i, 50) and that Hamlet shall to England (III, i, 169ff.) while we shall see for ourselves that Polonius is going to hide behind the arras – and hardly needed to be told why. Of course

iii contain? Only the non-stabbing of Claudius at prayer; and two static, sermonising speeches on kingship by Rosencrantz and Guildenstern – speeches that might almost have wandered into the play text from one of the Histories. That of Rosencrantz, in particular, is peculiarly undramatic, holding up the action like an aria in an opera (Claudius does not even find it necessary to reply) just to embroider, in melodiously varied ways, upon an idea already presented by Guildenstern anyway. Together, the two speeches constitute only a sevenfold repetition, prefaced by insistence on its 'holy and religious' significance, of that received Tudor truth that the monarch is the hub of the wheel of society, upon which all else depends. Nowhere else – not only in *Hamlet*, but indeed in the whole Shakespeare canon – is there anything quite like the same limited, insistent repetition of this one particular point. Considering the general density of ideas which *Hamlet* otherwise manifests, it seems quite beyond belief that so enormous a punctuation mark occurs at this point just by chance. It has, surely, all the appearance of a cue or marker.

And what it points to is not obscure. Its very ominousness tilts the emphasis back to Old Hamlet. 'The cease of majesty dies not alone ...but doth draw / what's near it with it'; yet this, we know, the death of the late King has yet to do. More than that, the two speeches firmly re-state a crucial test, which the rest of the scene is devoted to showing that Claudius fails, but which Old Hamlet passes uniquely well: thus clearing the ground for the latter's reappearance in the next scene. For no aspect of the Renaissance concept of kingship had been more hammered home for Shakespeare's contemporaries than the notion of the monarch as God's vice-gerent. Yet Claudius, as we are carefully shown, cannot even communicate with God, cut off from prayer by the retention of a crown which for this very reason is not altogether a true crown – as he himself knows.

For 'above', as he tells us, 'there is no shuffling; there the action lies / In his true nature' (III, iii, 61–2). By contrast Old Hamlet, returning to his kingdom only because supernatural powers allow it, to pursue the (obviously divinely-approved) tasks of ending the pollution of the sacred 'royal bed of Denmark' and punishing a sinner above the reach of human law, fulfils this aspect of the royal role to a degree that, in fact, no *living* man could ever do. No-one suspects in III, iv that here, too, might be a player-king: truth lies with the illusion.

'The true king / at the true centre.' Again we come back to the double assertion. As has recently been made clear, it would be quite consonant with Elizabethan literary practice to mark a sovereign mid-point by a royal presence *without* necessarily constructing any wider pattern of supporting symmetries around it at all. Nonetheless, having inspected the (presumptive) keystone, it is natural to build up the rest of our arch. Take, then, the odd affair of Polonius' body: an element in the play on which the plethora of commentators have been unusually silent. Why is so much of the second half of act III taken up with looking for it? To the present writer, at least, this episode has always seemed to have about it a touch of perverse irrelevance.

True, that is precisely what makes it so dramatically effective: its very unexpectedness, and the bustle of the search, clearly help prevent too great an anticlimax after the excitement of the Closet scene. And certainly it is all plausible enough: Hamlet, presumably, drags the body into some neighbouring room and simply abandons – rather than hides – it there. Then in the ensuing alarm (and darkness? these elements of III, iii are not therefore just *redundant*: they do serve a dramatic purpose, as part of a build-up of excitement ensuring that we know before it begins that III, iv is going to be important. But that only reinforces the general case for III, iv's intended centrality.

...it is midnight) the obvious place is overlooked and the conclusion is jumped to that mad Hamlet has hidden the body deliberately, Hamlet himself ironically playing along with the assumption. An effective piece of naturalistic observation, it might be said, spiced with residual doubts that perhaps Hamlet did, half hysterically, hide the body on purpose: just the sort of unsuitable bye-comedy that real life does often generate.

Yet is there not still a seeming break here, for good or ill, with a certain decorum? For while individual Shakespearian tragedies certainly vary profoundly, they do at least all give one the sense that some process, some sort of ritual, is darkly going forward, to which every event along the main line of action contributes. Of course wryly humorous observation is also there; but it is normally either smelted into something quite different ('pray you, undo this button') or else is as it were 'encapsulated' (the Gravediggers). It is from this point of view that the business of 'Hamlet, where's Polonius?' seems faintly odd. For though it is interwoven into the main line of the action at a crucial moment of the play, nothing comes of it. 'Hamlet, where's Polonius?' Eventually, he tells them; and that is that. It does not seem to carry the 'ritual' forward and hence has at first sight no very obvious place in the rites. Why did Shakespeare bother with it? Just to meet the sort of technical needs sketched in above? These could have been met in a score of ways.

Whether such a *Problemstellung* is thought acceptable or not, the fact remains that this part of the action does fall more plainly into some sort of 'ritual' place when oriented in relation to a central crisis. Although those who would reject all 'centric-' or ritual-minded approaches to the play can perfectly well deny the fact to be of any significance, it is undeniable that up to III, iv Polonius *is* hidden from (or talking about plans to hide from) Hamlet for most of act III – except during the 'false' centre provided by the Mouse-trap scene – whereas after III, iv he is instead hidden from Claudius. Thus when Hamlet's rough demand of Ophelia, 'Where's your father?' converts into 'Hamlet, where's Polonius?' it is at least not absurd to feel that one movement of a sinister ballet is being completed.

Claudius's failure to achieve prayer in III, iii, too, surely finds its own place in this same sombre dance. Claudius, living, cannot make successful appeal to Heaven: but Polonius' murdered body must and will do so. No cliché is more familiar in the rhetoric of Elizabethan melodrama than that of the murdered man whose-every-wound's-a-mouth-to-cry-to-Heaven. How tidy, then, that the Closet scene, which is *preceded* by (abortive) *prayer*, should be *followed* by the order to convey the old man's corpse *to the chapel*. Hamlet's instinctive, slightly hysterical evasion of surrendering the body falls more into place when seen in this perspective, too.

In short, it does seem arguable that a centric view of act III (as here defined) better activates what might perhaps seem otherwise to be an unusually 'inactive' section of the tragedy. Meanwhile acceptance of even a few pairings of course automatically opens up further, more tentative possibilities. There is much in the play that, while it could hardly be used to demonstrate, in its own right, any centred symmetry underlying the drama, nonetheless does fit comfortably with such a concept if that concept once gains acceptance by other means.[1] Not that every line and passage locks into a dead symmetry: an apter image would

[1] An example of this in the part of the play we have just been analysing, is the attack on Rosencrantz and Guildenstern as 'sponges'. If this passage is put side by side with the praise of Horatio in III, ii, then one has something that might approximately be said to be the obverse and reverse of one coin...but only approximately, so that it is only in the context of other pairings that it catches the eye.

be that of a statue constructed upon a symmetrical armature – not every part of which is likely to be covered with an equal depth of 'flesh', if the statue is to have life and momentum. In *Hamlet*, this symmetry / asymmetry dichotomy precisely parallels (and is indeed, I would suggest, intimately related to) that other dichotomy which everyone sees in the play, between its ritual quality and its contrasting vein of naturalism.

Obviously one large question remains. Could the analogy thus traceable between the organisation of *Hamlet* and that of some non-dramatic Renaissance works 'simply' be the reflection of subconscious pressure upon Shakespeare's mind from the general artistic climate of the day? If not, does it concern only the play's 'back-stage carpentry'; or is it something meant to be discerned by the judicious spectator (. . . or reader)?

Hamlet's structural tidinesses do seem often too marked to have escaped at any rate the conscious attention of the playwright himself, working as he was for a theatre alive to scene-divisions. Moreover, play-texts were much read; while *Hamlet*'s unpractical length does suggest that for Shakespeare this play perhaps grew into something to be valued more nearly as an autonomous literary object than as an actor's production-script. It might thus not be necessarily absurd to envisage him composing partly with an eye to the 'wiser sort' of reader rather than spectator. (For that matter, a pro-duction carefully worked out for some special audience or occasion *could* have pointed-up the play's 'tidinesses', via groupings, costumes, hangings, music, etc.)

But that is mere speculation. Still, it is at least worth noting (i) that Shakespeare does show evidence at times of wishing to challenge more socially-advantaged intellectuals in their own arena; (ii) that one of the 'worlds' of Hamlet is very much that of young-gentlemen-around-a-university;[1] (iii) that for no other play is explicit boast made of production at both universities;[2] (iv) that Gabriel Harvey noted the esteem of university-educated connoisseurs for the play – which he brackets for praise, as it happens, with the work of several poets who seem to have used numerological or patterned centric structures.[3]

[1] One passing remark of Hamlet's, apparently not altogether understood by commentators, which contributes to this general flavour of what might be called 'fashionable intellectualism' in the play, is his mocking reference (v, ii, 115–16) to Renaissance memory systems. Any Elizabethan audience qualified to relish that sort of allusion were surely qualified, too, to appreciate centric patternings, the taste for which was very much part of the same intellectual climate as the interest in 'memory theatres', etc.

[2] In Ch. 11 of *Shakespeare's Occasional Plays* (New York, 1965), J. M. Nosworthy presents an extremely thorough review of all the reasons for thinking that the Q2 version of *Hamlet* must have been prepared at least partly with a potential academic audience in mind.

[3] See his comments as quoted in E. K. Chambers, *William Shakespeare* (Oxford, 1930), II, 197.

NOTE (1978)

Readers interested in pursuing the wider issues raised by this essay may find it useful to consult Mr Brown's review-article in *Essays in Criticism*, XXVII, no. 1 (Jan. 1977), a discussion of Mark Rose's *Shakespearean Design*.

Rose's book, an important trail-breaking study published more or less simultaneously with Mr Brown's *Shakespeare Survey* essay, also of course requires to be studied in its own right.

THE PRINCE OF DENMARK AND CLAUDIUS'S COURT

JULIET McLAUCHLAN

In *King Lear* and *Macbeth*, in different ways, the hero by his own actions sets tragic forces in motion; in *Othello* the hero is gradually 'wrought' to destructive passion; but when *Hamlet* begins, someone other than the hero has already violated the natural order of the kingdom, and the hero, although profoundly disturbed, is only partially aware of the evil which is entrenched. Hamlet's original 'intent' to go back to Wittenberg seems to reflect a feeling of helplessness and a desire simply to escape from Elsinore as it now is. Agreeing to stay, he rightly senses that 'it is not, nor it cannot come to good' (I, 2).[1] Thus, for the hero of *Hamlet*, the situation is from the very start one of tragic disruption: to see the play in terms of a conflict which shatters the prince when he is faced with life in the Denmark of Claudius constitutes a key approach – not a new one, but, as I hope to demonstrate, one which it is illuminating to carry further. In this play Shakespeare creates and intensifies the sense of tragic conflict by particularly subtle and oblique *presentation* of concepts of the universe, the state, and man, which were familiar in his day.[2] As they are also familiar to all students of Shakespeare I wish to draw attention only to points most relevant to subsequent discussion.

The first concept underlying my argument is that of the Great Chain of Being. In this imagined hierarchy of created things, man was thought to enjoy a unique potential: *ni ange ni bête*, he could move upwards, through the exercise and control of reason, towards angelic apprehension and even godlike qualities, or he could move downwards, through the dominance of passion, towards the level of the beast. In *Hamlet*, the inevitable tragic conflict begins with Hamlet's immediate and painful sense of the bestial qualities embodied in Claudius and, what to the prince is worse, his mother's faithlessness to her marriage vows through her hasty union with the 'satyr'. She, too, has been brought down to the brute level – or even lower, for 'a beast, that wants discourse of reason, / Would have mourn'd longer', he cries (I, 2). Hamlet's passionate feeling of revulsion (seemingly an intuitive thing) is further intensified when he is cruelly shocked into awareness of sheer evil, through the revelation that his father has been murdered. My argument will seek to show that Shakespeare presents in *Hamlet* a conflict between the humanistic Wittenberg ideal with its upward aspirations, and the negation of it at Elsinore. He shows this ideal to have been Hamlet's and to have been embodied for him in

[1] All references are to H. H. Furness, New Variorum *Hamlet* (Phila. 1879; rep. N.Y. 1963).

[2] I am not maintaining that there was ever any single universally accepted medieval, Renaissance, Elizabethan, or other view of the cosmos and man's place in it; nor am I maintaining that Shakespeare was deliberately presenting in *Hamlet* or any of his plays an 'Elizabethan view' known and accepted by himself and everyone in his audiences. I am suggesting that in *Hamlet* Shakespeare shows certain views (mainly in conflict) which had long been known and discussed, and were therefore familiar to his audiences.

the figure of his father, 'a man, take him for all in all, / I shall not look upon his like again' (I, 2).

Arthur Lovejoy has written of that

> plan and structure of the world which, through the Middle Ages and down to the late Eighteenth Century, many philosophers, most men of science and, indeed, most educated men, were to accept without question – the conception of the universe as a 'Great Chain of Being', composed of an immense, or – by the strict but seldom rigorously applied logic of the principle of continuity – of an infinite number of links ranging in hierarchical order from the meagrest kind of existents, which barely escape non-existence, through 'every possible' grade up to the *ens perfectissimus*.[1]

This unquestioning acceptance did not rule out widely divergent views on cosmography and on man's place in the order of things: sometimes a Ptolemaic universe with the earth at its centre was seen as beautiful and man's position as favoured; sometimes 'the centre of the world was . . . the place farthest removed from the Empyrean, the bottom of the creation, to which the dregs and baser elements sank'.[2] Whether in a Ptolemaic or a Copernican universe, however, man's position remained crucial, for 'this planet alone contained a race of free creatures half material and half spiritual – the middle link in the Chain of Being – for whose allegiances the celestial and the infernal powers compete'.[3] Medieval Christian philosophy, like Neoplatonism before it, was faced with a choice between two concepts of God: one, the goal of the 'way up' for the soul which aspired to regain changeless perfection and rest; the other 'the source of and the informing energy of that descending process by which being flows through all the levels of possibility down to the very lowest'. Choosing the former, it thus

> shaped the assumptions concerning man's chief end which dominated European thought down to the Renaissance, and in orthodox theology, Protestant as well as Catholic, beyond it. The 'way up' alone was the direction in which man was to look for the good.[4]

Hamlet has seen life in the idealistic light of this concept of following the 'way up'. To this exalted ideal he suffers a shattering blow, which proves tragic in its effects upon him: we see the disintegration of his own wholeness as a man and, worse, watch his responses to the evil around him, responses which are passionate and ultimately destructive to others and to himself, rather than rational. It is what Hamlet suffers, is, and does in the course of the play, which pre-eminently constitutes the tragedy of *Hamlet*.

The second concept basic to my argument is that the king served (under God) as head of the body politic, and the health of this body depended upon the virtue of the king. This is in line with the medieval and Elizabethan doctrine of the king's two bodies, which Anne Barton (paraphrasing Ernst Kantorowitz in *The King's Two Bodies*) defines as a '*body natural . . . which is mystically united* at the moment of coronation with a *body politic*', this 'dual identity' then belonging to the king for life (italics are mine).[5]

These long-held and much-discussed concepts involved the conviction that a violation of any one part of the natural order of things must bring disruption into the rest. By Shakespeare's day they had been challenged in many ways, but in particular (for the purpose of this discussion): the concept of man's noble potential by Montaigne's deeply cynical writings on the baseness of man's nature and the weakness, even 'imbecillitie of man's

[1] Arthur Lovejoy, *The Great Chain of Being* (Cambridge, Mass. 1936), p. 59.
[2] *Ibid.*, p. 101.
[3] *Ibid.*, p. 103.
[4] *Ibid.*, pp. 83–4.
[5] 'Shakespeare: His Tragedies', Sphere History of Literature in the English Language, vol. 3 (*English Drama to 1710*, ed. Christopher Ricks, London, 1971), p. 219.

reason';[1] the concept of the ideal ruler by Machiavelli's writings on practical and realistic statecraft.

In *Hamlet* we see, mainly through the two protagonists, the shattering of familiar Renaissance (and earlier) ideals through conflict with a Montaigne-Machiavelli world – a world where the weapon of man's reason is not adequately used (by Hamlet) and where, in any case, it seems that reason would be powerless to 'set it right'.

Emphasising the conflict, deep ironies arise from the fact that the traditional positives of kingship and of man's potential are often expressed at Elsinore by those whose behaviour and values are a negation of what is asserted. Furthermore, there is sometimes more than the usual degree of irony when a character speaks more truly than he realises. Claudius, for instance, refers to Fortinbras as:

> Holding a weak supposal of our worth,
> Or thinking by our late dear brother's death
> Our state to be disjoint and out of frame
>
> (I, 2)

His sarcastic words imply his own worth and the health of his state; yet a weak supposal of Claudius would be the right one, and his Denmark *is* 'disjoint' and 'out of frame' precisely by his brother's death – or rather by the manner of it. While the court is completely taken in, Shakespeare would not intend his audience to miss the irony. The appearance of the Ghost in scene 1 would, for Elizabethans, be enough to make these words suspect; they would thus stand out, and the empty claim would still be resonating as the truth of the situation soon became clear.[2] At the end of the play's first 'movement', Hamlet's words provide a direct echo: 'The time is out of joint' (I, 5), as it now obviously *is*. 'Disjoint' and 'out of frame' are exactly right to suggest painful bodily dislocation which must prevent normal functioning; 'out of frame' brings in the cosmological order, since such phrases as 'this universal frame',[3] 'this wonderful and incomprehensible huge frame of God's works',[4] 'the universal frame of this world' and 'worldly frame'[5] appeared in many contemporary works.[6]

By Claudius's violation of the natural order,

[1] 'An Apologie of Raymond Sebonde', Ch. XII, Bk Two in Montaigne, *Essays*, as translated by John Florio (London, 1603; Everyman Edition, London, 1935), p. 255. The Nonesuch Edition, ed. J. I. M. Stewart (London, 1936), is the most authoritative, but is not readily obtainable. Frances Yates, in her *John Florio* (Cambridge, 1934), p. 213, points out that Florio's translation was licensed for publication in June 1600, and she mentions written references to it as early as 1600, concluding that it 'must have been circulated in manuscript' around 1598. This means that it could well have been seen by Shakespeare before its publication. Although the whole matter is still the subject of scholarly controversy it is certain that, beginning with the Second Quarto of *Hamlet* (1604), many apparent 'echoes' of the Sebonde essay come into the text; study of these is of the greatest interest.

[2] I do not wish to imply that we should feel here anything like the full extent of Claudius's hypocrisy and villainy. However, the play's first scene (with its unnatural tension, and the foreboding which springs from the intrusion of the supernatural) has suggested strongly the rottenness of Denmark, to which Shakespeare adds important clues – clues which would be less likely to be missed by an Elizabethan audience than a present-day one.

[3] Pierre de la Primaudaye, 'Of Policy and the Good Ordering of Estates', from *The French Academy*, trans. T. Bowes, 1586, reprinted in James Winny (ed.), *The Frame of Order* (London, 1957), p. 113.

[4] Thomas Digges, *A Perfit Description of the Celestiall Orbes*, etc. (London, 1576), reprinted Winny, *ibid.*, p. 152.

[5] Annibale Romei, *The Courtier's Academy*, trans. J. Kepers (London, 1598), Winny, *ibid.*, pp. 200, 207.

[6] Two examples from Florio's translation of the Sebonde essay show (not the generally euphuistic style of his translation but) the general application of these terms. He renders 'toute cette machine' and 'ce grand bastiment' (Montaigne, *Essais*, Tome II (Paris (Nelson), 1934, p. 59 and p. 64) by, respectively, 'this vast world's frame' and 'the huge world's frame', Florio (trans.) *Essays*, p. 135 and p. 139.

his state is 'rotten' and evil is established. He has murdered the rightful king, who was also his brother; although his marriage to the dead king's widow has been sanctioned by the court, Elizabethans would see it as incest, and this in itself would cast doubt upon the king's smooth explanations; similarly, although his accession has been formally approved according to Danish custom, the Ghost soon reveals that he is, in the spirit if not the letter, a usurper. The force of the Ghost's words:

> so the whole ear of Denmark
> Is by a forged process of my death
> Rankly abused; (I, 4)

would be much greater to an Elizabethan audience than to us.[1] The deliberately ambiguous uses of 'Denmark' in *Hamlet* (now referring, as here, to the body politic, now to the murdered king, now to Claudius) work to emphasise the inseparable link between the king and the health, or otherwise, of his state. The most extraordinary thing about Claudius is the blandness with which he assumes that he has become, in the true sense, 'Denmark'. He speaks as if he sees himself firmly within the order which his deeds have grossly violated. Gertrude, too, entirely accepts this; true, she is not aware of his crime, but it is a serious indictment of a weak and obtuse nature that she can beg her grieving son to 'look like a friend on Denmark'. Claudius goes further, even imagining that Hamlet can and will stay on at Elsinore as 'our chiefest courtier, our cousin, and our son'. Publicly making the prince his heir, he appears to see himself as successfully assimilating into his court, and even into the closest family relationship, the devoted son of the king he has murdered. To Hamlet such a relationship can seem only a ghastly parody (and so it should seem to the audience), yet Gertrude again seconds her husband's words with her plea to the prince to stay with 'us'.

To Claudius appearance is the reality of the situation. His murderous plot having gained him the throne, he operates as the epitome of smooth courtly condescension. The court accept the appearance of kingship with no apparent reservations. As 'Denmark' Claudius has a quick success in his diplomatic move *vis à vis* Norway. According to Machiavelli:

fortune, especially when she wants to build up the greatness of a new prince, whose need to acquire standing is more pressing than that of a hereditary ruler, finds enemies for him, so that he may have reason to triumph over them and ascend higher on the ladder his foes have provided.[2]

Fortune provides Claudius with just such an external threat: his triumph comes, characteristically, through a strong diplomatic stand. His manner is such as to reassure the court immediately (long before it is known that his move has succeeded) and this adds much to his appearance of kingship, even to the quite

[1] I am grateful to Nigel Alexander for giving me permission to quote a comment in which he develops what he calls the 'enormous dramatic implication' of my 'two bodies' argument: 'Claudius, as usurper (although the legally elected monarch) is trying to take over the body politic of Denmark. The only visible sign that this take-over is unlawful is his clearly unlawful and incestuous taking-over of the body of "the imperial jointress to this state" Queen Gertrude. The rape of the body politic of Denmark is thus truly symbolised by the lustful seduction of the body of Denmark's queen – and Hamlet's deep disgust at that act is partly because he can sense the deep political disorder of which it is so clear a sign.'
[2] Nicolò Machiavelli, *The Prince*, trans. George Bull (London, 1961), Ch. 20. I prefer this translation, but others are readily available, notably the World's Classics, trans. Luigi Ricci (London, 1903), revised E. R. P. Vincent (1935); and the Everyman's, trans. W. K. Marriott (London, 1958). The date of the first known English translation is 1640, so it is impossible to know how Shakespeare became familiar with Machiavelli's ideas. The English notion of Machiavellism was unquestionably 'in the air' in his day and that is enough, although Vincent suggests the existence of manuscript translations, and refers to a known Scots translation between 1580 and 1590.

erroneous belief (accepted by some critics) that he might have made a good ruler if only the Ghost and Hamlet had let well alone. The natural order has been violated in *Hamlet* as surely as in *Macbeth*. If the violation seems less blatant, it is simply because of the 'plastering art' which 'beauties' the 'harlot's cheek' of Claudius and his kingdom. In *Macbeth* the murderous usurper soon turns tyrant and his crimes are so evident that supporters begin to mistrust him, hate him, and desert his service, while Claudius continues to be surrounded by loyal courtiers.

The nature of loyalty at Elsinore is, however, very searchingly investigated. Horatio, alone, is truly loyal (to Hamlet as friend and prince); otherwise loyalty is, unquestioningly, to the *throne*, the worth of its occupant being simply assumed. The suggestive way in which the imagery works in *Hamlet* to show underlying corruption of the accepted ideal is very clear in Claudius's words to Laertes:

> The head is not more native to the heart,
> The hand more instrumental to the mouth,
> Than is the throne of Denmark to thy father.
>
> (I, 2)

The body of Claudius's Denmark functions and is sustained precisely through interdependence of usurper and blind supporters. Significantly, the support which Claudius enjoys is purely *court* support. The people hardly figure at all in the play: that they are not loyal to Claudius is apparent from their readiness to make Laertes king, and the love of the 'general gender' for Hamlet.

Polonius sees and expresses his loyalty in elevated terms:

> Assure you my good liege,
> I hold my duty as I hold my soul,
> Both to my God and to my gracious king
>
> (II, 2)

– unexceptionable words, if addressed to a truly gracious king by a courtier less blind in his loyalty, and less forgetful of past loyalty, for surely he has very recently served another 'Denmark'? Polonius is no Machiavel; he is simply obtuse, and when he maunders on about the folly of expostulating 'what majesty should be, what duty is', he clearly has no conception of either.

When Rosencrantz and Guildenstern arrive they vie with each other in piling phrase upon obsequious phrase. Rosencrantz declares that the 'majesties' of Denmark could by their 'sovereign power' put their 'dread pleasures' into commands instead of simply requesting service. Guildenstern rushes to add: 'But we both obey', finishing off Rosencrantz's line, and the rest of his words follow headlong:

> And here give up ourselves, in the full bent,
> To lay our service freely at your feet,
> To be commanded.   (II, 2)

Embodied in the very movement of this verse is their eagerness to throw themselves, literally if need be, at the feet of the king and queen: the positioning of 'bent' and 'commanded' gives the words weight, and the progressive shortening of the lines, with the breathless repetition of 'To lay . . .', 'To be . . .' adds to the effect. Blind sycophancy is the more blatant since we learn from Claudius that these young men have been 'of so young days brought up with Hamlet'; the prince first welcomes them warmly as 'My excellent good friends' and 'Good lads', and later appeals to them 'by the consonancy of our youth'; they have long known Hamlet, his parents, and the 'fair state' of the past, yet they know as little as Polonius how to value friendship and love or to assess true worth or majesty. It is part of the subtlety of Shakespeare's presentation of Claudius's court and state that these two consummate toadies should try to express the true positives of kingship, and particularly (again) the mystical unity between king and body politic:

Most *holy and religious* fear it is
To keep those *many many* bodies safe
That *live and feed* upon your majesty.

Rosencrantz immediately takes up this assertion of Guildenstern's and among other fulsome protestations, sees the king as:

That spirit upon whose weal *depends and rests*
The lives of many.

(III, 3; italics are mine)

The most obvious effect of this oblique presentation of the traditional ideal is to force the audience to see the contrast between these declarations and the realities of Elsinore, but the language itself makes this effect more interesting. With one exception, the italicised phrases (and others, 'strength and armour', 'singular and peculiar', even 'mortis'd and adjoin'd') are noticeably less forceful than are many of Shakespeare's complementary phrases (as Granville Barker has noted).[1] They are intentionally banal, spinning out and weakening the accepted positives, so that in their very words the toadies devalue what they say. The phrase 'live and feed' works differently: it provokes in the audience a response opposite to anything Guildenstern intends. He means the words to describe positive interdependence of people and king;[2] what they actually suggest is the sort of gross parasitism which Rosencrantz and Guildenstern represent. Moreover, what is really living and feeding upon the 'majesty' of Claudius is the 'imposthume' of his crime. Claudius himself (and this is again characteristic of the presentation in *Hamlet*) states the true position, though seeing it in the context of his own need to get rid of Hamlet:

but so much was our love,
We would not understand what was most fit,
But like the owner of a foul disease,
To keep it from divulging, let it *feed*
Even on the pith of *life*. (IV, 1; italics are mine)

Exactly. Claudius, trying to keep secret the foul disease which he owns, has been letting it

devour the living substance of his state: 'food' and similar words, recur throughout *Hamlet*, to suggest gross sensual appetite, ugly parasitism, or devouring disease.

If it were not already plain just what sort of courtiers Rosencrantz and Guildenstern are, it would become so when they speak as they do of Claudius, whom they see as a true king in fruitful relationship to the body politic – Claudius, whose guilt has just been confirmed in the play scene, who *is* now to the audience a 'damned smiling villain'. Hamlet's taunting words place the toadies exactly:

Hamlet. Besides, to be demanded of a sponge, what replication should be made by the son of a king?
Rosencrantz. Take you me for a sponge, my lord?
Hamlet. Ay, sir, that soaks up the king's countenance, his rewards, his authorities. (IV, 2)

Claudius's appearance of kingship is shown here in all its worthlessness. Hamlet is, of course, putting into precise perspective the extravagant words of Rosencrantz and Guildenstern, but what is more interesting is that the audience has no need of a nudge from Hamlet in order to judge them. What it does need is to see Hamlet's awareness of the nature of their relationship to the king and to see that this is part of his justified loathing of all that Elsinore has come to stand for since his father's death.

The full title of the play is *The Tragedy of Hamlet, Prince of Denmark*: much of the tragedy lies in the fact that the *prince* has been 'rose' of his father's 'fair state' and its 'expectancy', whereas he is now, against all inclination, crown prince of Claudius's Denmark.

[1] *Prefaces to Shakespeare, Hamlet* (London, 1930 and (Batsford Paperback) 1968), p. 170.
[2] Cf. *Macbeth*, I, 4 for the finest expression of this: the ideal king grateful and bountiful, has 'planted' and will 'labour' to make his loyal subjects 'full of growing'. Malcolm later acknowledges the same ideal, which is also embodied in the saintliness of the English king.

IA Gertrude's bedroom (III, iv): James Bailey's design for Michael Benthall's production,
1948. The platform and arches were permanent features of the set

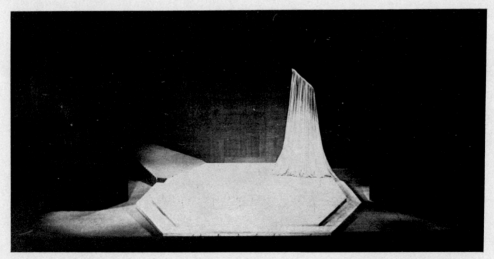

IB A view from the dress-circle of the permanent set (known as 'the bread-board') designed by
Michael Northen for Michael Langham's 1956 production, in which Alan Badel played Hamlet

II Leslie Hurry's basic set for Peter Wood's production, 1961, as arranged for
the graveyard scene (v, i)

IIIA 1, iii: Ophelia (Helen Mirren), Polonius (Sebastian Shaw), and Laertes (Christopher Gable)
in Trevor Nunn's production, 1970. The lutes provided an ironic foreshadowing of Ophelia's mad
scene (see Plate XI)

IIIB 1, iii: Polonius (André van Gyseghem) with Laertes (Stuart Wilson) and Ophelia (Yvonne
Nicholson) in Buzz Goodbody's modern-dress production at The Other Place, 1975

IVA II, ii: Hamlet with the players in Peter Wood's production, 1961. *L.* to *r.*, Ian Richardson as Guildenstern, David Buck as Rosencrantz, Ian Bannen as Hamlet, Tony Church as First Player

IVB III, ii: Hamlet's advice to the players: Robert Helpmann in Michael Benthall's production, 1948

V A III, ii: The play scene in Michael Benthall's production, 1948, in which Paul Scofield (seen here) alternated as Hamlet with Robert Helpmann. Diana Wynyard (*l.*) as Gertrude, Anthony Quayle as Claudius, and Claire Bloom (*r.*) as Ophelia

V B The same scene in Buzz Goodbody's production, 1975. *L.* to *r.*, Terence Wilton as Second Player, Bob Peck as First Player, Stuart Wilson as Fourth Player, Charles Dance as Third Player

VI III, iii: The prayer scene in Michael Benthall's production, 1948: Robert Helpmann as Hamlet and Anthony Quayle as Claudius

VII III, iii: The prayer scene: David Warner as Hamlet and Brewster Mason as Claudius
in Peter Hall's production, 1965

VIIIA III, iv: 'Look here, upon this picture, and on this': Michael Redgrave, with coin and locket, in Glen Byam Shaw's production, 1958; Googie Withers as Gertrude

VIIIB The same scene in Peter Wood's production, 1961; Ian Bannen and Elizabeth Sellars

IXA III, iv: The closet scene: Ben Kingsley as Hamlet and Mikel Lambert as Gertrude in Buzz Goodbody's production, 1975

IXB III, iv: Hamlet (David Warner) and Gertrude (Elizabeth Spriggs) on the Queen's bed; Peter Hall's production, 1965

X IV, v: The mad Ophelia: Dorothy Tutin in Glen Byam Shaw's production, 1958

XI iv, v: The mad Ophelia, obeying the 'bad' quarto's direction 'playing on a lute' (cf. Plate III A). *L.* to *r.*, David Waller as Claudius, a courtier, Christopher Gable as Laertes, Helen Mirren as Ophelia, and Brenda Bruce as Gertrude, in Trevor Nunn's production, 1970

XII v, i: The Gravedigger (David Waller) and Hamlet (David Warner) in the 1966 revival of Peter Hall's 1965 production

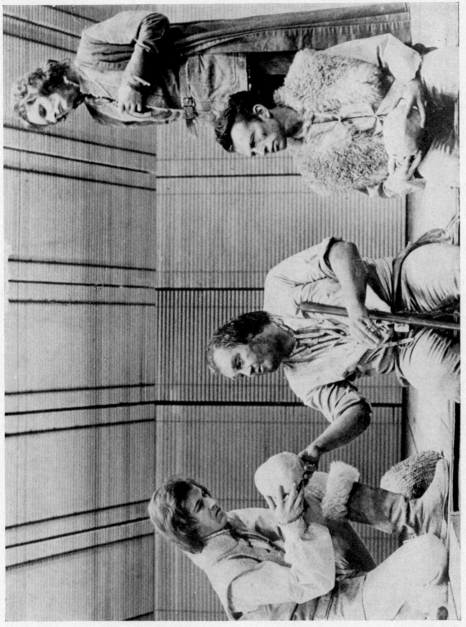

XIII v, i: The graveyard scene in Trevor Nunn's production, 1970. Alan Howard as Hamlet, Barry Stanton as First Gravedigger, Ralph Cotterill as Second Gravedigger, and Terence Taplin as Horatio

XIVA v, ii: 'Come, begin,/And you, the judges, bear a wary eye': the beginning of the duel in Trevor Nunn's production, 1970. Christopher Gable as Laertes, Peter Egan as Osric, Alan Howard as Hamlet

XIVB v, ii: The duel, in Peter Wood's production, 1961: Peter McEnery as Laertes, Ian Bannen as Hamlet

XV v, ii: The dying Hamlet: Terence Taplin as Horatio, Alan Howard as Hamlet in
Trevor Nunn's production, 1970

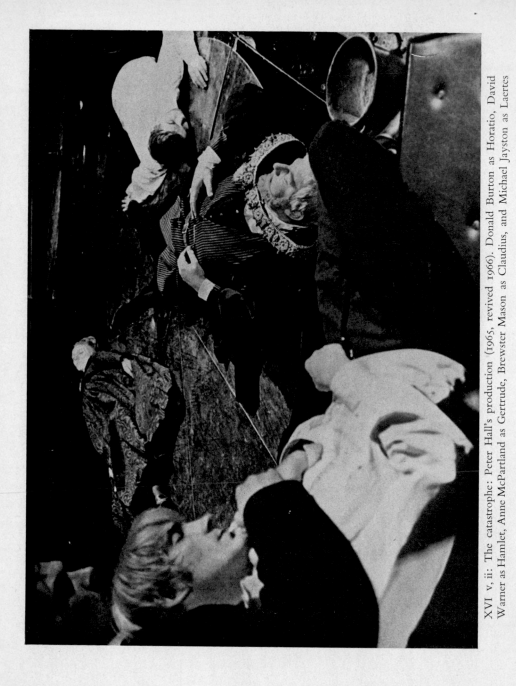

XVI v, ii: The catastrophe: Peter Hall's production (1965, revived 1966). Donald Burton as Horatio, David Warner as Hamlet, Anne McPartland as Gertrude, Brewster Mason as Claudius, and Michael Jayston as Laertes

While he cannot and should not acquiesce in such a denial of the natural order as would make him truly heir to a murderous usurping 'uncle-father', he must remain virtually imprisoned in this false court situation so long as he fails to come to terms with the duty laid upon him by his father's spirit. Conflicts within himself delay this so that the state is not finally purged until after Ophelia is dead (largely by Hamlet's fault, although she is not herself blameless) – too late, that is, for any restoration of the 'fair state' with Hamlet at its head, for the link between Ophelia and Hamlet (as the state's 'expectancy') is crucial to the future. Nigel Alexander sees the graveyard scene as one of the play's 'most tragic', precisely 'because the characters are burying the future'.[1]

The court obviously accepts Hamlet as crown prince. Because of Hamlet's position, Laertes warns his sister, and once again the image is of the body politic:

> for on his choice depends
> The safety[2] and health of the whole state.
> And therefore must his choice be circumscribed
> Unto the voice and yielding of that body
> Whereof he is the head. (I, 3)

Polonius's warning has been in similar terms (II, 2).

Hamlet sees the underlying court situation as evil because his ideal of kingship is inseparable from his ideal of 'a man'. The sort of a king a man will make depends upon the sort of man he is. Hamlet mourns his father as 'so excellent a king', with all the force of the word 'excellent', but it is his father as a man and as his mother's husband that he most reveres in memory. Horatio recalls him as 'a goodly king', and 'goodly' goes beyond external appearance to connote the admirable and worthy, but to Hamlet:

> He was a man, take him for all in all,
> I shall not look upon his like again. (I, 2)

Later Hamlet speaks to Gertrude in terms which lift his father's human qualities to the god-like: majesty (Jove, king of gods); valiance (Mars, god of war); old Hamlet's bearing has seemed to his son like that of the gods' messenger at the moment of touching the earth, the earth where it is nearest heaven, the verse suggesting aspiration upwards in 'heaven-kissing hill'. The old king has:

> A combination and a form indeed,
> Where every god did seem to set his seal
> To give the world assurance of a man

> (III, 4)

To Hamlet the god-like is a seal set upon the human when man attains his highest potential.

How far is this ideal really established in relation to old Hamlet? How much is it simply the son's idealisation of a beloved father? The words used of the Ghost, 'majestical', 'slow and stately', 'fair and warlike', 'valiant' (while living), 'solemn', 'courteous', 'more in sorrow than in anger', suggest a martial figure of regal dignity. There is little in the text to suggest that his own reference to his 'foul crimes' is more than a formal protestation of general guilt by one who has died without absolution. Some critics hold that the Ghost's demand for vengeance is evil and robs the old king of any nobility. Two points seem relevant: the 'rotten' state must somehow be purged of its evil; the demand of the soldier-king is made in terms of an accepted code, such as is followed without question by Laertes, and which is not questioned even by Hamlet himself. Old Hamlet takes on some of the attributes of the ideal king (and man) simply through deliberate contrasts with Claudius. Claudius's acknowledgement of his crime and his own realisation of its ugliness give weight to the Ghost's assessment of him, and to

[1] *Poison, Play and Duel* (London, 1971), p. 151.
[2] First Folio reads 'sanctity'; Theobald, Hanmer, *et al.* 'sanity'.

Hamlet's. It is clear that old Hamlet is *not* invested with the sort of value Shakespeare gives to Duncan; but, perhaps, whether or not he was all that Hamlet believes is less important than the simple existence of Hamlet's ideal, and the ways in which crucial details in the play's imagery link old Hamlet with this ideal.

Most significantly, value is associated with him chiefly through his love for Gertrude, which Hamlet recalls as a sort of gentle and protective devotion:

> so loving to my mother,
> That he might not beteem the winds of heaven
> Visit her face too roughly   (I, 2)

The Ghost's own description (I, 5) is very much in the same key (and see below).

The ideal and the negation of it, which the prince immediately senses at Elsinore, are evoked in his first soliloquy. The 'excellent' king and 'loving' husband was to Claudius 'as Hyperion to a satyr': this lifts the brightness and glory of the rightful king towards the god-like, while the usurper is brought down to the lecherous and beastlike. At the very beginning, therefore, Hamlet links his father with man's upward potential, his uncle with man's potential debasement. By contrast to his father's love, Hamlet recalls his mother's response in grossly sensual terms: 'as if increase of appetite had grown by what it fed on', and then in a key passage links her, too, with man's potentiality for debasement:

> O, God! a beast that wants discourse of reason
> Would have mourn'd *longer* ...
>   (I, 2; italics are mine)

Debasement occurs when 'reason panders will', in his later words (III, 4).

This recalls Montaigne's contention that not only was man not superior to beasts, he was indeed inferior to them in some ways, hence my italicised 'longer'. Montaigne wrote:

Brute beasts are much more regular than we, and with more moderation containe themselves within the compasse which nature hath prescribed them ... As some of our nations have wives in common ... so have some beasts; yet some there are that observe their marriage with as great respect as we do ours.[1]

Montaigne tells also of beasts which so mourned the death of masters as to be inconsolable and even to seek their own deaths.[2] We should note that it is for Hamlet, not the audience, that the dichotomy between a bestial Claudius and a godlike father is absolute. Claudius is complex and interesting, precisely because he is not a beast but a man, with considerable human potential, who slips towards the bestial through failure to control passion with reason.

Returning to the Ghost's speech, we can see how Shakespeare contrasts most dramatically, through the pattern of the language, man's upward and downward potential:

> O, Hamlet, what a falling-off was there!
> From me, whose love was of that dignity
> That it went hand in hand even with the vow
> I made to her in marriage: and to decline
> Upon a wretch, whose natural gifts were poor
> To those of mine!
> But virtue, as it never will be moved,
> Though lewdness court it in a shape of heaven,
> So lust, though to a radiant angel link'd,
> Will sate itself in a celestial bed,
> And prey on garbage.
>   (I, 5)

The note of pain and grief, coupled with the deliberately shocking contrasts in the imagery, lift this above the vaunting of an unworthy and complacent husband or the whinings of a cuckold. Hamlet's earlier description of his father's love and of his mother's appetite is taken up here in stronger terms. The first line sets the tone, after which the words flow smoothly, complementing one another until,

---

[1] Florio (trans.), *Essays*, p. 166, p. 174.
[2] *Ibid.*, p. 165.

in the middle of the passage, comes a direct contrast of values, which is intensified and rendered concrete by sharply antithetical words *within the lines* that follow. There is also a movement *from line to line* upwards: 'love', 'dignity', 'hand in hand', 'vow', 'marriage', 'virtue', 'shape of heaven', 'radiant angel', 'celestial'; human values come first and rise to the heavenly. This parallels an ugly movement downwards, which details the 'falling-off': 'decline', 'wretch', 'gifts' . . . 'poor', 'lewd-ness', 'lust', 'sate', 'prey on garbage'.

The Ghost's mention of the marriage vow is echoed twice by Ophelia (I, 3 and II, 1): '. . . almost all the holy vows of heaven' and 'music vows' which Hamlet has made to the 'celestial' Ophelia, his 'soul's idol' suggest that his idealistic sense of love has followed his father's. Hamlet later rebukes Gertrude for her broken vows, which her actions have made 'as false as dicers' oaths'. (Throughout Shake-speare great value is attached to vows and oaths.) The Ghost's last words seem to con-firm the value of this husband's love, and the validity of Hamlet's view of it. He forgets his desire to spur his son to revenge and pleads with Hamlet to show compassion to his mother, his last words, 'Speak to her, Hamlet'.

The significance of this is that Hamlet's ideal of his father, and thus of man, seems to have been based upon his ideal view of his parents' marriage; his deep disillusionment with man and with life springs *primarily* from the shock to this ideal. Hamlet rightly sees an ugly degeneration from love to lust in Gertrude's second marriage, and it is certainly this, rather than the political disruption of Denmark, which disturbs Hamlet most and rouses his most passionate outbursts.

Hamlet's magnificent prose speech on the universe and man, in which he evokes a familiar Renaissance ideal in noble terms, is a key passage:

I have of late, – but wherefore I know not, – lost all my mirth, forgone all custom of exercises; and indeed it goes so heavily with my disposition that this goodly frame, the earth, seems to me a sterile promontory; this most excellent canopy, the air, look you, this brave o'erhanging firmament, this majestical roof fretted with golden fire, – why, it appears no other thing to me than a foul and pestilent congregation of vapours. What a piece of work is man! how noble in reason! how infinite in faculty! in form and moving, how express and admirable! in action,[1] how like an angel! in apprehension, how like a god! the beauty of the world! the paragon of animals! And yet, to me, what is this quintessence of dust?

(II, 2)

The words in which Hamlet reveals his own distaste for the beauty and splendour of the universe are meant to shock: the earth now seems not a fruitful and admirable 'frame', framed in turn in an ordered universe, but a 'promontory', exposed and 'sterile'. The air and heaven seem (with the suggestion of a positive stench of corruption) to be 'foul' and plague-ridden 'vapours'. The paradox, 'quin-tessence of dust' works in a remarkable way. 'Quintessence' first creates the expectation of the distillation of something rare and fine, following on from the high human potential which Hamlet has been outlining. Then comes the terrible deflating effect of the mono-syllables, 'of dust' – with all the connotations of mortality, decomposition, and utter worth-lessness carried by the word 'dust'.

So, in contact with Elsinore, the Wittenberg student's whole view of the world and of man has degenerated. This accounts for Hamlet's growing obsession with the physical state of death and decomposition, with all that is im-plied in 'a king may go a progress through the

[1] John Dover Wilson adopts the Q2 punctuation in his *Hamlet* (Cambridge, 1934); in *Shakespeare and the Nature of Man* (Cambridge, 1934), Theodore Spencer calls this the punctuation 'which alone makes sense in terms of Elizabethan psychology'. I prefer it too: '. . . admirable in action; how like an angel in apprehension; how like a god!'

guts of a beggar'. He sees 'your fat king and your lean beggar' as being brought to 'one table', the worm's. 'Degree' has ceased to exist. In the reduction of the noble Alexander to something like 'this' (a stinking skull), and in the phrase 'your worm is your only emperor',[1] not only is there a reversal of man's aspiration (man no longer striving upwards in the chain of being, with the emperor looked upon as highest and most admirable in the human hierarchy) but there is a downward movement, from emperor to base dust. Hamlet has come to see the noble 'piece of work' as fragmented into its component parts or as reduced to its ultimate state of decomposition. He questions the purpose of human birth and life:

> and did these bones cost no more the breeding,
> but to play at loggats with them?
>
> (v, i)

and his next words, 'Mine ache to think on't', bring his sense of futility and mortality so close that he feels it deep within his own body. Similarly, politician, courtier, lawyer, jester, all are seen as coming to one end, rotting in the earth. By now, Hamlet has made and remade the point, but he goes on musing on a possible ignoble end for the 'noble dust' of Alexander and, against the mild protest of Horatio, stubbornly follows in detail the processes of Alexander's death, burial, return to 'dust', 'earth', his 'loam' finally being used 'to stop a beer-barrel'. And he must still go on to consider in similar fashion the possible fate of 'Imperious Caesar'. This insistence and repetition emphasise his obsession with the negative 'progress' of man. Just then he sees the arrival of the funeral procession, with the king and queen. This rounds off the point ironically: Hamlet had just brought all earthly power and glory down into a precise and infinitely belittling perspective: it is in fact the nature and behaviour of this 'king' ('a thing...

Of nothing') and of his wife, especially the nature of their 'love', which have brought Hamlet's view of kingship and of man so low.

Part of the tragedy of *Hamlet* lies then in our suffering with the prince in his deepening awareness of evil and in his consequent agonising loss of belief in man's potentialities. This is not the whole of it. In Elsinore, Hamlet's own personality, his embodiment of his own ideal, suffers disintegration. Ophelia's words of mournful remembrance are as crucial to the play as is Hamlet's great speech on the Renaissance ideal:

> Oh, what a noble mind is here o'erthrown!
> The courtier's, scholar's, soldier's, eye, tongue,
>   sword,
> The expectancy and rose of the fair state,
> The glass of fashion, and the mould of form,
> The observed of all observers, quite, quite down!
> And I, of ladies most deject and wretched,
> That suck'd the honey of his music-vows,
> Now see that noble and most sovereign reason,
> Like sweet bells jangled out of tune, and harsh;
> That unmatch'd form and feature of blown youth
> Blasted with ecstasy
>
> (III, i)

The more we imagine the whole man, as she recalls him, the more we feel the tragedy. Courtier, soldier, scholar – of this Renaissance prince there are only glimpses.

Soldier – on the battlements Hamlet draws his sword and is ready to use it in order to break free from restraint; he acts quickly in the encounter with the pirates, and fights creditably in the duel. Most significantly, Fortinbras, the soldier-prince who becomes 'Denmark', judges that Hamlet would have 'proved most royally had he been put on', and at the end lays repeated emphasis on the fact that Hamlet is to be accorded the treatment and rites due to a soldier.

[1] Montaigne wrote: 'The heart and life of a mighty and triumphant Emperor, is but the break-fast of a seely little Worme.' Florio (trans.), *Essays*, p. 155.

Scholar – most clearly Hamlet is (or has been) the scholar; above all, the scholar of Wittenberg, that great centre of Renaissance humanistic thought, the first university north of the Alps to go beyond medieval patterns of belief and teaching. We often see the inquiring, active, even playful aspects of Hamlet's mind; much less, as will be seen below, of its reasoning powers.

Courtier – the prince should be Denmark's 'chiefest courtier', not Claudius's, for we cannot imagine Hamlet with the 'candied tongue' capable of 'licking the absurd pomp' of the Danish court. There are flashes of princely behaviour, of a characteristic combination of gracious dignity with frankness and informality, but at Elsinore, where Claudius and his courtiers are parodies of true courtliness, Hamlet's behaviour is deliberately most uncourtly. In keeping with the oblique presentation of positives in this play, we have from Claudius, Elsinore's consummate 'courtier', a view of Hamlet which is revealing:

> he being remiss
> Most generous and free of all contriving,
> Will not peruse the foils.
>
> (IV, 7)

Towards the end of the famous passage in which Machiavelli counsels princes on the necessity of combining the attributes of the lion (strength and courage) and the fox (cunning), he also says that the prince must know how to:

act according to the nature of both man and beast . . . he cannot survive otherwise . . . those princes who have known best how to imitate the fox have come off best. But one must know how to colour one's actions and to be a great liar and deceiver. Men are so simple . . . that the deceiver will always find someone to be deceived.[1]

This is the way Claudius operates; again Shakespeare's presentation is striking. In Claudius's words we recognise at once Hamlet's nature, with an accompanying shock

of horror and revulsion, for the 'fox' will triumph through unscrupulous use of knowledge of his victim. There is the usual obvious dramatic irony here, but it is painfully intensified when we see the unsuspecting Hamlet with Laertes a little later, apologising for having hurt his 'brother' and (doubtless offering his hand) agreeing that he 'will this brother's wager play'. Here is a glimpse of Hamlet, courtier of the 'fair state' – generous, frank, trusting.

Shakespeare emphasises the disintegration of the prince by images which show in the world around Hamlet fragmentation of the whole man. Farthest from the prince in every sense, is the soldier; the unreflective, aggressive, forthright man of action, Fortinbras. But old Hamlet, too, is mainly shown as a *soldier*-king, with only minimal suggestions of the courtier, none of the scholar. Perhaps a significant element in the tragedy is that the *whole man* is asked to carry out a command based on the code of the soldier-king. Closest to Hamlet is the scholar: the rational, devoted man of thought, Horatio. All around Hamlet is the courtier: appropriately not compressed into a single figure, but multifaceted, even caricatured, especially in its last incarnation, Osric. Superficial, affected, chameleon-like in his views, a rich land owner, and only one of many on whom the 'drossy' time 'dotes', this 'waterfly' is placed exactly by Hamlet's words; these show the depths to which courtly standards are sinking under Claudius, and the metaphor echoes once again the dominant conflicts of the play:

> let a beast be lord of beasts
> and his crib shall stand in the king's mess
>
> (V, 2)

The tragedy of *Hamlet* goes further than the disintegration of the Renaissance prince. The evil, the 'imposthume' in the Danish royal

[1] *The Prince* (trans. Bull), Ch. 18.

family and state, so horrifies Hamlet that it evokes evil in response. The corruption of personality, family, and state is as ugly as Hamlet thinks it is, but the upsurge of evil within him is ugly too and destructive. Hamlet, whose ideal is 'that man that is not passion's slave', who believes that reason and moderation (like Horatio's) should control passion, becomes almost obsessed by hatred of evil, and is more often swayed by passion than ruled by reason. How can we account for this? Montaigne expressed the desire to make men feel: 'the emptinesse, vacuitie, and no worth of man; and violently to pull out of their hands the silly weapons of their reason'.[1] Is it this 'silly weapon' that fails Hamlet? In his last soliloquy, he passionately and half-despairingly asserts, in very characteristic terms, the value of reason:

> What is a man,
> If the chief good and market of his time
> Be but to sleep and feed? a beast, no more;
> Sure, he that made us with such large discourse,
> Looking before and after, gave us not
> That capability and god-like reason
> To fust in us unus'd.   (IV, 4)

Surely, he asks, man should not be just a beast? Surely he must use his reason? And Hamlet has been using his reason. Or has he? Later in this soliloquy he wonders if he may have been thinking 'too precisely upon the event'; if so, there is little evidence of it when we see Hamlet in thought or action, nor have we often seen him reasoning out alternative courses of action. The first soliloquy is no reasoned assessment of the situation but a passionate outpouring of deep grief and bitter disgust, culminating in resigned acceptance of heartbreak and silent inactivity. To the encounter with the Ghost he responds more passionately than rationally. The second soliloquy includes a passionate response to the player's speech, a passionate denunciation of himself, a passionate outburst against Claudius,

then more self-denunciation before he finally does set his brain to work on the idea of the play. 'To be or not to be' leads into a prolonged and complex meditation, rather than to concrete reasoning on specific problems. In the short soliloquy (III, 2) there is little reasoning, for Hamlet characteristically finds here some outlet in words, but is clearly swept by a passionate desire to act violently against his mother. Fear that he may actually do so leads him to resolve to exercise control. What happens as he debates the killing of Claudius, at prayer? Nigel Alexander argues very persuasively that Hamlet has at this stage every intention of acting as Pyrrhus and Lucianus do, and that, ironically, it is only the very blackness of his hatred and of his desire for total revenge which holds him back and saves him from sinking to the level of this type of revenger.[2]

Do we then see in *Hamlet* a twofold failure of reason: (1) to show the prince how to deal with evident external evil and (2) to enable him to control evil within himself? I would argue, rather, that his passionate response to evil is so intense that for the most part reason is simply not invoked at all. Instead of reasoning, Hamlet habitually verbalises the emotions which spring from his deeply-felt failure to come to terms with the problem – *with a problem which in fact reason cannot solve.*[3] Can reason show Hamlet any action which will restore an order which has been brutally and permanently destroyed? Old Hamlet is dead, Gertrude is 'one flesh' with the satyr who murdered him. Can the irreversible be reversed by any rational action? Even if reason should sanction the revenge to which passion prompts Hamlet (and this is never reasoned out) will this put things right?

In this situation Hamlet reacts not with

[1] Florio (trans.) *Essays*, p. 137.
[2] Alexander, *Poison, Play and Duel*, pp. 115–18; 196.
[3] David Daiches and L. C. Knights, Sussex Tape on *Hamlet*, discuss this in an illuminating manner.

reason, but swings from passionate outbursts to wry mockery to weary apathy. This last seems to spring from a partial awareness of the hopelessness of any action. His sense of evil and his obsessive hatred of it dominate him and sometimes carry him almost beyond rational control. Gertrude doubtless needs a brutal shock to make her see 'black and grainèd spots' within herself, but Hamlet revels in his rage and disgust, renewing his ugly attack in gross detail even after his mother's conscience has been roused. Much sadder, indeed crucial to the tragedy, is Hamlet's failure to use his reason in the one direction where reason could set something right. Sickened by totally imaginary evil and corruption in Ophelia, Hamlet rails pitilessly at the innocent, infinitely vulnerable girl who loves him. A touch of reason would lead Hamlet to some understanding of her behaviour. His failure to understand her is crucial to the tragedy, because from the moment that he in effect rejects her, there can be no hope of eventual re-establishment of the 'fair state' with Hamlet at its head.

Nigel Alexander, too, sees the Hamlet–Ophelia relationship as crucial and treats it fully and sensitively. Reproducing Titian's painting (Plate 4) *Amor-Pulchritudo-Voluptas*, which he sees as portraying 'an initiation of Beauty into Love',[1] he shows how Hamlet's pervasive sense of evil causes him to take a distorted view of the natural sequence 'from *Pulchritudo* through *Amor* to *Voluptas*'. Similarly, in Raphael's *The Three Graces*, which Alexander also reproduces (Plate 2):

The different qualities of these three female figures together make up the feminine principle... [and] just as each man must strive, in his choice of life, to be a union of wisdom, power, and pleasure, so every woman must be a combination of chastity, beauty, and passion... They [the Graces] must all be pursued if the individual is to acquire within his own soul the harmony of the dance which is also in tune with the music of the spheres and the divine order of the world.[2]

Alexander points out that in the nunnery scene the natural progression of Beauty from Chastity to the fullness of sensual pleasure, is perverted to the honesty–beauty–bawd sequence, Hamlet's three terms corresponding to the three Graces (Chastity, Beauty, Pleasure), except that the third becomes lust. Hamlet sees as inevitable 'a progression to lust'.[3]

This provides a splendid and original insight, and once again, from this rather different standpoint, we see the reversal in Hamlet of a familiar Renaissance ideal – another aspect of his obsession with man's *downward progression*. It emphasises, again, the fact that Hamlet's total ideal has been based upon an ideal of love. Once this has been shattered by his mother's 'falling off', he never stops to question his certainty that all women share the same corruption. Significantly, he rails passionately against his mother and the innocent Ophelia. Towards the corrupt court he turns only a mocking wit, never losing control as he does when he thinks of his mother's behaviour.

Hamlet's sense of evil extends, of course, to himself. It is in no sense a pretence (as is Malcolm's in *Macbeth*), but deeply felt, and again he sees it as springing from his mother's corruption. In the nunnery scene, he says he could accuse himself of 'such things', that 'it were better my mother had not borne me', and asks 'what should such fellows as I do crawling between earth and heaven?' Hamlet's disillusionment with man has gone so far that he has come face to face with evil within himself, and by this stage it seems to have paralysed any capacity for love. Real remembrance of his love (involving a kind of realisation of its value) comes only when it is too late: at Ophelia's graveside.

Does *Hamlet*, then, show the failure of

[1] Alexander, *Poison, Play and Duel*, p. 138.
[2] *Ibid.*, p. 139.
[3] *Ibid.*, pp. 140–1.

'Renaissance man' to master through reason the Machiavellian and the beastly in man? Montaigne insists that man's reason alone must fail; he contends (though some doubt his sincerity) that God's grace is essential if 'wretched' man is to raise himself above the brute. The Renaissance ideal did not, as Hamlet seems to do, stop at reason. Reason, working downwards upon sense data, had the task of abstracting from them: 'the immaterial forms which they contain. These forms are then apprehended intuitively, by the *understanding*, or intellect, which is akin to the pure intellect of the angels, and which is therefore a higher power than the "discourse of reason"'. And finally, there is *will*, 'which we use', says Raleigh ('A Treatise of the Soul', in *Works*, ed. Oldys and Birch, (London, 1829), VIII, 586), 'to stir us up to seek God and heavenly things, and are delighted and satisfied in them . . .' (my italics).[1] Hamlet, then, classes reason too high when he calls it 'God-like'. Unnecessary to higher beings, reason was man's distinguishing quality, and was, even so, only a tool to enable him to rise higher. Castiglione puts it like this:

And because in our souls there be three manner waies to know, namely, by sense, reason, and understanding: of sense there arises appetite or longing, which is common to us with brute beastes; of reason ariseth election or choise which is proper to man; of understanding by the which man may be partner with Angels ariseth will.[2]

Hamlet's failure to invoke even reason necessarily prevents his attaining to understanding or to a true sense of will, on which action might properly be based.[3]

There is a curious inversion of the reason–understanding–will sequence in Claudius's long speech to Hamlet (I, 2). Hamlet's grief shows 'a will most incorrect to Heaven', 'an understanding simple and unschooled', and is finally, 'to reason most absurd'. Why does Shakespeare do this? There are obvious ironies in the plain reversal of the traditional

upward order by one who personifies man's downward potential. Furthermore, the whole speech constitutes an example of careful but completely specious reasoning, characteristic of Claudius. '[Reason's] cry' cannot be 'This [death of fathers] must be so' when death is murder, disruptive of family and state. Claudius's understanding of himself and of the whole natural order is gravely at fault; his will is 'incorrect to Heaven', incorrigible, indeed, as we see when he fails to pray.

As the truth is presented so obliquely in *Hamlet*, more may be implied even than this. Will Hamlet's will be basically incorrect to Heaven, in that he does not subject it to higher control? Will his understanding remain simple and unschooled, not for the reason that Claudius adduces (his unmanly grief), but because Hamlet simply does not follow the upward course from reason to understanding (a crucial failure in Ophelia's case)? Is Hamlet's grief, with its concomitant bitterness and hatred of evil 'to reason most absurd' (senseless that is) because reason will not be able to control his passion, or to order the situation, or make any sense of it?

Any discussion of *Hamlet* must raise more

[1] Spencer, *Shakespeare and the Nature of Man*, pp. 12–13.

[2] Baldesar Castiglione, Book IV of *The Book of the Courtier*, trans. Sir Thomas Hoby (London, 1588); Everyman edition (London, 1928, 1948). A modern translation, Charles S. Singleton (New York, 1959), renders Hoby's 'understanding' (Italian 'intelletto') by 'intellect'. The whole of Book IV is of the greatest interest in the study of *Hamlet*.

[3] As a useful qualification, or corrective, to my whole view here, I quote another comment from Nigel Alexander: 'Hamlet frequently acts on his instincts rather than his reason – but his instincts have led him to the presentation of that union of intellect and emotion, a stage play. It is this act of "conscience" in every sense of that term which I think puts revenge-murder for ever beyond him (despite his instincts) in the prayer scene – it's the catching of the conscience of Claudius, which he had set out to do, which defeats the murderous intentions of Hamlet'.

questions than it answers. One large question will be: how much is put right or changed (in Hamlet) after his return from his voyage? He indulges in no more inconclusive verbalising of his conflicts, no more railing against evil. Although he is still acutely conscious of evil, he now thinks of it in terms of 'perfect conscience' and asks:

> is't not to be damned
> To let this canker of our nature come
> In further evil   (v, 2)

– which is to come much nearer the point, for the state must somehow be purged.

Most significantly, instead of the many references early in the play to Fortune (and indeed Hamlet's tragic situation, so far as he is concerned has been brought about by 'slings and arrows of [a particularly] outrageous fortune'), there are references to Heaven as 'ordinant', to 'divinity', to 'special providence', which seem to show some acceptance of the workings of a higher power. Here is the speech which contains Hamlet's most positive affirmation:

> Rashly,
> And *praised be rashness for it* . . . let us know
> Our indiscretion sometimes serves us well,
> When our deep plots do pall, and *that should teach us*
> There's a divinity that shapes our ends
> Rough-hew them how we will.
>   (v, 2; my italics)

To this Horatio gravely replies 'That is most certain'. Curiously Hamlet seems here to link divine guidance with his own rashness and even 'indiscretion' (the very opposite of reasoned action). He also explains that his brain had begun the 'play' 'Ere I could make a prologue' – that is, he acted without planning or reflecting. It is as if, abandoning the rational, he has come to feel the activity of something beyond and above human endeavours; it is after his similarly unreflecting action in killing Polonius that he refers to himself as having been punished by being made 'heaven's scourge and minister'.

There is, however, no such positive sense of heavenly control of affairs in *Hamlet* as we see in, say, *The Winter's Tale*. Despite Hamlet's few positive affirmations, we do not come to the end of the play with any conviction that the prince has attained higher understanding, or even regained wholeness as a human being. In the storm of evil, external and internal, in which he has been caught up, too much has been destroyed. This is not to say that 'the readiness is all' implies merely a fatalistic resignation or exhaustion, but Hamlet does seem in a sense spent. There is simplicity and beauty (but of a very ambiguous kind) in his last words, 'The rest is silence', no real affirmation. It is left to Horatio to confirm our feelings: despite all the degradation, the 'falling off' which we have watched in Hamlet in the course of the play, it is a 'noble heart' which has cracked; a 'sweet prince' has died. These comments do not sentimentalise Hamlet, but like Horatio's last prayer that 'flights of angels sing thee to thy rest', serve directly to link Hamlet once more with the great potential envisaged for Renaissance man. Indeed the whole man is once more evoked as both soldier and scholar praise in their own ways the dead prince. This constitutes a final and infinitely sad irony: in *Hamlet* the waste which is characteristic of tragedy is seen as a failure to fulfil a noble and precisely defined potential.

© JULIET McLAUCHLAN 1974

'HAMLET' AND THE 'MORIAE ENCOMIUM'

FRANK McCOMBIE

Perhaps the most impressive feature of Shake-speare's *Hamlet* is the way he has managed to transform a crude Norseman of the heroic age into a Renaissance prince of such impressive presence. Speculation about how it was done has led commentators a merry dance through sixteenth-century history and ideas. The place of Erasmus there, which no one familiar with the century would wish to dispute, has not really been taken into sufficient account in such speculation, considering first, how inescapable his influence was in general, and second, how much evidence there is in the plays that Shakespeare was familiar with his work[1] – and especially with the *Moriae Encomium*. Positive proof of first-hand acquaintance has, of course, been lacking; but circumstantial evidence is of sufficient weight to command attention. The *Moriae Encomium* was a grammar-school text in the 1570s and 1580s,[2] and it is perfectly possible that Shakespeare knew it as early as that, having perhaps been set to translate it himself. Schoolboys who were able to get hold of a copy must have been tempted to consult the Chaloner translation as a crib (it was first published in 1549, with subsequent editions in about 1560 and 1577); but there is, of course, no reason to think that Shakespeare did, though in later years he may well have known it. Whatever the truth of that, his acquaintance with the *Moriae Encomium* is supported by a wide range of what seem to be direct echoes of not only its thinking, but also its illustrative material. To mention only a few of the more

obvious which have drawn notice. There is a fairly direct relationship between Shakespeare's presentation of wisdom-in-folly in *King Lear* and the particular exposition of that philosophy in the *Moriae Encomium*,[3] both works finding a basis of thought, generally, in paradox, with particularly the animal imagery cast in very similar terms. There are general echoes in the love's-madness theme of *A Midsummer Night's Dream*; in the general conception of the wise fool in *As You Like It*;[4] in the world-as-a-stage motif in *As You Like It* and

---

[1] On Shakespeare's general acquaintance with the work of Erasmus, see Kenneth Muir, *Notes and Queries* (October 1956), pp. 424–5. John W. Velz, in *Shakespeare and the Classical Tradition* (Minneapolis, 1968), lists many suggestions from critics over the past hundred years, echoes notably being discovered in *As You Like It* and *Troilus and Cressida*, plays roughly contemporaneous with *Hamlet*. A recent instance of such detection – of, apparently, a direct echo of the *Moriae Encomium* – is offered by Jürgen Schäfer in *Notes and Queries* (April 1969), pp. 135–6.

[2] See T. W. Baldwin, *Shakespere's Small Latine* (Urbana, 1944), I, 436. There is further evidence in an unpublished dissertation by William Charles McAvoy on 'Shakespeare's Use of the *Laus* of Aphthonius' (Illinois, 1952). See *Dissertation Abstracts*, XIII (1953), 97.

[3] This has been much discussed; the argument is presented at length by Enid Welsford, *The Fool: His Social and Literary History* (London, 1935), pp. 236ff. A more recent discussion appears in Robert H. Goldsmith, *Wise Fools in Shakespeare* (East Lansing, 1955).

[4] See Welsford, *The Fool*, pp. 251–2 *et passim*; also John D. Rea, 'Jaques in Praise of Folly', *Modern Philology*, XVII (1919), 465–9.

The Tempest;[1] and a rather more precise echo in the implications and terminology of Gonzalo's speech on the nature of the island in *The Tempest*, II, i.[2] The general similarity of the turn of thought in the *Moriae Encomium* (probably Lucianic in origin) has always struck readers as being quite startlingly Shakespearian.[3] What I want to suggest, however, is something rather more particular than general similarity.

Although a variety of sources for Shakespeare's humanistic ideas makes better sense than a single source, and though one should not wish to argue for anything so patently absurd, it is nevertheless intriguing that so many of those ideas should echo the *Moriae Encomium* so insistently. It would not, for instance, be absurd to speculate upon how far the *Moriae Encomium* – which was only one example out of a whole field of 'fool' literature – owes its sustained popularity in this country to the fact that Shakespeare has attuned us to its characteristic modes of thought. The relationship is that close.

In proposing Hamlet, then, as a student of Wittenberg, a man in most ways at odds with the atmosphere of his uncle's court, as also – it is at least arguable – he had been with that of his heroic father, Shakespeare required a touchstone. Hamlet had to be given a humanist's turn of mind, even of phrase, to contrast, on the one hand, the world of chivalric heroics voiced by the Ghost and still sustained by Fortinbras, and on the other, that of Machiavellian political chicanery and treachery represented by Claudius and, in the event, by Laertes. What I want to suggest is, quite simply, that Shakespeare knew the *Moriae Encomium*, knew it well, and knew also that it precisely served the need.

The *Moriae Encomium*, written in 1509, first published in 1511, was valued in reformation England for its vigorous attack upon the abuses of the Church of Rome. There was a good deal more to its popularity than that, however. Quite notoriously (as the editing hand of Chaloner found), it was anti-chivalric, anti-heroic, and non-patriotic, in much of its content; and in proposing a specifically Christian view of the roles and duties of the prince, it was anti-Machiavellian. Although Erasmus often regretted the particular fame it brought him (watching propagandists carving it up piece-meal was galling), the *Moriae Encomium* did in fact epitomise the intellectual and moral convictions of the Christian humanists, ranged widely in support of its arguments, and powerfully illustrated a charac-

[1] See, for example, Thomas Woodhouse, 'All the World's a Stage', *Notes and Queries* (October, 1881), p. 311.

[2] Gonzalo plays with the thoughts that led men to name the West Indies 'The Fortunate Isles'. He projects a kind of paradise in impractical terms which could only have a rationale in paradise itself, and is thus an easy target for the wit of worldlings like Antonio and Sebastian. The irony is that the foolish prating old man proves his wisdom, first by showing a holy disposition that may win him salvation, second by recognising that what he is doing is merely (judged in practical terms) a 'merry fooling'. The line of thought followed by Erasmus when he makes the Fortunate Isles the birthplace of Folly (Sir Thomas Chaloner (trans.), *The Praise of Folie*, ed. Clarence H. Miller (EETS, London, 1965), pp. 12–13) is very close to all this, even as to imagery: 'I was brought foorth . . . euen amiddes the Ilandes, whiche of their synguler fertilitee and fruitefulnesse, are called Fortunatae, where as all thynges grow vnsowed and vntilled. In whiche iles neither labour, nor age, nor any maner sickenesse reigneth, nor in the fieldes there dooe either Nettles, Thistles, Mallowes, Brambles, Cockle, or suche lyke bagage grow, but in steede therof Gylofloures, Roses, Lilies, Basile, Violettes, and suche swete smellyng herbes, as whilom grew in Adonis gardeins, dooe on all sides satisfie bothe the sente, and the sight.' We note that of the three plants mentioned in the exchange between Gonzalo and his tormentors (nettles, docks, and mallows), two are in Folly's list; and that mallows are mentioned nowhere else in the plays.

[3] There is an essay on this by Alexander H. Sacton, 'The Paradoxical Encomium in Elizabethan Drama', in *University of Texas Studies in English*, XXVIII (1949), 83–104.

teristically humanist approach to the practical business of day-to-day living. Much of what Erasmus propounded there became, of course, the humanistic small change of the century; but the breadth and complexity of the echoes in *Hamlet* argue a relationship deeper than any mere echoing, and more significant than any echo could be. If, as I shall argue, Shakespeare consciously selected it as a touchstone of humanist thinking for his portrait of a humanist prince, he did particularly well; for the *Moriae Encomium* afforded him not merely a wealth of characterising detail, but a whole ethos of which to make him typical. He derived, in other words, not only a large part of Hamlet's character, but a world out of which he might act: not only a *persona*, but a place for him to stand.

In what follows, I have drawn for quotations particularly upon Kennet's translation (published by Woodward in 1709), as I do not wish to hang any part of the central argument upon Shakespeare's intimate acquaintance with the Chaloner, which at many points is less reliable in any case. Where it seems useful, however, I quote additionally from the Chaloner, in square brackets, sometimes from him instead of from Kennet, where the tone seems to me to have been more nicely caught. I have kept the Wilson translation (published 1668) in mind too, though it is altogether too free (and too politically coloured) to be much use here. The Erasmus text I have occasionally quoted directly, using the Basle edition of 1515.

To start, then, in the most familiar place. The precise quality of Hamlet's mind, it has been commonly felt, is revealed in some of its complexities in the 'To be, or not to be' soliloquy. Here, I hope we can take it, Hamlet is reflecting in a specifically, but also traditionally, humanistic way, less perhaps upon particularities than upon generalities. Quotation of his actual words is scarcely required to see how the drift and quality of his thinking is broadly similar to that of the following:[1]

And now were any one plac'd on that Tower, from whence *Jove* is fancied by the Poets to Survey the World, he would all around discern how many Grievances and Calamities our whole Life is on every Side encompassed with: How Unclean our Birth, how Troublesome our Tendance in the Cradle, how liable our Childhood is to a Thousand Misfortunes, how Toilsome and full of Drudgery our Riper Years, how Heavy and Uncomfortable our Old Age, and lastly, how Unwelcome the Unavoidableness of Death. Further, in every Course of Life how many Wracks there may be of torturing Diseases, how many unhappy Accidents may casually occurr [*sic*], how many unexpected Disasters may arise, and what strange Alterations may one Moment produce? Not to mention such Miseries as Men are mutually the Cause of, as Poverty, Imprisonment, Slander, Reproach, Revenge, Treachery, Malice, Cousenage, Deceit, and so many more, as to reckon them all would be as puzz'ling Arithmetick as the numbering of the Sands.

(Kennet, pp. 47–8)

Erasmus goes on to reflect that men can scarcely wonder that the Virgins of Milesia, contemplating such miseries, hanged themselves; and yet men cling to life most foolishly, 'unwilling to die, and mighty hardly brought to take their last Farewel of their Friends'. So far the thought follows that of the soliloquy very closely; but now Hamlet goes on to speculate for himself upon that unwillingness to die (not necessarily by suicide), rightly judging that it is the fear of the unknown that makes us foolish in this regard. What is remarkable here, of course, is not the sharing of the reflection, but the close similarity in the progress of the argument and in the choice of illustrations.

So, too, when Hamlet assures Rosencrantz and Guildenstern that Denmark is no prison for them, 'for there is nothing either good or

[1] See Harry Levin, *The Question of Hamlet* (New York, 1959), p. 72, where he notes this similarity.

bad, but thinking makes it so', he is drawing –
as Dover Wilson pointed out[1] – on a humanistic commonplace. But the two points in the
Moriae Encomium at which this commonplace
was given a new currency (Erasmus was paraphrasing Horace, *Satires*, I, i, 66)[2] are relevant
in a broader way than the term 'commonplace'
would suggest: 'but alas, Slander, Calumny
and Disgrace, are no other Way Injurious than
as they are Interpreted; nor otherwise Evil,
than as they are thought to be so' (Kennet, p.
50). As Chaloner put it: '*For what hurteth thee,
the peoples hissing, as longe as thou clappest thy
selfe on the backe?*' (Chaloner, p. 43). It must, at
such a moment of confrontation with fellow-
students, have seemed a ludicrously inadequate
piece of consolation; and Hamlet's observation,
seen as deriving hence, carries a weight of bitterness not immediately perceptible, and perhaps
only perceptible when the peculiar appropriate-
ness of the source to his own case is understood.
And even more strongly may this be felt to be
true when the other reference is recalled:

What Difference is there between them that in the
darkest Dungeon can with a *Platonick* Brain Survey
the whole World in Idea, and him that stands in the
open Air, and takes a less deluding Prospect of the
Universe? If the *Beggar* in *Lucian*, that *dreamt* he was
a Prince, had never wak'd, his *imaginary* Kingdom
had been as great as a *real* one. Between him therefore
that *truly* is happy, and him that *thinks* himself so,
there is no perceivable Distinction . . .

(Kennet, p. 81)

Reading the passage between Hamlet and his
friends in the light of this, one might even feel
that Rosencrantz had picked up a precise
reference, which prompts his jibe about
Hamlet's ambition. It is interesting to note how
Chaloner renders Erasmus here, '*sittyng in a
caue vnder the grounde, to see nothyng but
shadowes [uariarum rerum umbras] and repre-
sentacions of thynges*' (p. 64), for Guildenstern,
this time, leads the talk almost at once to the
difference between reality and shadow.

Hamlet's surprise at the indifference of the
clowns in V, i to the humanistic reflections their
occupation might have been expected to
evoke – echoing his strange cry at IV, iv, 33ff.[3]
– is expressed in a passage which takes its place
in a long heritage of similar observations; it is
another humanistic commonplace. It is, nevertheless, curiously close to an extended passage
in the *Moriae Encomium*, in which Folly sets
out to show how fools are not afflicted by the
troubles endured by rational men. What is
arresting here is the list of illustrations Erasmus
gives of experiences which leave the insensitive
man untouched:

these Persons in all Circumstances fare best and live
most comfortably: As first, they are void of all Fear,
which is a very great Priviledge to be exempted from;
they are troubled with no Remorse, nor Pricks of
Conscience; they are not frighted with any Bugbear
Stories of another World; they startle not at the
fancied Appearance of Ghosts or Apparitions [old
wiues tales of sprites, of diuelles, of hobgoblyne and
the fayries];[4] they are not wrack'd with the Dread of
impending Mischiefs [neither mournyng to theim
selues for feare of euilles and aduersitees impendyng],
nor bandied with the Hopes of any expected Enjoy-
ments: In short, they are unassaulted by all those
Legions of Cares that War against the Quiet of
Rational Souls [thousande thousand cares, wherwith
other men are oppressed] they are ashamed of nothing,
fear no Man, banish the Uneasiness of Ambition,
Envy, and Love . . .

(Kennet, p. 57)

Again, one feels that Shakespeare has borrowed
not simply a sentiment, but the entire climate
in which it blossomed forth.

Immediately following upon this, the Clown
turns up the skull of Yorick, and we might
wonder by what curious turn of thought

---

[1] *Hamlet*, the New Cambridge edition (Cambridge,
1934), p. 173.
[2] See Chaloner (trans.), *Praise of Folie*, p. 154.
[3] All references are to the *Complete Works*, edited
by Peter Alexander (London and Glasgow, 1951).
[4] Chaloner (trans.), *Praise of Folie*, p. 48.

Shakespeare should have chosen to make the gruesome illustration of humanistic reflection the skull of a court jester: our familiarity with the scene tends to obscure the fact that it was anything but an obvious choice. Whether or not it affords us an explanation, Erasmus, too, proceeds from a discussion of what the insensitive are protected against to a lengthy consideration of the privileges accorded to court fools: 'Yet Fools have so great a Priviledge as to have free leave, not only to speak *bare* Truths, but the most *bitter* ones too [not onely true tales, but euin open rebukes are with pleasure declared]' (Kennet, p. 60).[1] Taken as a whole, the passage presents a remarkably accurate summary of the Fool's role in Shakespearian drama; more immediately, we note how both Hamlet and Erasmus go on to remark how even women will take from a fool what they would not take from others: 'Now get thee to my lady's chamber . . .'

Closely following upon all this in the *Moriae Encomium*, there is Erasmus's famous passage upon the 'two kyndes of madnesse', as Chaloner renders it[2] (*duplex insaniae genus*). 'Shakespearian madness' is here described in some detail, and its relevance is commonly acknowledged. More immediate to our present purpose, however, is the fact that it offers a truly Erasmian gloss upon various kinds of madness in *Hamlet*. These are, first, the true (moral) madness of Old Hamlet and Claudius (*ab inferis*):

the one that which the Furies bring from Hell; those that are herewith possess'd are hurried on to Wars and Contentions, by an inexhaustible Thirst of Power and Riches, inflamed to some infamous and unlawful Lust, inraged to act the Parricide, seduced to become guilty of Incest, Sacrilege, or some other of those Crimsondy'd Crimes; or, finally, to be so prick'd in Conscience as to be lash'd and stung with the Whips and Snakes of Grief and Remorse [in pectora mortalium inuehunt, siue cum nocentem & conscium animum, furijs ac terriculorum facibus agunt] . . .

(Kennet, p. 62)

second, the assuaging (pathological) madness of Ophelia (*mentis error*): 'the Mind is freed from those Cares which would otherwise gratingly afflict it . . .' (Kennet, p. 63), this being, in the way Erasmus describes it, also the third, Hamlet's semi-feigned (politic) madness.[3] There is a fourth kind of madness proposed by Erasmus in a passage which comes very close to the picture we are given of Polonius, conspicuously in the exchange with Reynaldo in II, i:

There is another very pleasant Sort of Madness, whereby Persons assume to *themselves* whatever of Accomplishment they discern in *others*. Thus the Happy *Rich Churl* in *Seneca*, who had so short a Memory, as he could not tell the least Story without a Servant's standing by to prompt him . . .

(Kennet, p. 74)

Especially as Hamlet sees him, Polonius is ridiculous in his foolish and inefficient aping of his master, Claudius.

An interesting gloss on Hamlet's eulogy upon Horatio is also provided by the *Moriae Encomium*. Critics over the years have dwelt lovingly upon this passage (much quoted out of context), in which Hamlet expresses his high regard of a man who can take all that comes to him and do nothing about it; yet the same critics have spent considerable effort in accounting for Hamlet as a prince who, under pressure to act, does nothing. The fact is, surely, that it is rather a curious thing that a man like Hamlet should wish to be a man like Horatio. Explanations are not lacking, of course: under the complex of pressures he has to endure, Hamlet might well catch himself envying the sort of man who seems to bear pressures better. That it is no more than such a

[1] *Ibid.*, p. 50.
[2] *Ibid.*, p. 52.
[3] Levin (*The Question of Hamlet*, p. 125) points the conscious adoption by Hamlet of the Erasmian role – 'stooping to folly in the grand Erasmian manner' – in IV, iii, 17 ff.

localised sentiment, however, is suggested by the fact that its expression does not have any verifiable effect upon Hamlet's proceeding. The following expression of a typically humanistic view of stoicism suggests why. Erasmus has spoken of passions as 'diseases of the mynde',[1] but then goes on to say:

This, I suppose, will be stomach'd by the Stoical *Seneca*, who pretends, that the only Emblem of Wisdom is *the Man without Passion*; whereas the supposing any Person to be so, is perfectly to Unman him, or else Transforming him into some fabulous Deity that never was, nor ever will be [*qui nusquam nec extitit unquam, nec extabit*]; nay, to speak more plain, it is but the making him a meer *Statue*, immoveable, sensless, and altogether unactive.
(Kennet, p. 46)

Here is Hamlet's difficulty crystallised: to act in passion is absurd, even diseased, 'like a whore unpack my heart with words'; to be stoical is to be wooden, 'bestial oblivion'. Yet it is not difficult to see how a man with this dilemma, who fears on the one hand to be less than a man, but on the other to become a raving beast in the excess of action, must sometimes envy the stoic, however arid and circumscribed the humanist believes his philosophy to be – 'There are more things in heaven and earth, Horatio . . .'

Hamlet tries to steer a middle course, true humanist that he is, neither denying human feeling nor falling victim to its excessive pressures. It sounds easier in theory, however, than it is in practice: 'In the undertaking any Enterprize the Wise Man shall run to consult with his Books, and doze himself with poring upon musty Authors, while the dispatchful Fool shall rush bluntly on, and have done the Business, while the other is thinking of it' (Kennet, p. 42). To be guilty either way in the pursuit of a crown, even when one has been preparing oneself against the day – the *nouus homo* now to be the *nouus imperator* – must strike the humanist as a particular folly; but

to sin for it, folly in the extreme: 'For certainly none can Esteem Perjury or Parricide a Cheap Purchase for a *Crown*, if he does but seriously reflect on that Weight of Cares a Princely Diadem is *loaded* with' (Kennet, p. 124). Parricide (taken in its broadest sense) is condemned almost as regularly as stoicism throughout the *Moriae Encomium*; but living in a court where none is to be trusted, a wise man, we are told, might well learn to play the dissembling game as others play it, for his own safety: 'First then it is confest almost a Proverb, that the Art of Dissembling is a very necessary Accomplishment . . .' (Kennet, p. 139). And perhaps the safest guise under which to conceal onself is that of a fool: 'Ite alibi, Dulce est desipere in loco . . . delirius, inersque uideri, quam sapere, ringi.' Which is Hamlet's policy, as it had been Hal's in the *Henry I V* plays.

Erasmus goes on to describe the world of the court, in which such policies are called for. It is all familiar to us, of course, but once again the importance of the parallels lies less in the thought than in the mode of expression, and in the choice of illustration. Erasmus pictures the courtier as an ignorant and servile flatterer, skilled in the use of impressive-sounding language, extravagantly dressed, empty-headed, yet with a gift for concealing his true nature, nevertheless: 'If you make a stricter Enquiry after their other Endowments, you shall find them meer Sots and Dolts' (Kennet, p. 127). Kennet's rendering of a passage a few lines later is interesting: 'I have many times took great Satisfaction by standing in the Court, and seeing how the tawdry Butterflies vie upon one another . . .' (Kennet, p. 128). 'Butterflies' doesn't appear in the Chaloner; nor is there any such specific reference in the Erasmus text. What Kennet is taking up, clearly enough, however, is the tone of the whole passage, in which it is the self-display of the courtiers, before each other, but especially before the ladies, that is being

[1] Chaloner (trans.), *Praise of Folie*, p. 39.

satirised: the sense of 'butterfly' is very strong. It is interesting to note, then, Shakespeare's use of the term 'water-fly' to describe Osric, who is the personification of all the contemptible qualities Erasmus lists. Shakespeare never uses 'butterfly' in this sense; and 'water-fly' occurs only three times in the plays: once neutrally (in *Antony and Cleopatra*), and twice in Kennet's way, once by Hamlet of Osric, once by Thersites of Patroclus. Of itself, this coincidence is nothing: in the pattern of echoes in which it occurs, it seems entirely natural.

The prince ought, at any rate, to be sharply aware of how deceptive appearances can be, Erasmus reminds him, going to some lengths to show how a 'profess'd Enemy to Liberty and Truth, careless and unmindful of the common Concerns, taking all the Measures of Justice and Honesty from the false Beam of Self-interest [geuin onely to his peculier profite, addicted all to voluptuousnesse]' (Kennet, p. 126)[1] may dress himself in the regalia and look in no way different from the prince himself, 'whan he hath no maner part of a prince in hym, sauyng onely the clothyng', as Chaloner puts it (p. 94). Erasmus is here returning to an issue which, perhaps above everything else, alarmed him, as it did Shakespeare, that 'all humaine thynges lyke the *Silenes or duble images of Alcibiades*, haue two faces muche vnlyke and dissemblable'. The passage continues (taking here the Chaloner, which is less free than the Kennet):

that what outwardly seemed death, yet lokyng within ye shulde fynde it lyfe: and on the other side what semed life, to be death: what fayre, to be foule: what riche, beggerly: what cunnyng, rude: what stronge, feable: what noble, vile: what gladsome, sadde: what happie, vnlucky: what friendly, vnfriendly: what healthsome, noysome. Briefely the Silene ones beyng vndone and disclosed, ye shall fynde all thynges tourned into a new semblance.

(Chaloner, p. 37)[2]

In order to expound the matter the more plainly, Erasmus goes on to picture court life in terms of a play enacted in a theatre:

If one at a solemne stage plaie, woulde take vpon hym to plucke of the plaiers garmentes, whiles they were saiyng theyr partes, and so disciphre vnto the lokers on, the true and natiue faces of eche of the plaiers, shoulde he not (trow ye) marre all the mattier? and well deserue for a madman to be peltid out of the place with stones?

Here we have, I believe, a significant light upon Hamlet's being 'idle' at the court performance of 'The Mouse-trap', by which he clearly intends 'acting the madman', though we should not in fact think anything he does or says during the performance warrants such a description. The passage continues: 'ye shoulde see yet straightwaies a new transmutacion in thynges: that who before plaied the woman, shoulde than appeare to be a man: who seemed youth, should shew his hore heares: who countrefaited the kynge, shulde tourne to a rascall...' (Chaloner, p. 37). Erasmus, of course, goes on to philosophise upon the world as a stage, in the now familiar manner; but here we have, I believe, the origin of the players in *Hamlet*. 'He that plays the King shall be welcome', Hamlet delightedly cries, though at the time of his making it the remark might well strike us as odd, even inexplicable: it is in the sequel that it becomes clear. Hamlet sets up in play form the drama of Elsinore, and then reduces it, in the manner suggested in the Erasmus passage, even as it is being performed, forecasting the outcome of the living drama, when Claudius, the player-king, 'a king of shreds and patches', will be exposed as the rascal he really is. For, as Erasmus says, quoting the proverb, 'an Ape will be an Ape, tho' clad in Purple' (Kennet, p. 24); and Claudius, Hamlet would

[1] *Ibid.*, pp. 93–4.
[2] This passage is also cited by Levin (*The Question of Hamlet*, p. 74).

willingly believe, is no more, keeping Rosencrantz and Guildenstern 'like an ape in the corner of his jaw, first mouthed to be last swallowed' (IV, ii).

The world of the court is a debased world, where 'fawning Courtiers' (Kennet, p. 134) will find a way of condoning the murders done by their princes, 'having found out the Way how a Man may draw his Sword, and sheath it in his Brother's Bowels . . .' Such men, nevertheless, play with fire, to their own damnation; and here it may be as well to quote Erasmus in the original, since the translations tend to mask his sharpness: 'Etenim siquis beatum existimet principibus placuisse uiris, & inter meos illos, ac gemmeos deos uersari, quid inutilius sapientia, imo quid apud hoc hominum genus damnatius?' The fate of Polonius, Laertes, Rosencrantz, and Guildenstern could scarcely be forecast more plainly than this, nor could the manner of their deaths more graphically illustrate the point Erasmus was making.

This passage follows hard upon Erasmus's discussion of Fortune in the *Moriae Encomium*. We note that there is some slight gesture towards personification of Fortune, and to the extent that there is, it is towards portraying her as an asinine creature, fit companion to Folly, pouring wealth and success into the laps of fools, while wise men go in fear of her. The rash, the foolhardy, the adventurous, these are her favourites, and these she rewards; the wise go (in Erasmus's own words) '*neglectos, inglorios, inuisos*'. Direct references to Fortune in *Hamlet* number eighteen: six of these are by the First Player and need not concern us further here; of the rest, that by the Queen, that by Fortinbras, and four references by Hamlet simply refer to Fortune as luck, the turn of events. Three others of Hamlet's picture Fortune as a meddlesome fool – 'outrageous fortune', 'Fortune's buffets and rewards', 'a pipe for Fortune's finger / To

sound what stop she please'. What we tend to remember, however, is the conversation between Hamlet and his fellow-students, Rosencrantz and Guildenstern, when Fortune is described as a strumpet. It is not characteristic of Hamlet so to picture her, though he is clearly familiar – and bored – with this particular analogy, one propounded, significantly for the sixteenth century, by Machiavelli. For him, Fortune (*fortuna*) was ruthless, daemonic, overwhelming, and characteristically he portrayed her as a whore playing with her wheel. The difference between this pagan view and the Erasmian view typified by Hamlet is caught in the German in the difference between *Rückschlag* and *Glückschlag*. It is significant that the only typically Machiavellian use of the word should occur in Hamlet's brief exchange with two amateur Machiavels. It is a distortion of memory if we recall this use rather than the others, for Hamlet's own view of Fortune is thoroughly Erasmian.

It is not, of course, to luck in any sense that Hamlet resigns himself, but to Providence – 'There is special providence in the fall of a sparrow', says Hamlet, as he goes, sword in hand, to meet his fate, reflecting that, 'If it be not now . . . yet it will come.'

It is curiously close to the drift of Erasmus's argument in the *Moriae Encomium*, where he rebukes those who mistake Christ's injunction to the Apostles to buy a sword, on the night of Gethsemane, for a recommendation to arms. Such a person, Erasmus says, speaks: 'As if he had forgot that he encouraged them by the Examples of *Sparrows* and *Lillies* to take [no – omitted in error] Thought *for the Morrow* [the small care that thei shuld take for theyr liuyng]' (Kennet, p. 150).[1] We might well think that the tragedy of Hamlet lies as much as anywhere in his singular failure to learn how to live till that fateful hour when he learned how to die. Yet he goes to his fate with the

[1] Chaloner (trans.), *Praise of Folie*, p. 113.

whole force of Erasmus's treatise supporting his spirits;[1] as we might see in a remarkable passage in which so much of the situation as well as the thought of this play is set forth. Erasmus (through Folly) pictures a heavenly messenger come to earth to rebuke certain men for foolish *affections*, and asks what sort of reception he would get. I quote here from Chaloner, who has, I feel, captured the mood of the original most aptly:

Here nowe if one of these wisemen, come (I wene) from heauen, did sodeinly appeare, and saie, *howe euin this great prince, whom all men honor as their god and soueraigne, deserueth skarce to be called man, seyng like the brute beastes, he is trained by affections, and is none other than a seruaunt of the basest sort, seyng willyngly he obeith so many, and so vile vices his maisters. Or thanne againe, woulde bidde some other, who mourned for his fathers or friendes decease, rather to laughe, and be merie, because suche diyng to this worlde is the beginnyng of a better life, wheras this here, is but a maner death as it were. Furthermore, wolde call an other gloriyng in his armes and auncestrie, bothe a villaine, and a bastarde, because he is so many discentes disalied from vertue, whiche is the onely roote of true nobilitee.*

(Chaloner, p. 38)

Here, in turn, Claudius, Hamlet, and Old Hamlet are – typically – arraigned: but, as it were, unavailingly. Old Hamlet remains, even beyond the grave, a man 'gloriyng in his armes', crying for the vindication of his 'auncestrie', one for whom the rarer action is in vengeance than in virtue; Claudius dies, we might well think, deserving 'skarce to be called man', obeying to the last those 'vile vices his maisters'; and Hamlet, by a bitter irony, dies a man of chivalry, avenging his too-much-mourned father with poison and the sword. The story of these three Shakespeare has set forth as an investigation into 'the onely roote of true nobilitee'.

Other reflections in *Hamlet* of the *Moriae Encomium* may be no more than reflections, distant and, taken just in themselves, accidental

– the inevitably shared data of two works of Christian humanism. But they cannot, I believe, be taken 'just in themselves', and so are worth indicating here for the support they lend to the general contention.

Hamlet's attitude towards the women in his life, for instance, interestingly echoes that expressed in the *Moriae Encomium*, which was not in fact specially typical in this respect of the humanist tradition. Hamlet is not hostile and unaccommodating so much as patronising, once his horror at woman's disloyalty is out of his system. His manner is at all times superior: he is contemptuous of the weaknesses he sees so clearly but cannot find sympathy enough to forgive. Erasmus presents Folly as a woman, and the characteristic note of the work is sounded when he says, 'a Woman will be a Woman *i.e.* a Fool, whatever Disguise she takes up' (Kennet, p. 24). He refers to '*mulierum genus*', speculating upon what likelihood there could be of this species belonging to that of rational man.

A curious reflection of the *Moriae Encomium* may be found in the appearance Hamlet makes at the court gathering (I, ii), and at the play (III, ii). Folly castigates serious, or wise, men for being poor mixers:

For place a formal Wise Man at a *Feast*, and he shall, either by his morose Silence put the whole Table out of Humour, or by his frivolous Questions disoblige and tire out all that sit near him . . . Invite him to any Publick Performance, and by his very Looks he shall damp the Mirth of all the Spectators . . .

(Kennet, pp. 36–7)

Hamlet, trapped in a court where what is serious can find no obvious place, may well feel that he has been tricked into playing a caricature of the scholar in insisting upon observing proper respect for the recently deceased king

[1] Perhaps even consciously. See Levin (*The Question of Hamlet*, pp. 118–19); he supports the speculation that the book Hamlet is reading in II, ii is the *Moriae Encomium*.

his father. And Claudius, we may well believe, is playing most adroitly on the caricature when, in a long and disreputable speech, he cold-bloodedly debases Erasmus's humanistic argument against undue mourning for the dead and undue elevation of parents ('for what did they more than Generate a Body?' (Kennet, p. 165)).

In his first soliloquy, Hamlet compares his father with Hercules, a suitable analogy for one who seems to have been pre-eminently a man of action. There is no hint of irony: nor is there, curiously enough, in Erasmus's references to Hercules; we might reasonably have expected that there would be: 'Ye shall heare therfore the praise set foorth, not of Hercules, nor yet of Solon, but rather of myne owne selfe, That is to saie of Folie' (Chaloner, p. 8). Hamlet, though he never uses the term 'fool' of himself – reserving it as an expression of contempt for others – nevertheless sees himself most gallingly cast in the role of the fool ('Why, what an ass am I') both in the eyes of the court, and in his own. Hamlet does not himself share Shakespeare's later enthusiasm for the paradox of wisdom-in-folly, though he does begin to approach it, we might think, in v, i. His exaggerated view of his father's merits, however, partakes of his general reaction to the picture he entertains of himself:

> Hyperion's curls; the front of Jove himself;
> An eye like Mars, to threaten and command;
> A station like the herald Mercury
> New lighted on a heaven-kissing hill –
> A combination and a form indeed
> Where every god did seem to set his seal,
> To give the world assurance of a man.
>
> (III, iv, 56–62)

No more than Hal could swallow the exaggerated stories about Hotspur can we accept this: no such man ever existed. And almost point by point, the claim is rebuked by Folly:

Few haue the gyfte of beautie through Venus fauour. Fewer haue eloquence at Mercuries handes. Hercules maketh not all men riche. Iupiter graunteth not kyngdomes to euery bodie. Oftentymes Mars fauoureth neither partie. Many retourne discomforted from Apollos oracle. Not seeldome Ioues thunder destroieth men . . . But I Folie am she, that egally dooe comprehende all men vnder the compasse of my so great a good gifte. (Chaloner, pp. 65–6)

Here, too, one can appreciate the gall for Hamlet in being cast – by the need he feels to confirm his faith in his father and to reprove his myopic mother – in a role so remote from the one he would have chosen for himself.

There are, further, several striking verbal echoes of the *Moriae Encomium* in *Hamlet*, striking, more often than not, because the words in question are uncommon in Shakespeare generally, and, where they are not particular to this play, are rarely much removed from it in the time of writing. For example, Shakespeare's choice of a name for Polonius's son may have been dictated by a wish to use Greek names for both son and daughter, and he may have already lighted upon Ophelia. But why Laertes, particularly? The classical Laertes was one of the Argonauts, but Shakespeare may have known him as the father of Odysseus: perhaps the connotations of the name were sufficiently evocative of an adventurous life to seem appropriate. It is interesting, nevertheless, that the name occurs in the *Moriae Encomium*, in a list Erasmus offers of Greek names typical of those appropriated by contemporary authors in a current affectation for things Greek, and perhaps with the hope of sounding more impressive than they would otherwise.

We find Hamlet speaking of some act 'That has no relish of salvation in't' (III, iii). In the *Moriae Encomium*, we find Erasmus using 'gustus' in just this way, rendered by Chaloner as 'taste' sometimes, but more usually as 'smacke'. Both 'smack' and 'relish' are common enough in Shakespeare, but only in *Hamlet* with the sense of 'fore-taste', as in the following, where the context is exactly the same: 'tamen quoniam piorum uita, nihil aliud est, quam illius uitae meditatio, ac uelut umbra quaedam, fit ut praemii quoque illius aliquando gustum aut odorem aliquem sentiant'.[1]

The *Moriae Encomium* may possibly shed some light too upon Shakespeare's sole dramatic use of the term 'quietus', which Steevens (quoted in the Variorum edition) describes as: 'the technical term for the acquittance which every sheriff receives on settling his accounts at the Exchequer' (Variorum, I, 212n). This reading might well sound a little strained to the modern reader, who is so determined to think of death in this soliloquy in terms of a release into peace and quiet; but Steevens, in fact, seems to be much closer than this to the truth. Erasmus (thinking perhaps of Henry VII and his death-bed amnesties) pours scorn on those who think they can wipe out the sinful excesses of a life-time by some slight gesture of reparation, and imagine that all is (as Chaloner put it, p. 57): 'therby as vpon a Quites est redeemed . . .' Erasmus has '*uelut ex pacto redimi*', where '*pactum*' clearly calls for some appropriate technical term in the translation; and Chaloner found an obvious one. If Shakespeare knew the Chaloner, his attention would be drawn to the '*Quites est*' on the page, as it was printed in roman. Whatever the truth of that, Shakespeare is clearly using 'quietus' as a version of '*quites est*', and with exactly the same sense of 'contract'.

Other words appearing in Chaloner, and notable in *Hamlet* for their relative rarity are: 'quidditee' – only twice in the plays, once in I *Henry IV* (I, ii), and once in *Hamlet*, in a passage strongly reminiscent of the passage in the *Moriae Encomium* castigating the affectations of lawyers; 'tropologically' – appearing in *Hamlet* as 'tropically', the only use of this word in the plays: 'Niobe' – only two occurrences in the plays (*Troilus and Cressida* and *Hamlet*); 'camel' – three times in the plays (*Troilus and Cressida*, *Hamlet*, and *Coriolanus*); 'satyr' – occurs only in *Hamlet*; 'quintessence' occurs only twice in the plays (*As You Like It* and *Hamlet*); and Shakespeare's 'the front of Jove' is his only use of Jupiter as a source of description, and is very reminiscent of a similar use by Erasmus: 'Iupiter hym selfe, *with all his depe dissembled chere*, lokyng so sternly, as geueth terrour . . .' (Chaloner, p. 21).

In conclusion, I can only express my personal conviction that in proposing to himself a Renaissance prince, cast in the humanist mould, confronting the long-familiar but still painful humanist dilemma, Shakespeare turned to an obvious source, and one with which he had probably been long acquainted. The precise nature of the relationship that indubitably exists between these two works suggests to me that the *Moriae Encomium* was drawn upon by one who knew it very intimately, had absorbed a great deal of its feeling into his own outlook and thinking, but who now consulted it again, on the brink, as it were, of his new creation, to see what it might afford him in terms of basic data. The use he made of it was masterly, his absorption of it entire: hence the laborious business of tracing even a little of it out.

[1] The words occur in the Chaloner trans. on pp. 126, 127, and 128.

© FRANK McCOMBIE 1974

'TO SAY ONE': AN ESSAY ON 'HAMLET'

RALPH BERRY*

The beginning of act v, scene ii finds Hamlet in a trough between action, released for once from the immediate stimuli of events. He is merely discussing his affairs with Horatio. It is a still moment, not with the felt danger of the moment that follows the acceptance of Laertes' challenge, but freer, less constrained. Horatio reminds him gently that the English authorities must shortly report on the death of Rosencrantz and Guildenstern. And Hamlet responds with these words:

> It will be short,
> The *interim's* mine, and a mans life's no more
> Then to say one.

That is what we have, and I reproduce it exactly in the terms that the Folio, our sole authority for this passage, supplies. 'A man's life's no more than to say one.' What does it mean? The editors – with, I think, a single major exception – pass the line by, its meaning being so obvious as to warrant no commentary. But I find that to explain the line, if I can, requires me to explain the play.

An editor can look the other way, but a translator cannot. We can usefully glance at two distinguished translations. Schlegel appears to stonewall successfully with 'Ein Menschen-leben ist als zählt mans eins': in fact he has given the phrase a decisive inclination, for 'zählen' is to count, not utter. André Gide makes this rendering even clearer:

> Et la vie d'un homme ne laisse même pas compter jusqu'à deux.

Since the tendency of French is always to be reductive of meanings, and of Shakespeare to expand possibilities, we can start with Gide's –

single – meaning. He takes Hamlet to be saying that man's life is brief, and that one must be ready for action. That is a legitimate meaning. John Dover Wilson suggests, in his New Cambridge edition, that 'one' is the fencer's word, the exclamation that one utters at the climax of the lunge: 'a single pass, then, will finish Claudius off'.[1] I think he must be right, but here too the single meaning pauperizes the riches of Shakespeare's wordplay here. 'One' is of all numbers the most resonant. It bears the implications of unity and self-hood, and it has moreover a significant past in *Hamlet*. Is not Hamlet saying that man's life is a quest for unity, for a profound accord between self and situation? But let us explore some of the ways in which the final scene permits Hamlet to say 'one'.

Hamlet is not a play that admits of ready, or final, description. I find L. C. Knights's term 'the Hamlet consciousness'[2] helpful, and I prefer to think of the play as a prolonged description of a single consciousness. At the beginning, that consciousness is aligned against its situation. It rejects external events, it lacks a stable base of self-hood: it is profoundly disturbed. At the end of the play, the consciousness is fully aligned with its situation. It is sufficiently self-aware, it has a base for judgment and action. Hamlet is, so to speak, *comfortable*. That, in broadest outline, is what happens in *Hamlet*.

[1] John Dover Wilson, *What Happens in Hamlet* (Cambridge, 1935), p. 272. References are to *The Complete Works*, ed. Hardin Craig (1951).
[2] L. C. Knights, *Some Shakespearean Themes and An Approach to Hamlet* (Stanford, 1966), pp. 191 ff.

* Professor Berry's article appears, with minor revisions, as a chapter in his book, *The Shakespearian Metaphor*, published by the Macmillan Press Ltd, 1978.

(i) Certain elements predominate in the Hamlet consciousness, and can be identified here. We might, I think, begin by discarding a misleading term that figures in the commentaries, 'intellectual'. Hamlet is not an intellectual, in the sense that he is given to rational analysis of a problem. The formulation of categories and issues is not his forte. He has a superb, intuitive intelligence, but that is something quite different. This type of mind is especially good at perceiving meanings reflected back from the environment. A flair for symbolism is central to a poet, dangerous (if still vital) to a thinker. I instance the Danish drinking practices, the player's emotions, Fortinbras' march to Poland: events supply their meaning for Hamlet. But they have meaning only to the receiving mind, and to find 'sermons in stones' has always a certain intellectual naiveté. There is no such thing as a symbol *per se*. The crucial sampling of Hamlet's powers as intellectual is the 'To be or not to be' soliloquy. It is unreasonable to treat it as a philosophical disquisition – it is an associative meditation, the mind reviewing a diorama of concepts and images. But it is fair to point out that it suggests, in outline, a logical structure. Harry Levin, indeed, has stressed that Hamlet is using 'the method preferred by Renaissance logicians... the dichotomy, which chopped its subjects down by dividing them in half, and subdividing the resultant divisions into halves again'.[1] Nevertheless, there are so many questions left hanging in the air that the soliloquy appears to me quite unlogical in essence, if not in form. I instance a few: 'To be, or not to be: that is the question' surely implies another question. This is true whether (a) one accents 'that', implying the rejection of a preceding question, (b) one accents 'is', re-affirming the proposition after a previous doubt, (c) renders 'that is' as a spondee, thus more subtly re-affirming the question after a doubt. Then, is 'in the

mind' a tautology ('nobler' is a mental quality) or a meaningful choice, 'suffering' to occur to the body or the mind? Does 'And by opposing end them' mean that the forces of outrageous Fortune can be physically defeated, or that the act of opposition in itself is a means of dispersing them, or that the act of opposition must mean death, with its own resolution of the problem? Again, 'puzzles the will': this I take to be a fusion of 'puzzles the mind' and 'inhibits the will'. Is Hamlet aware of this fusion, or confusion? Presumably not, since he arrives at 'Thus conscience does make cowards of us all; / And thus...' as though a logical terminus of argument had been arrived at. He is, like his twin Brutus, a poor reasoner – just as Brutus *begins* with his conclusion ('It must be by his death') and then goes on to discover reasons, Hamlet begins with the reasoning, and then – more subtly – ends with what looks like a conclusion but is in fact the unacknowledged premise of the meditation. A good argument may be circular, as may a bad: the line of Hamlet's argument is not known to geometry. Whatever else Hamlet is, he is not an intellectual.[2]

The foundation of the play is precisely this separation between premise and conclusion, between action and awareness. This remains true even though the acknowledged premises – belief in ghosts, questions of damnation, conscience, and so on – may be, objectively, perfectly sound. The play is not concerned to identify the sources of this disjunction: it states the fact. And it presents a final situation in which the disjunction has either ceased to exist, or ceased to be important. Until then, Hamlet

[1] Harry Levin, *The Question of Hamlet* (New York, 1961), p. 69.
[2] The complement to Hamlet here is, as so often, Claudius. We have only one opportunity to observe his mind at close quarters, but he uses it to think hard – and accurately – about the issues. 'May one be pardoned and retain the offence?' (III, iii, 56) is a brutally precise way of defining the problem.

has at times appeared uncommonly reminiscent of Nietzsche's idealist: 'The creature who has reasons for remaining in the dark about himself, and is clever enough to remain in the dark about these reasons.'

(ii) The Hamlet consciousness is strongly egocentric, with an impulse to self-protection that takes several forms. A vein of self-vindication, which is a part of self-affirmation, runs throughout the play. The occasions on which Hamlet blames himself are obvious enough. Not so well understood are the passages in which Hamlet is providing a kind of alibi for himself. His opening words (after a muttered aside) negative the King, placing Claudius in the wrong: and his first speech of any length is a sustained justification of his appearance and conduct to the Queen, and Court:

> Seems, madam! nay, it is: I know not 'seems'.
> . . .these indeed seem,
> For they are actions that a man might play:
> But I have that within which passeth show;
> These but the trappings and the suits of woe.
>
> (I, ii, 76–86)

There is here not only a defence, but an implicit appeal to the verdict of the Court. Then, in his discourse to Horatio and Marcellus on the sentry-platform, comes:

> So, oft it chances in particular men,
> That for some vicious mole of nature in them,
> As, in their birth – *wherein they are not guilty*,
> *Since nature cannot choose his origin –*

A man is guiltless of his genetic heritage: but note the conclusion:

> Shall in the *general censure* take corruption
> From that particular fault
>
> (I, iv, 23–36)

A curious word, 'censure', and a curious conclusion. Hamlet does not say that mankind is, of its origins, condemned to err or sin. He says that *public opinion* will regard the man as stained by the single fault. And that consider-ation troubles him. (The final word in the speech, 'scandal', drives home the point.) 'Censure', moreover, is a word that reaches out, for Hamlet uses it later of an audience ('the censure of the which one must in your allowance o'erweigh a whole theatre of others' (III, ii, 31–3)). Is there not a strong hint here of what is plain elsewhere, that a part of Hamlet's self is derived from the opinion of others, that is to say, his audience, and that he is aware of this?

The existence of this audience is vital to the elucidation of 'That would be scann'd' (III, iii, 75). There is a problem here, and the editors have closed their ranks around it. All modern editions which I have consulted punctuate this passage with a colon or period after 'scann'd' and the universal gloss is that 'would be' here means 'requires to be'. 'Scann'd' is given as 'scrutinized', and the statement is thus rendered 'That needs to be scrutinized/considered carefully'. I propose an entirely different reading here. 'Scan', in sense 4 listed by the *O.E.D.*, means 'to interpret, assign a meaning to'. If we accept this, 'would be' takes on its normal modern conditional meaning. The reading looks stronger if we refer back to the pointing of the Second Quarto and the Folio, so often superior to modern punctuation. The Second Quarto gives no punctuation at all after 'scann'd':

> Now might I doe it, but now a is a praying,
> And now Ile doo't, and so a goes to heaven,
> And so am I revendge, that would be scand
> A villaine kills my father, and for that,
> I his sole sonne, doe this same villaine send
> To heaven.

The Folio gives a comma, thus:

> Now might I do it pat, now he is praying,
> And now Ile doo't, and so he goes to Heaven,
> And so am I reveng'd: that would be scann'd,
> A Villaine killes my Father, and for that
> I his soule Sonne, do this same Villaine send
> To heaven.

This rapid, fluent pointing makes the syntax and meaning perfectly clear. 'A Villaine killes my Father' is now a noun clause subordinate to 'scann'd', and not an autonomous unit of thought. I claim no originality for this reading: the *O.E.D.* actually cites the above passage in support of its sense 4. (It cites other contemporary passages for this sense.) But we have to conduct this exercise to jettison a useless (and, in my view, erroneous) meaning that has established itself over the years. For 'that would be scann'd' now means: 'that is how public opinion would interpret the matter', and the centre of the play shifts slightly but unmistakably. Hamlet's conscience increasingly takes on the aspect of the approval conferred on the self by others.

Allied to this consideration are Hamlet's uses of the 'antic disposition'. He exploits it with a certain elemental calculation. He indeed, with a premonitory awareness of the possibilities of madness, introduces the subject to his immediate audience:

> As I perchance hereafter *shall think meet*
> To put an antic disposition on
>
> (I, v, 171–2)

And this disguise has notable defensive qualities, throughout the manoeuvring of Acts II and III. At the same time, it takes on a therapeutic function. 'In personating a mad Hamlet, Hamlet is in fact personating a chaos of his inner self. It both is and is not Hamlet.'[1] But Hamlet is perfectly capable of distancing himself from his madness, when it suits him. 'Lay not that flattering unction to your soul, / That not your trespass, but my madness speaks' he tells Gertrude (III, iv, 144–5). To Laertes, before the Court, he proclaims:

> This presence knows,
> And you must needs have heard, how I am punish'd
> With sore distraction. What I have done,
> That might your nature, honour and exception
> Roughly awake, I here proclaim was madness.
> Was't Hamlet wrong'd Laertes? Never Hamlet:

> If Hamlet from himself be ta'en away,
> And when he's not himself does wrong Laertes,
> Then Hamlet does it not, Hamlet denies it.
> Who does it, then? His madness
>
> (v, ii, 239–48)

This speech is normally taken as a handsome, indeed noble, offer of amends. On the contrary, I regard it as an adroit (and largely successful) attempt to win over public opinion, and to place the responsibility for his actions on to his 'distraction'. It is disingenuous to plead the 'antic disposition' which he himself chose. The speech is an *apologia pro vita sua*, disguised as an apology. If this reading seems too harsh, I ask for an explanation of 'I'll be your foil, Laertes: in mine ignorance / Your skill shall, like a star i' the darkest night, / Stick fiery off indeed' (v, ii, 266–8). Hamlet knows perfectly well, and has told Horatio earlier, that he is in excellent training and will win at the odds. He is, in fact, exhibiting a widely-encountered trait, that of the player who cries down his skill either to lull his opponent or to magnify his achievement. We should today call it gamesmanship: we should certainly not sentimentalize Hamlet's conduct. Hamlet – and here we move to the existential truth of the situation – is presenting himself to the Court as the flower of Renaissance chivalry, an illustration stepped forth from the pages of Castiglione, the fencer whose success comes always as a surprise to himself. Besides, the Queen has let him know, through a messenger, that some kind of graceful gesture ('some gentle entertainment to Laertes') would be in order. And he now divests himself of his responsibility for outrageous conduct. He is, then, starring in the drama about to be played. And the drama ends, for Hamlet, with his concern for his 'wounded name', i.e. his reputation.

I am suggesting, then, that Hamlet's consciousness exhibits a profound concern for

[1] David Horowitz, *Shakespeare: An Existential View* (1965), p. 39.

himself, for his *self*. This is far more than a simple concern to protect his body, though it includes that consideration. It is rather a consistent desire to present his actions in the most favourable light, an awareness that the 'censure of the judicious' is what matters. Horatio is several things for Hamlet: a friend and aide, a sounding-board, an instrument for communication with the world, a participant in the self-dialogue. It is to himself, as well as to Horatio, that Hamlet says 'is't not perfect conscience, / To quit him with this arm?' (v, ii, 67–8). Hamlet needs the approval of himself and of others. He does not get it in the passage I have just cited, for Horatio turns the subject instead of answering directly. But it is with others that the final appeal lies, and to others that the consciousness of this supreme egotist is directed.

(iii) And this is contained within the final element in Hamlet's consciousness that I wish to touch on, his awareness of self as that of the actor. Maynard Mack is, I am sure, right in taking '"Act"... to be the play's radical metaphor... What, this play asks again and again, is an act? What is its relation to the inner act, the intent?'[1] Michael Goldman has also written well of the play as a search for the significance of action.[2] I want here, however, merely to stress the psychological implications of 'actor' for Hamlet.

An actor, as Mr Goldman observes, is a man who wants to play Hamlet.[3] Hamlet, I would continue, is an actor profoundly dissatisfied with his part, now that he has got it. His opening scene (I, ii) is consistent with this view. It is one of the classical paradoxes of theatre: '*Flourish. Enter Claudius King of Denmark, Gertrude, the Queen; Council, as Polonius, and his son, Laertes, Hamlet and others.*' An impressive entrance: but no audience has ever looked at Claudius, or ever will. It is looking at the still, aloof figure who alone of the Court has not abandoned mourning, and

is effortlessly accomplishing that most exquisite of actors' satisfactions, wordlessly upstaging a whole cast. In context, indeed, he is destroying the production, Claudius' first speech from the Throne. But that is not how it appears to Hamlet. *He* is upstaged by Claudius. We must remember how Hamlet reacts to bad acting – the directive to the players, the explosion at Ophelia's funeral, 'Nay, an thou'lt mouth/ I'll rant as well as thou' (v, i, 306–7) followed by the later admission 'But, sure, the bravery of his grief did put me / Into a towering passion' (v, ii, 79–80). And in his opening scene Claudius is *bad*, as he never is again. His speech is a series of contorted subordinate clauses, collapsing into main clauses that themselves crumple into further subordinates. Claudius is, of course, nervous – the jumpy, slightly illogical transitions give him away. ('now follows ... So much for him. / Now for ourself...' Claudius has earlier talked of himself; in fact he goes on to talk of further action in the Fortinbras affair, a matter he has just seemed to dismiss.) Claudius gives the impression of continually backing into meaning, a process which continues until 'But now, my cousin Hamlet, and my son' (I, ii, 64). I labour the point, which is made vastly more subtly in the text, that Claudius is not doing too well in I, ii. And this is the man who has dispossessed Hamlet. May we not add, to the ferment of emotions expressed in the first soliloquy, an inchoate rage that this far from well-graced figure has annexed *his* role?

We may, of course, reject the possibility, on the grounds that the first soliloquy can only express what is there. In this most devious of all plays, that is scarcely an adequate position; for we have then to explain away Hamlet's

[1] Maynard Mack, 'The World of *Hamlet*', *Yale Review*, XLI (June, 1952), 513.
[2] Michael Goldman, *Shakespeare and the Energies of Drama* (Princeton, 1972), pp. 74–93.
[3] *Ibid.*, p. 74.

later, and perfectly unequivocal, statement to Horatio, that Claudius 'Popp'd in between the election and my hopes' (v, ii, 65). There are really only two ways of taking this reference, which is presumably a crystallization of the earlier 'Excitements of my reason and my blood' (IV, iv, 58). Either Hamlet is providing a pseudo-motive, a rounding-out of the indictment against Claudius to make it respectable to Horatio and himself: or a genuine motive, slowly rising from the depths of his mind, has now broken surface and can be formulated and uttered. I take the second possibility to be the right one. Hamlet, then, is enmeshed in a central paradox. His role requires him to 'act' – to feign, put on an antic disposition, to produce and introduce a play, to assume different styles of speech, to plot and deceive – and moreover to *act*, to resolve the whole Claudius problem: yet the role is the wrong one for him. And what, then, is the right role? It is the function of the play to answer that question.

The features of the Hamlet consciousness, then, I take to be these: an intuitive though not wholly rational intelligence, an egocentricity that is especially concerned with the protection of his self as it appears to others, and an actor's capacity to appreciate that self in its manoeuvrings. The course of the play demonstrates, I suggest, the truth of what that 'strange fellow' whom Ulysses has been reading has to say:

> Who, in his circumstance, expressly proves
> That no man is the lord of anything,
> Though in and of him there be much consisting,
> Till he communicate his parts to others;
> Nor doth he of himself know them for aught
> Till he behold them form'd in the applause
> Where they're extended.
> (*Troilus and Cressida*, III, iii, 114–20)

'Applause': that is a part of the resolution of the *Hamlet* issues. Now: my central contention is that Hamlet is a man moving towards the final awareness and affirmation of self. We must, therefore, regard the death of Hamlet as his final statement, and while it is tedious to work backwards from it – progressive chronology has too many uses to be lightly discarded – I think we ought to take note of the quality of that final position. Hamlet's death is curiously gratuitous, actorish. All the other deaths (of the protagonists) in Shakespeare's major tragedies have an elemental, obvious necessariness. A continued living (*pace* Johnson) is unthinkable for Lear, as for Othello, Macbeth, Coriolanus, and Antony. There is, simply, nothing to add to their lives. But Hamlet has, as it seems, much to live for. He is young, greatly gifted, likely to have proved most royal. His death is unfortunate and premature. It certainly appears to be of a different order from the other major tragic figures. But is it? I prefer to advance the hypothesis of the necessary death, that is, the completed life-statement. I regard the final position as the consummation (Hamlet's own word) of his life, one that combines the notions of significant and expressive action, duties accomplished, and the assurance that the 'mutes or audience' will be given the full information necessary for the understanding and appreciation of the spectacle they have just witnessed. This latter is the only point that seems to concern Hamlet at the last. He raises the matter, and elaborates it after Horatio's impulsive gesture of suicide. The Court/audience must applaud, and approve. The death scene of Hamlet is, then, satisfying in a double sense. Hamlet the actor, and the actor playing Hamlet, fuse in the climax of the drama.

That is the situation at the moment of Hamlet's death. We can now read more closely the movement leading up to it, that is to say the final scene (v, ii). Since Hamlet's drive towards significant action takes the mode of the duellist and fighter, we can note that the metaphor of fighting virtually opens the scene. There is much imagery of war throughout the play, now much better understood than it used to be;[1] the point of Hamlet's metaphor here is that it reflects a change of mental orientation:

> Sir, in my heart there was a kind of fighting,
> That would not let me sleep.
>
> (v, ii, 4–5)

'Sleep': the threat to sleep, in the 'To be or not to be' soliloquy, and the admission to Rosencrantz and Guildenstern (II, ii, 262), is bad dreams. Now it is 'a kind of fighting'. That is action, and aggressive action. Hamlet goes on to tell the story. He tells it well, with a relish of its dramatic possibilities and his own role:

> Being thus be-netted round with villanies, –
> Ere I could make a prologue to my brains,
> They had begun the play.
>
> (v, ii, 29–31)

This is an obvious and characteristic concept of the self as hero. Less obvious is the import of his action: he imitates Claudius, he becomes Claudius in his pastiche of the King's tumid rhetoric:

> As England was his faithful tributary,
> As love between them like the palm might flourish,
> As peace should still her wheaten garland wear
> And stand a comma 'tween their amities,
> And many such-like 'As'es of great charge
>
> (v, ii, 39–43)

(The style of this missive is assimilated into his later note to Claudius, details of which we have already been given (IV, vii, 43–8). It is florid, politic, dangerous. Hamlet is taking on the persona, or the assumptions, of Claudius.) And, in a moment of exquisite symbolism, he ratifies his action with his father's seal:

> I had my father's signet in my purse,
> Which was the model of that Danish seal.
>
> (v, ii, 49–50)

Hamlet now becomes Hamlet senior. Is it possible that Hamlet, with his flair for sym-bolic interpretation, has no inkling of what he is doing? The central fact is clear: Hamlet is now moving towards the mode of his father, as politician, fighter, and – the encounter with Fortinbras comes to mind – as duellist. This is the vital metaphor, the self-conceptualization that Hamlet projects:

> Why, man, they did make love to this employment;
> They are not near my conscience; their defeat
> Does by their own insinuation grow:
> 'Tis dangerous when the baser nature comes
> Between the pass and fell incensèd points
> Of mighty opposites.
>
> (v, ii, 57–62)

In the immediate context, this is a further piece of self-justification: the point is that it is dangerous to come between two duellists, and thus Hamlet acquits himself of any guilt in the deaths of Rosencrantz and Guildenstern. But the justification pushes Hamlet a little more firmly in the direction in which he is moving anyway. To be guiltless, he must be a duellist. Horatio's exclamation, 'Why, what a king is this!', leads Hamlet to his vindication of his future conduct:

> Does it not, thinks't thee, stand me now upon –
> He that hath kill'd my king and whored my mother,
> Popp'd in between the election and my hopes,
> Thrown out his angle for my proper life,
> And with such cozenage – is't not perfect conscience,
> To quit him with this arm? and is't not to be damn'd,
> To let this canker of our nature come
> In further evil?
>
> (v, ii, 63–70)

That is the bill of indictment against Claudius, and it is the basis of the appeal to Horatio's sense of 'conscience', as to Hamlet's own. It is, even its final image, a call to action, for whether 'canker' means 'ulcer' or 'maggot' it implies a positive course of remedial action. The question

---

[1] See especially Maurice Charney, *Style in Hamlet* (Princeton, 1969), pp. 6–30: and Nigel Alexander, *Poison, Play, and Duel* (London and Lincoln, Nebraska, 1971).

is not one for Horatio to comment directly on, and he reminds Hamlet that the time for effective action is limited:

Horatio.
　It must be shortly known to him from England
　What is the issue of the business there.
Hamlet.
　It will be short: the interim is mine;
　And a man's life's no more than to say 'One'.

(v, ii, 71–4)

'Man's life's no more than to say "One"': in the brevity of life, one can at least achieve a moment of significant, aggressive action. The affirmation of self is the end of life: and 'one' denotes, among other things, the unity of self. The word harks back to the meditation on the sentry-platform, and its recognition of the 'one defect' which may 'Soil our addition; and indeed it takes / From our achievements, though perform'd at height, / The pith and marrow of our attribute' (I, iv, 20–2). M. M. Mahood's commentary is especially valuable here: 'Addition, besides being our applied title, is the sum total of our natures, what we add up to in ourselves. Attribute, according to the N.E.D., can mean not only a quality ascribed or assigned but an inherent or characteristic quality'.[1] The final implications of these terms, then, are that the 'one' of self must include the 'one defect', together with the sum of our inherent and attributed parts. Clearly, this 'one' cannot be adequately stated with the mere vulgar striking of a blow. Nor can it be expressed through the arts of the stage, though Hamlet had once, in a moment of devastating self-revelation, indicated that these would express him:

Hamlet. Would not this, sir, and a forest of feathers –
　if the rest of my fortunes turn Turk with me – with
　two Provincial roses on my razed shoes, get me a
　fellowship in a cry of players, sir?
Horatio. Half a share.
Hamlet. A whole one, I.

(III, ii, 286–91)

Identity can only be an experimental truth. It is confirmed in the moment of equipoise between self and situation, which must include the will to action and the public awareness of the act. The problem, then, is to encounter the moment that offers the opportunity of significant action. And this moment will present itself in the essential form of a challenge.

The challenge takes on the actuality of the King's wager. It is a formal, and symbolic, solution to Hamlet's predicament. Hamlet has previously indicated no plan, but a determination to use the time at his disposal: and his 'I am constant to my purposes, they follow the King's pleasure' is no less than the truth. He will react to the situation that 'special providence' supplies. He must have a dark awareness that in fencing with Laertes he is opposing the 'pass and fell incensèd point' of his adversary, the King. The challenge, then, gives Hamlet this: it is an opportunity for the duel, a symbolic yet real combat; it provides an audience, before which he can both vindicate and dramatize himself; and it is the imitation of a great act once performed by his father. The 'union' which is the central pun of the final scene is that of Hamlet himself, as – in death – with Laertes, with Claudius, with his father and mother, the 'one flesh' to which he had once referred (IV, iii, 54). The sword-play itself proceeds through the phases of symbolic contest, genuine fighting, and the ultimate act of killing the King. We should note that Hamlet does not kill Claudius until Laertes has gasped out the truth. The Court, therefore, knows it too – and apart from cries of 'Treason!' it does nothing to impede Hamlet in his regicide. He acts, then, upon the implied state of public knowledge and sanction – to which his last words enjoin Horatio. In the final minutes of

[1] M. M. Mahood, Shakespeare's Wordplay (1957), pp. 116–17.

his life, Hamlet has become King: and tragic hero. 'Il est devenu ce qu'il était.'

And perhaps this, the final position in Hamlet's life, is the answer to the kingly summons of the first scene, 'The bell then beating *one*...' Or perhaps we reflect back the soldierly rites of the conclusion into the prime meaning of Hamlet's 'one'. For Hamlet does say it. After the courtesies that precede the duel, Hamlet willing as ever to react rather than act invites Laertes to the first attack, 'Come on sir', and Laertes returns the invitation, 'Come my lord'. The rapiers touch then, and we may conceive of Hamlet, after that, launching the first attack. The dialogue of the foils, with its staccato interrogations and metallic elisions, is Hamlet's final scanning of his universe. Sooner or later he will pose Laertes a question to which the stock answer will come a fiftieth of a second too late. And then the counter-thrust slides inside its parry, and travels through free space home to its target, *one*.

'HAMLET' AND THE POWER OF WORDS

INGA-STINA EWBANK

If the first law of literary and dramatic criticism is that the approach to a work should be determined by the nature of that work, then I take courage from the fact that *Hamlet* is a play in which, in scene after scene, fools tend to rush in where angels fear to tread. That such fools also tend to come to a bad end – to be stabbed behind the arras or summarily executed in England, 'not shriving-time allowed' – I prefer at this point not to consider.

The area into which I propose to rush is the language of *Hamlet*. The method of entry is eclectic. If there is any timeliness about the rush it is that – just as ten years or so ago King Lear was Our Contemporary – Hamlet is now coming to the fore as one of the inhabitants of No Man's Land. A recent book on Shakespeare's *Tragic Alphabet* speaks of the play being about 'a world where words and gestures have become largely meaningless', and even as long as twenty-five years ago an article on 'The Word in *Hamlet*' began by drawing attention to 'the intensely critical, almost disillusionist, attitude of the play towards language itself'.[1] Against these, I must confess a firm (and perhaps old-fashioned) belief that *Hamlet*, the play, belongs not so much in No Man's as in Everyman's Land: that it is a vision of the human condition realized in the whole visual and verbal language of the theatre with such intensity and gusto that from any point of view it becomes meaningless to call that language meaningless; and that in the play as a whole speech is something far more complex, with powers for good and ill, than the 'words, words, words' of Hamlet's disillusionment. My

aim is to explore the part which speech plays in the life of this play *and* the function of speech as part of Shakespeare's vision in the play. I must start with an example.

At the opening of act IV – or, as some would prefer to describe it, at the close of the closet scene – Claudius pleads with Gertrude, whom he has found in considerable distress:

There's matter in these sighs, these profound heaves,
You must translate; 'tis fit we understand them.

Of course he thinks he knows what the 'matter' is, for he also immediately adds 'Where is your son?'. Gertrude has just been through the most harrowing[2] experience: Hamlet's words to her have 'like daggers' entered into her 'ears' and turned her 'eyes into [her] very soul' where she has gained such unspeakable knowledge of her 'black and grained spots' as might well have made her feel unable to comply with Claudius's request for a 'translation'. Indeed, in a modern play, where husbands and wives tend to find that on the whole they don't speak the same language, the shock of insight might well have led her to make some statement of non-communication – some version of the reply by Ibsen's Nora (that early non-communicat-

[1] Lawrence Danson, *Tragic Alphabet: Shakespeare's Drama of Language* (New Haven and London, 1974), p. 48; John Paterson, 'The Word in *Hamlet*', *Shakespeare Quarterly*, II (1951), 47.
[2] Though Gertrude herself does not use the verb 'harrow', I use it advisedly, as it seems to be a *Hamlet* word. It occurs once in *Coriolanus*, in its literal sense, but Shakespeare's only two metaphorical uses of it are in *Hamlet*: by the Ghost (I, v, 16) and by Horatio describing the impact of the Ghost (I, i, 44).

ing wife) to her husband's wish to 'understand' her reactions:

You don't understand me. Nor have I ever understood you.[1]

In fact, of course, Gertrude does the opposite. She provides a translation of the preceding scene which manages to avoid saying anything about herself but to describe Hamlet's madness, his killing of Polonius, and his treatment of the body. As so often in this play,[2] we have a retelling of an episode which we have already witnessed. And so we can see at once that Gertrude's translation is a mixture of three kinds of components: first, of what really happened and was said (including a direct quotation of Hamlet's cry 'a rat', though she doubles it and changes it from a question to an exclamation);[3] secondly, of what she thinks, or would like to think, happened and was said. She is prepared to read into Hamlet's behaviour such motivations, and to add such details, as she would have liked to find – as Polonius suspected when he appointed himself 'some more audience than a mother, / Since nature makes them partial' (III, iii, 31–2), though even he could not have foreseen that her partiality would come to extend to a fictitious description of Hamlet mourning over his corpse.[4] Thirdly, but most importantly, as it most controls both what she says and how she says it, her translation consists of what she wants the king to think did happen: that the scene demonstrated what Hamlet in a doubly ironic figure of speech had told her not to say, i.e. that he is 'essentially' mad and not 'mad in craft'. Her emotion is released, and her verbal energy spends itself, not on the part of the recent experience which concerns herself most radically, but on convincing her husband that her son is

Mad as the sea and wind, when both contend
Which is the mightier.

Claudius may end the scene 'full of discord and dismay', but – and this seems usually to be the most Gertrude can hope for – things are not as bad as they might have been. She has in a manner protected her son by sticking to her assurance to him that

if words be made of breath
And breath of life, I have no life to breathe
What thou hast said to me;

she has at least not added to Claudius's suspicions of Hamlet's 'antic disposition'; and she has paid some tribute to the victim of the game between the two, the murderer and the revenger: 'the unseen good old man'. I do not think that Gertrude's design is as conscious as this analysis may have suggested, but her translation has worked.

In so far as anything in this play, so full of surprises at every corner, is typical of the whole, the scene seems to me a model for how language functions within much of the play: communicating by adapting words to thought and feeling, in a process which involves strong awareness in the speaker of who is being spoken to. Of course there has not been much truth spoken and on that score, no doubt, the

---

[1] *A Doll's House*, act III (*Et dukkehjem*, in *Henrik Ibsens Samlede Verker*, Oslo, 1960, II, 474).

[2] Some other examples of 'translated' versions of an episode we have already seen are: Rosencrantz and Guildenstern's slanted report, in III, i, 4 ff., of their meeting with Hamlet in II, ii; Polonius's to Claudius and Gertrude, in II, ii, 130 ff., of how he admonished Ophelia in I, iii; and Polonius's attempt to bolster up Claudius, in III, iii, 30 ff., by attributing to him his own plan hatched at III, i, 184–5. Significantly, at the end of the nunnery scene Polonius and Claudius specifically do not want a report from Ophelia: 'We heard it all' (III, i, 180).

[3] That is, in the punctuation of modern editors (e.g. Alexander and Dover Wilson). In Q 2 Hamlet says 'a Rat,' and Gertrude 'a Rat, a Rat,'; in F 1 the readings are, respectively, 'a Rat?' and 'a Rat, a Rat,'.

[4] As Dover Wilson points out in his note on 'a weeps for what is done', 'the falsehood testifies to her fidelity' (New Cambridge Shakespeare, *Hamlet*, 1934, p. 218).

scene is a thematic illustration of that dreaded pair of abstracts, Appearance and Reality; and the author's attitude is 'disillusionist' enough. And of course the scene in one sense speaks of non-communication between husband and wife. Gertrude has drawn apart, with her unspeakable knowledge and suspicion, much as Macbeth has when he bids his wife 'Be innocent of the knowledge, dearest chuck' (*Macbeth*, III, ii, 45). But, in its dramatic context, the language does a great deal more than that. There is, as Polonius has said, 'some more audience' in the theatre, and to them – to us – the language speaks eloquently of the strange complexities of human life, of motives and responses and the re-alignment of relationships under stress. It speaks of Gertrude's desperate attempt to remain loyal to her son but also (however misguidedly) to her husband and to his chief councillor. Ultimately the power of the words is Shakespeare's, not Gertrude's, and it operates even through the total muteness of Rosencrantz and Guildenstern who, like parcels, are, most Stoppard-like, sent out and in and out again in the course of the scene.

Claudius's verb for what he asks Gertrude to do is apter than he knew himself: 'You must translate'. Presumably (and editors do not seem to feel that annotation is needed) he simply wants her to interpret her signs of emotion in words, to change a visual language into a verbal. But, as anyone knows who has attempted translation in its now most commonly accepted sense, the processes involved in finding equivalents in one language for the signs of another are far from simple. There is a troublesome tension – indeed often an insoluble contradiction – between the demands of 'interpretation' and those of 'change', between original meaning and meaningfulness in another language. That Shakespeare was aware of this – although, unlike many of his fellow poets and dramatists, he was apparently

not an inter-lingual translator – is suggested, in the first place, by the various ways in which he uses the word 'translate' in his plays. Alexander Schmidt's *Shakespeare-Lexicon* separates three clearly defined meanings: 1. to transform or to change, as Bottom is 'translated', or as beauty is *not* translated into honesty in the nunnery scene; 2. 'to render into another language (or rather to change by rendering into another language)', as Falstaff translates Mistress Ford's inclinations 'out of honesty into English', or as the Archbishop of York translates his whole being 'Out of the speech of peace . . . Into the harsh and boist'-rous tongue of war' (both these examples being rather demanding in the way of dictionaries); and 3. to interpret or explain, as in the Claudius line I have been discussing, or as Aeneas has translated Troilus to Ulysses.[1] Not only do Schmidt and the *OED* disagree over these definitions,[2] but, as the examples I have given indicate, meanings seem to overlap within Shakespeare's uses of the word – so that all three hover around the following lines from Sonnet 96:

So are those errors that in thee are seen
    To truths translated and for true things deem'd.

That sonnet is in a sense about the problem of finding a language for the 'grace and faults' of the beloved – a problem which haunts many of the Sonnets and can be solved, the poems show, only by fusing change and interpretation into a single poetic act. In much the same way, *Hamlet* is dominated by the hero's search for a way to translate (though Shakespeare does not use the word here) the contra-

[1] See *A Midsummer Night's Dream*, III, i, 109; *Hamlet*, III, i, 113; *The Merry Wives*, I, iii, 47; 2 *Henry IV*, IV, i, 46–8; *Troilus and Cressida*, IV, v, 112.
[2] The *OED*, for example, uses both Claudius's line and the one from *The Merry Wives* to illustrate the meaning 'to interpret, explain' ('Translate' II.3. *fig.*)

dictory demands of the Ghost:

> If thou hast nature in thee, bear it not;
> . . . .
> But, howsomever thou pursuest this act,
> Taint not thy mind . . .
>
> (I, v, 81, 84–5)

Claudius, we are going to see, finds that his position translates best into oxymorons; and Troilus feels the need to be bilingual – 'this is, and is not, Cressid' – or simply silent: 'Hector is dead; there is no more to say'.

If, then, to translate means both to interpret and to change, it also usually means being particularly conscious of the words used in the process. All of us, surely, are prepared to claim with Coleridge that we have 'a smack of Hamlet' in us; but those of us who have approached the English language from the outside may perhaps claim a special kind of smack. For lack of sophistication we may share that alertness to a rich, hybrid language, to latent metaphors and multiple meanings waiting to be activated, which Hamlet has by an excess of sophistication. With still fresh memories of looking up a word in the English dictionary and finding a bewildering row of possible meanings, or an equally bewildering row of words for a supposedly given meaning, we are also peculiarly prepared to give more than local significance to Claudius's line: 'You must translate; 'tis fit we understand'.

I would not indulge in these speculations if I did not believe that they applied directly to *Hamlet*. George Steiner, in *After Babel*, maintains that '*inside or between languages, human communication equals translation*'.[1] *Hamlet*, I think, bears out the truth of this. Hamlet himself is throughout the play trying to find a language to express himself through, as well as languages to speak to others in; and round him – against him and for him – the members of the court of Elsinore are engaging in acts of translation. The first meeting with Rosencrantz and Guildenstern, in II, ii, would

be a specific example of this general statement. Hamlet's speech on how he has of late lost all his mirth – mounting to the much-quoted 'What a piece of work is man! . . . / And yet, to me, what is this quintessence of dust?' – is only partly, if at all, a spontaneous overflow of his mythical sorrows (let alone of Shakespeare's). Partly, even mainly, it is his translation, in such terms of *fin-de-siècle* disillusionment as clever young men will appreciate, of just as much of his frame of mind as he wants Rosencrantz and Guildenstern to understand. And the verbal hide-and-seek of the whole episode turns what might have been a simple spy / counterspy scene into a complex study of people trying to control each other by words. Here, and elsewhere in the play, the mystery of human intercourse is enacted and the power of words demonstrated: what we say, and by saying do, to each other, creating and destroying as we go along.

No one in the play seems to regret that it is words they 'gotta use' when they speak to each other. Hamlet, unlike Coriolanus, never holds his mother 'by the hand, silent'; and his only major speechless moment is that which Ophelia describes to Polonius, when

> with a look so piteous in purport
> As if he had been loosed out of hell
> To speak of horrors – he comes before me.
>
> (II, i, 81–4)

The Ghost does indeed hint at unspeakable horrors – 'I could a tale unfold' – but he is very explicit about the effects its 'lightest word' would have, and the only reason he does not speak those words is a purgatorial prohibition on telling 'the secrets of my prison-house' to 'ears of flesh and blood' (I, v, 13 ff.). Words govern the action of the play, from the ironical watchword – 'Long live the King!' – which allays Francisco's fears

---

[1] *After Babel: Aspects of Language and Translation* (1975), p. 47 (Dr Steiner's italics).

at the opening, to Hamlet's 'dying voice' which gives the throne of Denmark to Fortinbras at the end; and, beyond, to the speech which will be given by Horatio when it is all over, explaining 'to th'yet unknowing world / How these things came about'. Words control the fates and the development of the characters, and not only when they are spoken by the Ghost to Hamlet and turned by him into a principle of action ('Now to my word': I, v, 110). Words can open Gertrude's eyes, help to drive Ophelia mad, unpack Hamlet's heart (however much he regrets it); and if Claudius finds that 'words without thoughts never to heaven go' (III, iii, 98), this merely validates those words which have thoughts. Sometimes the words deceive, sometimes they say what is felt and meant, sometimes they are inadequate – but the inadequacy reflects on the speaker rather than the language. In the study, where the play so readily presents itself spatially and thematically, it may be easy to speak of it as demonstrating the inadequacy of words. In the theatre, the words have to get us through the four-and-a-half hours traffic of the stage, and (when they have not been cut or played about with) they give us a play of relationships, of 'comutual' (as the Player King would call them) interactions and dialogues – a world where it is natural to ask not only 'What's Hecuba to him?' but also 'or he to Hecuba?'. *Hamlet*, for all its soliloquies, may well be the Shakespeare play which most confirms Ben Jonson's statement, in *Discoveries*, that language 'is the instrument of society'; and in exploring the function of speech in the play we may do well to listen to Henry James's words to the graduating class at Bryn Mawr College in June 1905:

All life therefore comes back to the question of our speech, the medium through which we communicate with each other; for all life comes back to the question of our relations with each other . . .
. . . the way we say a thing, or fail to say it, fail to learn to say it, has an importance in life that is impossible to overstate – a far-reaching importance, as the very hinge of the relation of man to man.[1]

Looking at the world of 'relations' in *Hamlet* from the outside, we can have no doubt that its hinges are well oiled, by the sheer size of its vocabulary. Long ago now, the patient industry of Alfred Hart demonstrated that *Hamlet* has 'the largest and most expressive vocabulary' of all Shakespeare's plays, and that it abounds in new words – new to Shakespeare and also, in many cases, apparently new to English literature – a considerable number of which do not recur in any later Shakespeare plays.[2] And a new language for new and unique experiences is suggested not only by the single words but by the new structures, images and figures into which they are combined – as indeed by the new uses of old syntactical patterns and rhetorical figures. (It is worth remembering that, seen through the eyes of T. W. Baldwin and Sister Miriam Joseph, Hamlet's forerunners are Holofernes and Sir Nathaniel.)[3] Language is being stretched and re-shaped to show the form and pressure of the *Hamlet* world. The extraordinary variety of language modes is important, too: we move, between scenes or within a scene or even within a speech, from moments

[1] See *Discoveries* CXXVIII, and Henry James, *The Question of Our Speech* (Boston and New York, 1905), p. 10 and p. 21.
[2] Alfred Hart, 'Vocabularies of Shakespeare's Plays', *Review of English Studies* XIX (1943), 128–40, and 'The Growth of Shakespeare's Vocabulary', *ibid.*, 242–3. The subject was freshly illuminated in the paper on 'New Words between *Henry IV* and *Hamlet*' given by Professor Marvin Spevack at the Seventeenth International Shakespeare Conference in Stratford-upon-Avon, August 1976, and by the booklet of word lists which he distributed in connection with his paper.
[3] T. W. Baldwin, *William Shakspere's Small Latine and Lesse Greeke*, 2 vols. (Urbana, Ill., 1944), *passim*; and Sister Miriam Joseph, *Shakespeare's Use of the Arts of Language* (New York, 1947), esp. p. 12.

of high elaboration and formality to moments of what Yeats would have called 'walking naked',[1] where speech is what the Sonnets call 'true and plain' and we call 'naturalistic'.

If we view the world of *Hamlet* from the inside, we find that what the still small voices in the play have in common with the loud and eloquent ones is a general belief in the importance of speaking. The play begins with three men repeatedly imploring a ghost to speak and ends with Hamlet's concern for what Horatio is going to 'speak to th'yet unknowing world', and in between characters are always urging each other to speak. It is as natural for Laertes to part from Ophelia with a 'let me hear from you' (I, iii, 4) as it is for Polonius to react to Ophelia's 'affrighted' description of Hamlet's appearance with 'What said he?' (II, i, 86). In this particular instance there is no speech to report, but the key-note of most of the character confrontations in the play could, again, have been taken from the *Discoveries*: 'Language most shews a man: Speak, that I may see thee.'[2] In *Hamlet*, unlike *King Lear*, seeing is rarely enough. Ophelia's lament at the end of the nunnery scene –

O, woe is me
T' have seen what I have seen, see what I see! –

follows upon an unusually (for her) eloquent analysis of both what she has seen and what she is seeing ('O, what a noble mind is here o'er-thrown!'); and Gertrude, we know, soon finds words to translate into words her exclamation, 'Ah, mine own lord, what have I seen tonight!' Often seeing has to be achieved through hearing. 'You go not till I set you up a glass', Hamlet tells his mother, but that 'glass' is not so much 'the counterfeit presentment of two brothers' as Hamlet's speech on Gertrude's lack of 'eyes'. Unlike Edgar, Horatio is left with the exact and exacting task of speaking not what he feels, but what he ought to say. One begins to feel that the ear is the main sense organ in *Hamlet*, and concordances confirm that the word 'ear' occurs in this play more times than in any other of Shakespeare's.[3] Through the ear – 'attent', or 'knowing' – comes the understanding which Claudius asks Gertrude for in IV, i; but through the 'too credent' or 'foolish' ear come deception and corruption. Claudius seems obsessed with a sense of Laertes's ear being infected 'with pestilent speeches' while he himself is being arraigned 'in ear and ear' (IV, v, 87–91). Well he might be, for in the Ghost's speech all of Denmark had, as in a Bosch vision, been contracted into a single ear:

so the whole ear of Denmark
Is by a forged process of my death
Rankly abus'd;   (I, v, 36–8)

and the ironic source and sounding-board of all these images is of course the literal poisoning by ear on which the plot of the play rests.

So the characters not only speak, they listen. Not only do we, the audience, marvel at the variety of idioms heard, from Gravedigger to Player King, from Osric, who has 'only got the tune of the time and the outward habit of encounter' (V, ii, 185), to Ophelia whose real fluency comes only in madness. But the characters themselves take a conscious and delighted interest in the idiosyncrasies of individual and national idioms, in how people speak, as Polonius says, 'according to the

---

[1] W. B. Yeats, 'A Coat'. (*Collected Poems*, 1933, p. 142).

[2] *Discoveries* CXXXII (*Oratio imago animi*).

[3] 'Ear' and 'ears' occur, together, 24 (16 + 8) times. The second largest figure is for *Coriolanus*: 17 (3 + 14) times. The different lengths, in lines, make comparisons somewhat unreliable; though *Coriolanus* is less than 500 lines shorter than *Hamlet*, and *King Lear*, with 3,205 lines as against *Hamlet*'s 3,762, has only 5 (4 + 1) occurrences of 'ear' and 'ears'. (I take my figures for lengths in lines from Hart, 'Vocabularies of Shakespeare's Plays', and for word frequencies from Marvin Spevack's *Harvard Concordance to Shakespeare*, Cambridge, Mass., 1973).

phrase and the addition / Of man and country' (II, i, 47–8). Hamlet's parodies of spoken and written styles are outstanding, but Polonius – in instructing Reynaldo – is just as good at imitating potential conversations. Seen from our point of view or the characters', the play is alive with interest in how people react to each other and to each other's language.

Like Claudius, in the scene from which I began, the characters, when they urge each other to speak, expect to understand the 'matter', or meaning, of what is said. Hence they are particularly disturbed by the apparent meaninglessness of 'antic' speech – 'I have nothing with this answer, Hamlet; these words are not mine', is Claudius's sharpest and most direct rebuke to his nephew / son (III, ii, 93–4) – and by the dim apprehension, again expressed by Claudius, after overhearing the nunnery scene, that the lack of 'form' in such speech may conceal 'something' (III, i, 162 ff.) Laertes does recognize that mad speech may reach beyond rational discourse – 'This nothing's more than matter' – and be more effectively moving (IV, v, 171 and 165–6). But the first we hear of Ophelia's madness is Gertrude's abrupt opening line in IV, v: 'I will not speak with her', followed by the Gentleman's long account of her language:

> Her speech is nothing,
> Yet the unshaped use of it doth move
> The hearers to collection; they yawn at it,
> And botch the words up fit to their own thoughts.
>
> (ll. 7–10)

Yielding to Horatio's cautiously applied pressure – ''Twere good she were spoken with' – Gertrude can attempt a dialogue only through the usual request for *meaning*: 'Alas, sweet lady, what imports this song?'; and even Ophelia knows through her madness the kind of question that will be asked about her: 'when they ask you what it means, say you this: . . .'

We have returned to the idea of translation, for in their intercourse the characters seem unusually aware of their interlocutors' tendency to 'botch the words up fit to their own thoughts'. One main aspect of this is the belief, demonstrated throughout the play, in the importance of finding the right language for the right person. The opening scene is a model of this. Horatio had been brought in as a translator ('Thou art a scholar; speak to it, Horatio')[1] but, though the Ghost's first appearance turns him from scepticism to 'fear and wonder', he is unsure of his language. His vocabulary is wrong: 'What art thou that usurp'st [a particularly unfortunate verb in the circumstances] this time of night . . .?' and so is his tone: 'By heaven I charge thee, speak!'. On the Ghost's second appearance, Horatio's litany of appeals – 'If . . . Speak to me' – more nearly approaches the ceremony which befits a king. The second 'If', with its sense of 'comutual' purpose, gets very warm –

> If there be any good thing to be done,
> That may to thee do ease and grace to me –

but Horatio then loses himself in the motivations of generalized ghost lore; and, in any case, Time in the form of a cock's crow interrupts any possible interchange. A 'show of violence' signals the hopeless defeat of verbal communication. Horatio now knows that none but Hamlet can find the language needed, and so the scene ends with the decision to 'impart what we have seen tonight / Unto young Hamlet', for:

> This spirit, dumb to us, will speak to him.

But the gap between speakers which – they are aware – must be bridged by translation is

[1] As Professor A. C. Sprague has pointed out to me, G. L. Kittredge exploded the idea (still adhered to by Dover Wilson; see his note on I, i, 42) that this line refers to the fact that exorcisms of spirits were usually performed in Latin. 'Horatio, as a scholar, knows how to address the apparition in the right way, so as neither to offend it nor to subject himself to any evil influence.' (G. L. Kittredge, ed., *Sixteen Plays of Shakespeare* (Boston, 1939), p. 1021).

not always as wide as the grave. The king appeals to Rosencrantz and Guildenstern as being on the same side of the generation gap as Hamlet –

> being of so young days brought up with him,
> And sith so neighboured to his youth and haviour –
> (II, ii, 11–12)

which should give them a language 'to gather,/So much as from occasion you may glean'; and Hamlet conjures them to tell the truth 'by the consonancy of our youth' (II, ii, 283). When the opening of the closet scene has demonstrated that Gertrude's language and her son's are in diametrical opposition –

> Hamlet, thou hast thy father much offended.
> Mother, you have my father much offended. –

and that he will not adopt the language of a son to a mother ('Have you forgot me?') but insists on a vocabulary and syntax which ram home the confusion in the state of Denmark –

> No, by the rood, not so:
> You are the Queen, your husband's brother's wife.
> And – would it were not so! – you are my mother –

then Gertrude can see no other way out of the deadlock but to call for translators:

> Nay then, I'll set those to you that can speak.

Hamlet's refusal to be thus translated is what leads to Polonius's death. Polonius spends much energy, in his last few days of life, on finding a language for a madman, trying – as in II, ii – at the same time to humour and to analyse Hamlet. But Rosencrantz and Guildenstern are perhaps even more supremely aware of the necessity of different languages for different persons. They take their colour, their style, tone and imagery, from their interlocutors, whether it is a question of speaking the snappy, quibbling dialogue of clever young students with Hamlet on first meeting him,

or enlarging before Claudius on the idea of 'the cease of majesty' so that it becomes an extended image of 'a massy wheel,/Fixed on the summit of the highest mount' (III, iii, 10 ff.). They are in the end chameleons rather than caterpillars, and it is naturally to them that Hamlet speaks the words in which the play's interest in suiting language to persons is taken to the extreme of parody:

> Besides, to be demanded of a sponge – what replication should be made by the son of a king?
> (IV, ii, 12)

It is natural, too, that when the programming has gone wrong in their language laboratory they are helpless and can say nothing but

> What should we say, my lord?
> (II, ii, 275)

The characters of the play, then, are on the whole very self-conscious speakers, in a way which involves consciousness of others: they believe in the word and its powers, but they are also aware of the necessity so to translate intentions and experiences into words as to make them meaningful to the interlocutor. And not only vaguely meaningful: they know the effect they want to produce and take careful steps to achieve it. Perhaps the Reynaldo scene is the best model of this. Polonius, in a dialogue of superb naturalism, with its stops and starts, doublings back and forgettings what he was about to say, gives Reynaldo a lesson in translation which is much closer to the heart of the play than any mere plot function might suggest. Anyone who thinks Polonius just a fool ought to look again at the almost Jamesian subtlety with which Reynaldo is instructed to control the *tone* of his indirect enquiries into Laertes's Parisian life, to

> breathe his faults so quaintly
> That they may seem the taints of liberty,
> (II, i, 31–2)

and, in case he has not got the point, to lay

'these slight sullies on my son,/As 'twere a thing a little soil'd wi' th' working' (ll. 39–40). This is a situation less Machiavellian than the Revenge *genre* might seem to demand, and more like the instruction of Strether where, as here, facts tend to refract into opaque impressions rather than moral certainties.

Perhaps I am now being seduced by the power of words – and Polonius's of all people. Not that Shakespeare allows this to happen for very long: the moment that Reynaldo exits, Ophelia bursts in, and the contrast is blatant between the urbanity of the preceding scene and the raw experience of her account – acted out as much as spoken – of Hamlet's speechless visit to her. Clearly, when the characters in *Hamlet* use their language, or languages, for purposes of persuasion and diplomacy, they are generally engaging in duplicity and deception. In the end, the evil underneath is (as James also knew) made more, not less, pernicious by the bland surface of the dialogue. An outstanding example of this is the 'witchcraft of his wits' (as the Ghost is to describe the usurper's 'power/So to seduce') practised by Claudius in the second scene of the play. His opening speech establishes him as a very clever chairman of the board. First he gets the minutes of past proceedings accepted without query, by a carefully arranged structure of oxymorons:[1]

> Therefore our sometime sister, now our queen,
> Th'imperial jointress to this warlike state,
> Have we, as 'twere with a defeated joy,
> With an auspicious and a dropping eye,
> With mirth in funeral, and with dirge in marriage,
> In equal scale weighing delight and dole,
> Taken to wife. (I, ii, 8–14)

The oxymorons, in a relentless series of pairings, operate to cancel each other out, smoothing over the embarrassment (or worse) involved in 'our sometime sister, now our queen', stilling criticism and enforcing acceptance of the apparent logic of the argument, so

that by the time we finally get to the verb ('Taken to wife') the 'Therefore' seems legitimate. Then he justifies chairman's action by suggesting that there have been consultations all along, spiking the guns of any potential rebel by thanking him in advance for his agreement:

> nor have we herein barr'd
> Your better wisdoms, which have freely gone
> With this affair along. For all, our thanks.
> (ll. 14–16)

Having dealt with the minutes, he then proceeds to the agenda and polishes off, in turn, the foreign policy problems with Norway, the home and domestic issue of Laertes, and finally the awkward business with Hamlet which – who knows – might be both personal and national, psychological and political. He intends to deal with Hamlet, too, through the technique of dissolving contradictions –

> But now, my cousin Hamlet, and my son –
> (l. 64)

but his briskness here comes to grief, as Hamlet becomes the first to raise a voice, albeit in an aside, which punctures such use of language:

> A little more than kin, and less than kind.
> (l. 65)

Intrepidly, Claudius continues in an image suggesting the tone of decorous grief which ought to be adopted – 'How is it that the clouds still hang on you?' – but this again founders on Hamlet's pun on sun/son. The pun, according to Sigurd Burckhardt in *Shakespearean Meanings*, 'gives the lie direct to the social convention which is language. . . . It denies the meaningfulness of words.'[2] But in their dramatic context here, Hamlet's puns do no

---

[1] Danson, *Tragic Alphabet*, p. 26, has some excellent comments on Claudius's use of the oxymoron.
[2] Sigurd Burckhardt, *Shakespearean Meanings* (Princeton, N.J., 1968), pp. 24–5, quoted also by Danson, p. 27, n. 2.

such thing: they deny the logic and sincerity and meaningfulness of Claudius's words but suggest that there is a language elsewhere.

The rest of the scene, until it closes on Hamlet's decision to 'hold my tongue', is a series of contrasts and clashes between different languages. Hamlet's 'common' is not the queen's and implies a far-reaching criticism of hers. Gertrude's reply suggests that she is not aware of the difference, Claudius's that he is trying to pretend that he is not, as he follows Hamlet's terrible outburst against seeming with an, in its way, equally terrible refusal to acknowledge any jar:

'Tis sweet and commendable in your nature, Hamlet,
To give these mourning duties to your father.
(ll. 87–8)

Hamlet has no reply to Claudius's appeal to the 'common theme' of death of fathers, nor to the request that he give up Wittenberg for 'the cheer and comfort of our eye'; his reply, promising to 'obey', is made to his mother. But it is Claudius who comments on it as 'loving' and 'fair', and it is he who sums up the conversation, translating the tense scene just past into an image of domestic and national harmony –

This gentle and unforc'd account of Hamlet
Sits smiling to my heart –   (ll. 123–4)

and an excuse for a 'wassail'. The incongruity is as if a satire and a masque by Jonson were being simultaneously performed on the same stage. The ultimate clash comes as, immediately upon Claudius's summing-up, Hamlet breaks into his first soliloquy, giving *his* version of himself and of 'all the uses of this world', particularly those involving his mother and uncle.

The different languages spoken in a scene like this clearly add up to a kind of moral map. That is, the adding up is clear, the map itself not necessarily so. It is not just a matter of Hamlet's words being sincere and Claudius's

not. In the dialogue Hamlet is striving for effect in his way just as much as Claudius in his. And Claudius is soon going to be sincere enough, when we learn from his own mouth, in an image that could well have been used by Hamlet, that he is aware of the ugliness of his deed as against his 'most painted word' (III, i, 50–4) and that his words are unable to rise in prayer (III, iii, 36 ff.). Morality and sensitivity to language are peculiarly tied up with each other in this play; and in trying to think how they are related I, at least, am driven back to James and 'The Question of Our Speech': to the importance of 'the way we say a thing, or fail to say it, fail to learn to say it'.[1] In a play peopled by translators, it is in the end the range of languages available to each character – those they 'fail to learn' as well as those they speak – which measures their moral stature. Both Claudius and Gertrude at various times have their consciences stung, but neither seems able to find a language for his or her own inner self. Even Polonius is able to learn and, up to a point, articulate what he has learnt. 'I am sorry', he says about having misunderstood the nature of Hamlet's love for Ophelia, 'that with better heed and judgment/I had not quoted him' (II, i, 111–12). Hamlet himself never has such a moment of recognition in regard to Ophelia. But typically Polonius at once takes the edge off any personal pain of remorse by translating it into a sententious generalization:

It is as proper to our age
To cast beyond ourselves in our opinions
As it is common for the younger sort
To lack discretion.   (II, i, 114–17)

Claudius similarly lacks a really private language. Even when he is alone and trying to pray, his speech retains the basic characteristics of his public 'translations'. Images which in content might seem to anticipate

[1] See note 1, p. 88, above.

Macbeth's,[1] are turned out in carefully balanced phrases – 'heart, with strings of steel' against 'sinews of the new-born babe'; his similes have the considered effect of earlier tragic verse:

> And, like a man to double business bound,
> I stand in pause where I shall first begin,
> And both neglect;   (III, iii, 41–3)

and the most trenchant self-analysis is as cleverly antithetical as anything he has to say before the assembled court in I, ii: 'My stronger guilt defends my strong intent'. Unlike Macbeth, Claudius seems to be talking *about* himself, not from inside himself, and his own evil seems to contain no mystery to him, nothing unspeakable. Gertrude has known less evil, and her moral imagination has an even narrower range. Even after the closet scene, her appearances suggest that, like Claudius and unlike Lady Macbeth, she is able to cancel and pass on. The woman who describes Ophelia's death, and strews flowers on her grave, is harrowed within her limits but not marked and changed by her experience, in language and being. The fact that Hamlet and Ophelia are thus changed (however variously) sets them apart. Each of them receives shocks and undergoes sufferings which are taken into their language; and at the extremest point each speaks – whether in madness or not – a language foreign to the other characters.[2]

And yet Hamlet's own language is in many ways that of Elsinore. As others, notably R. A. Foakes, have pointed out, his speech modes and habits are largely those of the court: wordiness, formality, sententiousness, fondness of puns and other forms of word-play, etc.[3] He too uses language in all the ways practised by Claudius and his entourage: for persuasion, diplomacy, deception, and so on. His sheer range, which is as large almost as that of the play itself, has made it difficult for critics to define his own linguistic and stylistic attributes. As Professor Foakes succinctly puts it, 'Hamlet seems master of all styles, but has no distinctive utterance of his own.' Up to a point we can explain this, as Professor Foakes does, by seeing Hamlet as 'the supreme actor who never reveals himself'.[4] But beyond that point we still need a way of talking about Hamlet's language which includes his uncontrolled and (surely) revealing moments, such as the nunnery scene or the leaping into Ophelia's grave, as well as his moments of deliberately antic disposition; and the simple statements in the dialogues with Horatio as well as the tortuous questioning in the monologues. It might be helpful, then, to think of Hamlet as the most sensitive translator in the play: as the one who has the keenest sense both of the expressive and the persuasive powers of words, and also and more radically the keenest sense both of the limitations and the possibilities of words. No one could be more disillusioned with 'words, words, words'. Even before he appears on stage, his mother's rush 'to incestuous sheets' has had an impact which he later describes as having (in contemporary parlance) deprived language of its very credibility:

> O, such a deed
> As . . . sweet religion makes
> A rhapsody of words;
>
>   (III, iv, 45–8)

and, though a Wittenberg scholar could hardly

---

[1] Claudius wonders whether there is not 'rain enough in the sweet heavens' to wash his 'cursed hand . . . white as snow', and he associates innocence with a 'new-born babe'.

[2] Marvin Spevack has a very interesting discussion of how Hamlet's imagery shows him transforming all he sees, and how he is thus isolated by speaking, as it were, a foreign language; see 'Hamlet and Imagery: The Mind's Eye', *Die Neueren Sprachen*, n.s. v (1966), 203–12.

[3] R. A. Foakes, '*Hamlet* and the Court of Elsinore', *Shakespeare Survey 9* (Cambridge, 1956), pp. 35–43.

[4] R. A. Foakes, 'Character and Speech in *Hamlet*', in *Hamlet: Stratford-upon-Avon Studies 5* (1963), p. 161.

have lived unaware of the general maxim that 'one may smile, and smile, and be a villain', the encounter with the Ghost proves it on his own pulses and leaves him permanently aware that language may be a cloak or masque. Yet no one could use his disillusionment more subtly or positively to fit his words to the action, the interlocutor and his own mood – so far indeed that the disillusionment is swallowed up in excitement at the power of words.

No other Shakespearian hero, tragic or comic, has to face so many situations in which different speakers have different palpable designs on him, and where he so has to get hold of the verbal initiative. No other hero, not even Falstaff or Benedick, is so good at grasping the initiative, leading his interlocutor by the nose while – as with Polonius and Osric – playing with the very shape and temperature of reality. Many of the play's comic effects stem from this activity, and the strange tonal mixture of the graveyard scene has much to do with Hamlet, for once, almost playing the stooge to the indomitable wit of the First Gravedigger. No other Shakespearian hero is so good at running his antagonists right down to their basic premisses and striking them dumb, as with Rosencrantz and Guildenstern in the recorder scene. He won't be played upon, and so he listens in order, with lightning speed, to pick up a key-word and turn it into a pun or some other device for playing upon others.

But, unlike many other Shakespearian tragic heroes, Hamlet also listens in a more reflective way – listens and evaluates, as Othello does not (but Hamlet surely would have done) with Iago. In some situations we begin to feel that his linguistic flexibility is founded on a sympathetic imagination. In him, alone in the play, the ability to speak different languages to different people seems to stem from an awareness that, in George Eliot's words, another being may have 'an equivalent centre

of self, whence the lights and shadows must always fall with a certain difference'.[1] Other characters meet to plot or to remonstrate, or they step aside for an odd twitch of conscience. To Hamlet, conversations may become extensions of moral sympathy. Even under the immediate impact of encountering the Ghost he can stop to realize and regret that he has offended Horatio with the 'wild and whirling words' which came out of a hysterical absorption in his own experience (I, v, 133 ff.). In retrospect the scene at Ophelia's grave is illuminated by the same sympathy:

> I am very sorry, good Horatio,
> That to Laertes I forgot myself;
> For by the image of my cause I see
> The portraiture of his;　　(v, ii, 75–8)

and the courtly apology to Laertes (v, ii, 218 ff.), which some critics have taken to be mere falsehood,[2] is surely a genuine attempt at translating his own 'cause' into the language of Laertes. In a case like this, his verbal virtuosity seems to aim at an interchange, a two-way traffic of language between selves. It is worth noting that Hamlet's most explicit tribute to Horatio is to call him 'e'en as just a man / As e'er my conversation cop'd withal' (III, ii, 52–3). Two senses of 'conversation' merge in that phrase – 'the action of consorting or having dealings with others; . . . society; intimacy' (OED 2) and 'interchange of thoughts and words' (OED 7) – and, one feels, in Hamlet's consciousness.

There is a kinship here between Hamlet and Cleopatra, another character who in her

---

[1] *Middlemarch*, end of chap. 21 (Penguin ed., p. 243).

[2] For a conspectus of these, see Dover Wilson's note on v, ii, 230, and the Furness *Variorum* edition of *Hamlet*, I, 440. Dr Johnson wished that Hamlet 'had made some other defence; it is unsuitable to the character of a brave or good man to shelter himself in falsehood'; and Seymour believed that the passage was an interpolation: 'The falsehood contained in it is too ignoble.'

language combines intense self-preoccupation with strong awareness of others. In North's Plutarch Shakespeare would have found an emphasis on her verbal powers, even at the expense of her physical beauty which,

as it is reported, was not so passing as unmatchable of other women, nor yet such as upon present view did enamour men with her; but so sweet was her company and conversation that a man could not possibly but be taken.

Not the least part of the power of Cleopatra's 'conversation' was her ability to speak different languages:

her tongue was an instrument of music to divers sports and pastimes, the which she easily turned to any language that pleased her. She spake unto few barbarous people by interpreter, but made them answer herself.[1]

It may not be wholly fanciful to imagine that North's comments on Cleopatra's inter-lingual dexterity have in Shakespeare been translated into an intralingual flexibility. Cleopatra is able to speak different languages to Emperor and to Clown as well as to forge her own variety of idioms according to situation and mood – and finally to create, through language, her own reality and Antony's ('Methinks I hear/Antony call.... Husband I come'). In her case, as in Hamlet's, the vitality which comes from superb handling of language affects us both aesthetically and morally. To measure it we need only turn to Octavia who is 'of a holy, cold and still conversation'.

Yet by the same measurement there is only a hair's breadth between moral sympathy and callousness, and *Hamlet* shows this too. Hamlet's awareness of others as autonomous beings with 'causes', and accordingly with languages, of their own also helps to explain why he despises Rosencrantz and Guildenstern so, and can so unflinchingly let them 'go to't', recounting his dealings with them as

'not near my conscience' only a few lines before he speaks to Horatio of his regret for what he did and said to Laertes. To him they lack any 'centre of self'; they are instruments used to turn others into 'unworthy' things (III, iii, 353); they are sponges whose only function is to be 'at each ear a hearer' (II, ii, 377). Hamlet's sympathetic imagination falls far short of Stoppard's, and of Christian charity. The killing of Polonius, whom he sees only as an over-hearer and a mouthpiece, affects him no more than a putting-down in verbal repartee:

> Take thy fortune;
> Thou find'st that to be busy is some danger.
> (III, iv, 32–3)

At this point, his whole sense of 'conversation' – of dealings with others – is narrowed onto speaking 'daggers' to Gertrude:

Leave wringing of your hands. Peace; sit you down,
And let me wring your heart. (III, iv, 34–5)

Everyone knows that Hamlet speaks rather than acts, and therefore delays; but it is worth pointing out that his peculiar involvement with words can be at the expense of humanity as well as of deeds. It is worth remembering, when we speak of Hamlet as an actor (who can 'act' but not act), that what he remembers from plays are great speeches; and that his own acting – as against his advice to the actors and his full admiration of their art – is almost entirely a matter of handling language: of the ability to control other people's reaction to his words. His self-reproach after the Hecuba speech is not that he can do nothing but that

> I ... unpregnant of my cause
> ... can say nothing. (II, ii, 562–3)

[1] *Shakespeare's Plutarch*, ed. T. J. B. Spencer in the Penguin Shakespeare Library (Harmondsworth, 1964), p. 203. Cleopatra, it is pointed out, differs from 'divers of her progenitors, the Kings of Egypt', who 'could scarce learn the Egyptian tongue only'.

Yet, less than twenty lines later he is reproaching himself for saying too much,

> That I, the son of a dear father murder'd,
> Prompted to my revenge by heaven and hell,
> Must, like a whore, unpack my heart with words.
>
> (ii, ii, 579–81)

There is no contradiction here for, while the words with which he unpacks his heart are merely therapeutic, even an anodyne, directed at no object and no audience, the 'saying' which he admires in the First Player is the absorption of the self in a purposeful act of communication, 'his whole function suiting / With forms to his conceit'. The language needed for his own 'conceit' is non-verbal, the act of revenge to which he is 'prompted'. Yet in the logic of this soliloquy, transferring his own 'motive' and 'cue for passion' to the Player and imagining the result, the act is translated into a theatrical declamation:

> He would drown the stage with tears,
> And cleave the general ear with horrid speech;
> Make mad the guilty, and appal the free,
> Confound the ignorant, and amaze indeed
> The very faculties of eyes and ears.
>
> (ii, ii, 555–9.)

It is natural for him to translate intention into language – into verbal rather than physical violence – hence the apparent relief as he finds gruesome reasons not to murder the praying Claudius, or as the 'bitter business' of the 'witching time' can, for the moment, be allowed to be resolved into a matter of words:

> I will speak daggers to her, but use none.

Hence, too, the play to be put on excites him beyond its detective purpose. It is going to speak for him, or he through it – and at least at the outset of ii, ii his hopes of the effect of the play seem to hinge on the speech 'of some dozen or sixteen lines' which he has composed himself – to Claudius, to form a translation fully and terribly meaningful only to Claudius.

If, besides, it means different things to the rest of the court,[1] all the better a translation. Murder speaks metaphorically in much Elizabethan-Jacobean tragedy, but rarely is the speaking so completely *heard* by the imagination as in Hamlet's plan for the effect of 'The Murder of Gonzago':

> For murder, though it have no tongue, will speak
> With most miraculous organ.   (ii, ii, 589–90)

Hamlet's excitement with speech as translation of deeds would help to explain, too, why in the graveyard scene it is Laertes's rhetoric which becomes the centre of Hamlet's grievance and object of his aggression. The leaping into the grave is a kind of act fitted to the word, a rhetorical flourish:

> Dost come here to whine?
> To outface me with leaping in her grave?
> . . . Nay, an thou'lt mouth,
> I'll rant as well as thou.
>
> (v, i, 271–2, 277–8)

We return here to the notion of human sympathy, as well as positive action, being absorbed and lost in speech. For it is in his dealings with Ophelia – which is as much as to say his language to Ophelia – that Hamlet most shows the destructive powers of speech. His vision of the world as 'an unweeded garden' ultimately drives Ophelia to her death, wearing the 'coronet weeds' of her madness. I do not wish to turn the play into a *Hamlet and Ophelia:* the love story is played down in the structure as a whole, its pre-play course known only by the odd flashback and infer-

---

[1] A. C. Bradley, *Shakespearean Tragedy* (paperback ed., 1955, p. 109, note), finds it strange that while everyone at court 'sees in the play-scene a gross and menacing insult to the King', no one 'shows any sign in perceiving in it also an accusation of murder'. Dover Wilson, in his note on iii, ii, 243, points out that 'Hamlet arranges *two* meanings to the Play, one for the King (and Horatio), the other for the rest of the spectators, who see a king being murdered by his nephew'.

ence, and it disappears altogether after the graveyard scene. All the responsibility that Laertes can remember to remove from Hamlet with his dying breath is 'mine and my father's death'. But I still believe that the Hamlet–Ophelia relationship reveals something essential to Hamlet's and his creator's vision of the power of words; and also that it illuminates the way in which Hamlet contracts what Kenneth Muir has called 'the occupational disease of avengers'[1] – how he is tainted by the world in which he is trying to take revenge.

The poisoning of that relationship within the play is full of searing ironies. Hamlet never says 'I love you' except in the past tense and to unsay it at once. By the time he tells the world 'I loved Ophelia', she is dead. The first time he refers to her it is antically, as the daughter of Polonius, the fishmonger. From Hamlet's love-letter – which we are surely meant to take more seriously than Polonius does – we learn that in his wooing he was both as exalted and as tongue-tied as any lover who hesitates to sully the uniqueness of his love by common speech. When he tries to write a love sonnet, the attempt to look in his heart and write turns into a touching version of the conventional idea that the beloved is inexpressible:

O dear Ophelia, I am ill at these numbers. I have not art to reckon my groans; but that I love thee best, O most best, believe it. (II, ii, 119–21)

When, his world shattered, he came to her in the scene she recounts to Polonius, he was speechless and, though he frightened her, he also, as her mode of telling shows, drew out all her sympathy. But when he actually confronts her on stage, he has translated her into a whore, like Gertrude, and he is only too articulate, in a language which is meaningless and yet desperately hurtful to her – one to which she might well have responded in Desdemona's words:

I understand a fury in your words,
But not the words.[2] (*Othello*, IV, ii, 32–3)

Hamlet's vision of Ophelia has changed with his vision of the world. The language to be spoken to her is that current in a world where frailty is the name of woman, love equals appetite, vows are 'as false as dicers' oaths' (III, iv, 45), and nothing is constant. It is a terrible coincidence, and a masterly dramatic stroke, that before Hamlet and Ophelia meet within this vision, Laertes and Polonius have been speaking the same language to her, articulating out of their worldly wisdom much the same view of their love as the one Hamlet has arrived at through his shock of revulsion from the world. In I, iii, while Hamlet off-stage goes to meet the Ghost, Ophelia meets with equally shattering (to her world) commands from her father, attacking her past, present and future relations with Hamlet.

Laertes is made to open the attack, all the more insidiously since it is by way of well-meaning brotherly advice, and since it is phrased in the idiom of the courtly 'songs' to which he is reducing Hamlet's love:

For Hamlet, and the trifling of his favour,
Hold it a fashion and a toy in the blood,
A violet in the youth of primy nature,
Forward not permanent, sweet not lasting,
The perfume and suppliance of a minute.

(I, iii, 5–9)

On highly reasonable social grounds he argues that Hamlet's language must be translated:

Then if he says he loves you,
It fits your wisdom so far to believe it
As he in his particular act and place
May give his saying deed. (ll. 24–7)

[1] Kenneth Muir, *Shakespeare's Tragic Sequence* (1972), p. 57.
[2] I have discussed some aspects of Ophelia's and Desdemona's language, especially the way in which the hero and the heroine in these tragedies become unable to speak the same language, in a short paper to the Second International Shakespeare Congress, held in Washington, D.C., in April 1976.

I need not point out how deeply rooted this is in the language assumptions of the play as a whole. Laertes's tone is not unkind in its knowingness; his final thrust has some of the ineluctable sadness of the Sonnets when contemplating examples of the precariousness of youth and beauty –

> Virtue itself scapes not calumnious strokes;
> The canker galls the infants of the spring
> Too oft before their buttons be disclos'd;
> And in the morn and liquid dew of youth
> Contagious blastments are most imminent –
>   (ll. 38–42)

and Ophelia, as her spirited reply suggests, is on the whole able to cope with both the matter and the manner of his preaching. But when Polonius picks up the attack, it is different. His technique is far more devastating: an interrogation where each answer is rapidly demolished. Ophelia does not have the speech-habits of most of the other characters; she is brief, simple and direct – and therefore particularly vulnerable. In a play where rhetorical units of measurement may be 'forty thousand brothers', there is a moving literalness about her statement that Hamlet has 'given countenance to his speech . . ./With *almost* all the holy vows of heaven'. She does not have the worldly wisdom to produce translations which protect her feelings and hide her thoughts. So to Polonius's opening question – 'What is't, Ophelia, he hath said to you?' – she simply, and vainly, tries to be non-specific:

> So please you, something touching the Lord Hamlet.
>   (l. 89)

Some fifteen lines later her confidence is already undermined:

> I do not know, my lord, what I should think.

Polonius's method is particularly undermining in that he lets Ophelia provide the key-words which he then picks up and translates by devaluing them – painfully literally so when Ophelia's 'many tenders/Of his affection' provokes:

> . . . think yourself a baby
> That you have ta'en these tenders for true pay
> Which are not sterling.   (ll. 105–7)

His translation is partly a matter of devaluation by direct sneer ('think' and 'fashion' are thus dealt with), partly a matter of using the ambiguities of the English language to shift the meanings of words (thus 'tender' is translated into the language of finance and 'entreatment' into that of diplomacy); and partly a dizzifying matter of making one meaning slide into another by a pun. In this last way Hamlet's vows are translated, first into finance, then into religion –

> Do not believe his vows; for they are brokers,
> Not of that dye which their investments show,
> But mere implorators of unholy suits,
> Breathing like sanctified and pious bonds –
>   (ll. 127–30)

but always in proof of their falsehood: 'The better to beguile'. What supplies the power of Polonius's words is also a logic which, like Iago's, strikes at the root of the victim's hold on reality:

> You do not understand yourself so clearly
> As it behoves my daughter and your honour;
>   (ll. 96–7)

and which has a kind of general empirical truth – such as in the comedies might have been spoken by a sensible and normative heroine:

> I do know,
> When the blood burns, how prodigal the soul
> Lends the tongue vows.   (ll. 115–17)

By the end of the scene, Polonius's words have left Ophelia with no hold on her love and with nothing to say but 'I shall obey, my lord'.[1] When there is no one left even to obey,

---

[1] To 'obey' (which is of course also what Hamlet promises his mother in I, ii, 120) is a troublesome matter in Shakespearean tragedy. Cf. *Othello*, I, iii, 180 and *King Lear*, I, i, 97.

she will go to pieces. But before then she has to be pushed to the limit by Hamlet's verbal brutality which doubly frightens and hurts her because it seems to prove both that Hamlet is mad and that Polonius was right. A first and last intimation of the intimacy and tenderness which might once have prevailed in their dialogues rings out of her greeting to Hamlet in the nunnery scene –

> Good my lord,
> How does your honour for this many a day? –

but by the end of that scene there is not even a dialogue. The two of them are speaking *about* each other, Hamlet's stream-of-consciousness circling around nuns and painted harlots and Ophelia appealing, twice, to an invisible and silent audience: 'O, help him, you sweet heavens!' and 'O heavenly powers, restore him!' She is left to speak her only soliloquy over the ruins of what used to be her reality, and to lament the most terrible translation of all: 'the honey of his music vows' is now 'like sweet bells jangled, out of time and harsh'.

Hamlet and Ophelia no longer speak the same language. I dwelt at some length on the Polonius–Ophelia scene because it brings out, ironically and indirectly, an important aspect of the 'tainting' of Hamlet. Though he does not know it, and would hate to be told so, his language has moved away from Ophelia's and towards Polonius's. It is a language based on the general idea of 'woman' rather than a specific awareness of Ophelia (to whom he now listens only to score verbal points off her, usually bawdy ones, too). Even his technique is like Polonius's as he picks up words only to demolish them, and her. Thus, in perhaps the cruellest stretch of dialogue in the whole play, Ophelia is allowed, briefly, to think that she knows what Hamlet means, only to have this understanding taken from her:

Hamlet. . . . I did love you once.
Ophelia. Indeed, my lord, you made me believe so.

Hamlet. You should not have believ'd me; for virtue cannot so inoculate our old stock but we shall relish of it. I loved you not.
Ophelia. I was the more deceived.   (III, i, 115–20)

Polonius turned her into an object, an instrument, by 'loosing' her to Hamlet in the nunnery scene; Hamlet turns her into a thing – as 'unworthy a thing' as he ever may accuse Rosencrantz and Guildenstern of attempting to make out of him – in the play scene where, in public and listening to a play which from her point of view must seem to be mainly about women's inconstancy and sexual promiscuity, she is all but sexually assaulted by Hamlet's language.[1] We have no evidence that Hamlet ever thinks of her again before he discovers that the grave he has watched being dug is that of 'the fair Ophelia', and no redeeming recognition that the power of his own words has helped to drive her into that grave. In their story speech functions, in the end, as part of a vision of man's proneness to kill the thing he loves.

So we seem in the end to be left with a long row of contradictions: Hamlet's use of language is sensitive and brutal; he listens and he does not listen; his speech is built on sympathy and on total disregard of other selves; his relationship with words is his greatest strength and his greatest weakness. Only a Claudius could pretend that these are not contradictions and only he could translate them into a simple unity. Hamlet's soliloquies are not much help to this end. Even they speak different languages and add up, if anything, to a representation of a man searching for a language for the experiences which are forcing themselves upon him, finding it now in the free flow of I-centered exclamations of 'O, that this too too solid flesh would melt', now in the

[1] I have found Nigel Alexander's study of Hamlet, *Poison, Play and Duel* (1971), esp. chap. 5, 'The Power of Beauty', the most illuminating analysis of Hamlet's relationship with Ophelia.

formally structured and altogether generalized questions and statements of 'To be, or not to be'. It is tempting to hear in Hamlet's self-analytical speeches a progression towards clarity, reaching its goal in the fusion of the individual and the general, of simple form and complex thought, in the speech about defying augury –

If it be now, 'tis not to come; if it be not to come, it will be now; if it be not now, yet it will come – the readiness is all –

and coming to rest on 'Let be'. It is tempting because many Jacobean tragic heroes and heroines were to go through such a progression, through tortured and verbally elaborate attempts at definition of their vision of life to simple statements of – as in Herbert's poem 'Prayer' – 'something understood'. But to me this seems too smooth a curve, too cathartic a movement, more indicative of critics' need to experience the peace which Hamlet himself happily appears to gain at the end than of the true impact of the language of the play as a whole. That impact is surely much closer to the sense that for a complex personality in an impossible situation – and in 'situation' I include a number of difficult human relationships – there is no single language. This does not mean that the play ultimately sees speech as meaningless, or that Shakespeare (or even Hamlet) is finally trapped in a disillusionist attitude to language. It means that we are given a very wide demon-stration of the power of words to express and communicate – it is, after all, words which tell Horatio and us even that 'the rest is silence' – but also, and at the same time, an intimation that there is something inexpressible and incommunicable at the heart of the play.

Shakespeare – whatever the true facts of the *Ur-Hamlet* – must have seen himself as pro-ducing a new 'translation' of what the title page of the second Quarto describes as 'The Tragicall History of Hamlet, Prince of Denmark'. Like Gertrude's translation, in IV, i, it meant both changing and interpreting his raw material. Like Gertrude, he concen-trated on the speech and deeds of the prince, and their ramifications, merging any personal pressure of experience in a concern for com-municating with an audience. The analogy ends here, for Gertrude was, even like Hamlet himself, only part of his translation – a trans-lation which T. S. Eliot criticized for trying to 'express the inexpressibly horrible'.[1] To me the final greatness of the play lies just there: in its power to express so much and yet also to call a halt on the edge of the inexpressible where, to misquote Claudius, we must learn to say ''Tis fit we do not understand'. This, I think, is the hallmark of Shakespeare as a trans-lator, into tragedy, of the human condition.

[1] 'Hamlet and His Problems', in *Selected Essays* (New York, 1932), p. 126.

CRITICAL DISAGREEMENT ABOUT
OEDIPUS AND HAMLET

BY

NIGEL ALEXANDER

'The art of representation', says Henry James in the Preface to *Roderick Hudson*, 'bristles with questions the very terms of which are difficult to apply and appreciate.'[1] Questions of dramatic representation almost invariably involve the critic in attempts to apply and appreciate terms first used by Aristotle in the *Poetics*. Critical controversy about Aristotle's exact meaning has tended to distract attention from the fact that, although his terms may not always be satisfactory, the questions that he asked are still important. In re-opening two old controversies I should like to try to demonstrate that there is a tradition of disagreement about certain passages in the *Oedipus Tyrannus* and in *Hamlet*. These disagreements are not simply an occupational hazard of criticism or further evidence of what Aldous Huxley has eloquently described as 'the prevalence of folly, its monumental unchanging permanence, and its almost unvariable triumph over the forces of intelligence'. So far from belonging to the *Dunciad Variorum* these disagreements are relevant to our own concerns and are part of the evidence for believing, with Sir John Myres, that:

Criticism, in spite of popular misapprehension, is a progressive and constructive study, tending not only to the discipline of a liberal education, but in the strictest sense to the advancement of science.[2]

As an example I should like to turn to the work of Henry James Pye, who is a poet laureate entirely without honour in his own country. Few Englishmen, apart from professional scholars, would recognize him as the man who succeeded Thomas Warton as poet laureate in 1790 and few, even among professional scholars, will have read his epic poem *Alfred* published, three years after *Lyrical Ballads*, in 1801. He claims my attention because he was involved in critical controversy about both Oedipus and Hamlet. In 1788 he produced the first respectable translation of Aristotle's *Poetics* in English, a translation which he revised and re-published with an extensive commentary in 1792, and in 1807 he published a small volume called *Comments on the Commentators of Shakespear. With preliminary Observations on his Genius and Writings*. There he warns the reader that:

After so much that has been written on this subject in the prolegomena to the various editions of Shakespear, and after the two luminous Essays of Mrs Montague and Mr Morgan, it is difficult to say anything new upon the subject,[3]

and continues to inform him that:

The chief faults of his commentators, besides this, arise from a desire to say everything they can say, not only on the passage commented on, but on everything that has been said in the comment, as well as from a too great display of black-letter reading.[4]

This last attribute of scholarship, he remarks, may be necessary, but only as dung is necessary to fertility, no one should want to make an ostentatious display of it. These formidable strictures do not, of course, inhibit Pye himself in any way when he feels that scholarship or comment are called for and so they need not prevent us from considering Oedipus's speech to Jocasta at line 771 of Jebb's edition, the forged commission which sends Rosencrantz and Guildenstern to their deaths in England, and the dumb show.

Pye comments on the first passage when he is dealing, in his *Commentary Illustrating the Poetic of Aristotle*, with Aristotle's remarks about the nature of the tragic hero in chapter 13 (1452b–1453a). Pye makes as reasonable an attempt as many of his more scholarly successors to explain Aristotle's meaning. But he is also a more thorough commentator than many of his successors and feels compelled to deal with the troublesome point, which they often pass over in simple silence, that Aristotle's two examples of the 'intermediate' kind of person who falls, not through vice or depravity but through some ἁμαρτία, are Oedipus and Thyestes. And, however we translate ἁμαρτία, and whatever we think of Oedipus, Thyestes appears to be the model of exceptional depravity. Pye reflects the disagreement about this point by quoting two most interesting and instructive opinions:

Metastasio is much dissatisfied with both these examples. He maintains that Thyestes is a character entirely vicious and that Oedipus, to use his own words, 'is a man of so sublime and pure a virtue that to avoid the risk of becoming, as the oracle had menaced, incestuous and a parricide he quits what he believes to be his parental house, hazards the succession of a crown, and goes alone and voluntarily into exile. He is a man of such exalted courage that, being attacked and insulted by a multitude of persons, instead of flying he valiantly defends himself though alone, kills one, wounds another, and disperses the rest'.

To this eulogy on Oedipus we may oppose the reasoning of Batteux: 'It was in his power to avoid his crime and his misfortune, although foretold by an oracle. This was the common belief of all Greece. Laius believed that by destroying his son he should avoid his destiny, Oedipus believed that by flying from Corinth, where he thought his father and mother then lived, he should avoid the fatal disaster with which he was threatened. Admonished as he was by the Oracle, should he have thought it sufficient to fly from Corinth? Should not he have respected the age of every man who was of a time in life to be his father? Should not he have been afraid of marrying any woman of an age to be his mother? So far from taking this precaution he no sooner leaves Delphi than he kills the first man he meets, which happens to be his father Laius: he arrives at Thebes, he triumphs over the Sphynx; elated with his victory and the offer of a crown he marries a woman who evidently might be his mother, since she actually was so. His unhappiness therefore was obviously the fruit of his imprudence and his passions and might serve for an example to all the Greeks.'[5]

More recent critical approaches to the play attempt to bypass this kind of disagreement by drawing attention to the fact that the play is a process of self-discovery which saves the city as well as revealing that the oracle has been fulfilled and that questions of moral guilt or innocence are not raised by Sophocles until the *Oedipus Coloneus*. The past history of Oedipus is, however, a vital part of the action and Metastasio and Batteux are clearly basing their opposed views on Oedipus's partial account of his past history to Jocasta at line 771. Sophocles is here engaged in one of the most necessary and difficult tasks that face any dramatist: the task that Henry James calls 'Harking back to make up'[6] and Arthur Miller 'the biggest single dramatic problem, namely, how to dramatize what has gone before'.[7] The account that Oedipus gives to Jocasta is designed to explain to her why the killing of an old man and his retinue at a place where three roads met, an event which had previously not been near his conscience because he had felt himself the injured party, should now, in the light of the evidence he has just uncovered, begin to trouble his mind. The speech looks before and after. It informs the audience of events that had occurred before the action began and it indicates or warns them of the future course of the action. Given the information in this speech the audience can now take an ironic or doubting view of Jocasta's statement that the actual murder of Laius, at least, can never be made to agree with the oracle which foretold that he should be killed by his son. This sense of irony or doom is then intensified by the following ode in which the Chorus virtually pray that the oracles may be fulfilled. The whole action of the play is then swung into its new, final and fatal direction by the arrival of the Corinthian messenger. The speech, then, is a point of balance in the play which sums up the action that is past and predicts, more or less, the action that is to come.

Disagreement about this speech, therefore, indicates a genuine disagreement about the entire structure of the play. And if the exact question of moral guilt or innocence is not directly raised, the question of responsibility surely is. Guilty or not, Oedipus accepts responsibility for his actions and, at the end of the play, demands the sentence of exile which will clear the city of pollution. The real disagreement between Metastasio and the Abbé Batteux is a disagreement about the degree and nature of that responsibility. The difficulty arises from the fact that, as Oedipus tells the story to Jocasta, it is an account of actions which are determined by his free will; as a speech within the context of the play it is part of a pattern which, if not pre-determined, has at least been predicted. Metastasio emphasizes the first of these elements and admires the driving will and courage of Oedipus; the Abbé Batteux stresses the second, respects the divine guidance of the Gods, and gives advice which is practically equivalent to the opinion of the Chorus: it would have been better for Oedipus never to have been born. This difference of opinion and emphasis continues to run through criticism of the play. For Cedric H. Whitman:

The action of the play itself, therefore, is motivated by the free will of the hero, which culminates in the act of self-blinding;[8]

while for Bernard M. W. Knox:

The play, in the simplest analysis, is a reassertion of the religious view of a divinely ordered universe, a view which depends on the concept of divine omniscience, represented in the play by Apollo's prophecy.[9]

The problem is that either view can, with a bit of scraping and shoving, be made to fit the case but that the play, as Sophocles wrote it, does not really contain enough definite information to allow us to say unequivocally that one view is correct and the other mistaken. Nor should we find this uncertainty entirely surprising. Anton Chekhov once wrote to I. L. Shcheglov:

As regards the ending of my *Lights* I take the liberty of disagreeing with you. A psychologist should not pretend to understand what he does not understand. Moreover, a psychologist should not convey the impression that he understands what no one understands. We shall not play the charlatan, and we will declare frankly that nothing is clear in this world. Only fools and charlatans know and understand everything.[10]

It would, I think, be unreasonable to expect Sophocles to have solved the question of determinism and free-will in his play since it still seems to come into the category of questions that no
one understands. His critics can only do him disservice if they attempt to show that he unquestionably favoured the solution that they find most appealing. Sophocles treated the question of
free-will and determinism in the only way that a dramatist can—he dramatized it. Such a
dramatization will not solve the problem for the audience but will leave them facing some
difficult questions whose significance they had perhaps previously only half realized. Critical
opinion is, therefore, so divided about the structure of this play because the structure of the
play is designed to divide critical opinion at precisely this point. Whether or not we accept a
Freudian interpretation we can hardly deny that the play is most delicately balanced at a critical
point for the human psyche. And this is why, in my opinion, it is so important to listen to the
views of those who are engaged with us in the common pursuit of true judgment and to listen
with more attention the more violently their judgments conflict with our own. In the dramatic
equation presented by the poet they may have guessed the value of certain terms undreamt of
in our philosophy.

Hamlet, like *Oedipus Tyrannus*, is an extremely finely balanced dramatic structure. Both
plays provide us with what Henry James has called the soul of drama, 'a catastrophe determined
in spite of oppositions'.[11] In both cases the chief opponent of catastrophe is the protagonist
who brings about the determined end in unpredictable fashion. These actions compel us to
ask for answers and seek emotional resolutions of problems which have remained difficult and
intractable. Here, too, I believe that an examination of the traditional disagreements allows us to
consider the problem in a more critical spirit.

One of the traditional disagreements about Hamlet has always been his method of transposing
the commission given to Rosencrantz and Guildenstern and sending them to execution in
England. In *Comments on the Commentators of Shakespear* Henry James Pye deals with the matter
in this way:

Steevens's note on Malone's observation on this passage is insolent and impudent, and he is, as usual,
positive in the wrong; there is not one word uttered by Rosencrantz and Guildenstern throughout the
play that does not proclaim them to the most superficial observer as creatures of the king, purposely
employed to betray Hamlet, their friend and fellow-student.[12]

The comments of George Steevens on the character of Hamlet had first appeared in his edition
of Shakespeare of 1773 as a note to Horatio's 'Good-night, sweet prince'. Malone had attempted
a refutation on historical principles in his edition of 1790 and Steevens had replied by asserting
that the critic must judge by what he found in the text in front of his eyes not by what he
could deduce from the 'black-letter history'. In 1963 Patrick Cruttwell[13] joined issue with L. C.
Knights[14] over the same question. Knights has written of the 'murder' of Rosencrantz and
Guildenstern but Cruttwell appeals to the military imagery as a guide to response. Hamlet is at
war and the language is a clear indication of this state of affairs to the audience. If Knights
ignores these indications it must be because, for him, war and murder are synonymous terms.

It is perhaps worth while to have a closer look at two of the passages involved. The first
occurs at III, iv, 205. At the end of the closet scene Hamlet mentions to his mother the scheme
of sending him to England, suspects that Rosencrantz and Guildenstern are involved in the plot,
and predicts that he will circumvent it:

> Let it work;
> For 'tis the sport to have the engineer
> Hoist with his own petar; and 't shall go hard
> But I will delve one yard below their mines
> And blow them at the moon. O, 'tis most sweet
> When in one line two crafts directly meet.

The imagery here certainly refers to a military operation. The operation is siege warfare and the mine and counter-mine which Hamlet describes were last used in Europe in 1917 under Messines ridge. The delving below an opponent's mine to blow him at the moon with the force of his own explosive charge implies secrecy in operation and terrible suddenness in execution. It is an apt metaphor for Rosencrantz and Guildenstern sent to execution, 'not shriving time allowed', by the forged commission. When Horatio challenges Hamlet's account of their deaths at v, ii, 56 with the quiet comment,

> So Guildenstern and Rosencrantz go to 't,

Hamlet changes his metaphor and provides a rather different defence:

> Why, man, they did make love to this employment;
> They are not near my conscience; their defeat
> Does by their own insinuation grow:
> 'Tis dangerous when the baser nature comes
> Between the pass and fell incensed points
> Of mighty opposites.

Rosencrantz and Guildenstern are not now caught in the tunnels under the hill and blown up with their own charge. They have openly intervened in a duel. In both cases the language used, the 'two crafts' which meet and the 'mighty opposites', implies that a war is being fought between two persons or parties but Rosencrantz and Guildenstern participate in significantly different ways. In the first they are servants of the King overwhelmed in the course of their muddy but necessary duty, in the second they are men aware that they have intervened in a deadly and desperate business. Their exact role depends on whether or not they knew the nature of their employment in England. Hamlet's words suggest that they did, but when the King finally reveals the journey-to-England plot to the audience Rosencrantz and Guildenstern are not on the stage. This is another occasion when we are simply not given enough information to be able to make up our minds. Disagreement between those who find Hamlet's actions culpable and those who find them excusable at this point is, therefore, inevitable. But this disagreement is again one which is forced on the audience by the entire structure of the play. Hamlet's references to the secret working of the counter-mine and the duel between mighty opposites fit into a recognizable pattern in the play. The mining image had already been used at I, v, 162:

> Well said, old mole! Canst work i' th' earth so fast?
> A worthy pioneer!

and he talks to his mother of 'rank corruption, mining all within'. I am not suggesting that these linked images could have even a subliminal effect on an audience across three-quarters of the play.

What I wish to emphasize is that the double description of the deaths of Rosencrantz and Guildenstern, as an unexpected secret explosion and as an incident in a duel, is part of a whole series of double descriptions and contrasted effects.

Hamlet's words, 'the fell incensed points of mighty opposites', are the only direct reference in the play to a duel with the King. Yet the image of the duel between Hamlet and Claudius is referred to by many commentators. Such an image depends not simply on the words but upon the whole stage action of the play. The play ends, and the final catastrophe is brought about, during the duel scene between Hamlet and Laertes. This is a duel scene, but it is also a play scene since the bout with foils is frequently referred to as 'play' and Hamlet himself has the significant line, 'And will this brother's wager frankly play'. It is also a poisoning scene, the poison of the anointed rapier and the poisoned union in the cup from which the Queen, the King and finally perhaps Hamlet himself all drink. These elements have all been in the play from the beginning. The play begins with the appearance of the Ghost, and the Ghost is first referred to as the majesty of buried Denmark who had fought the famous duel with Fortinbras of Norway. The Ghost reveals the secret of his murder, by poison, to Hamlet who has already, in the hearing of the audience, defended himself against the charge of playing one part, the over-intense mourner, and now deliberately announces that he will adopt another, the antic disposition. The use of the antic disposition leads on naturally to the presentation of *The Murder of Gonzago* or *The Mousetrap*. This is certainly a 'play' scene. It is also a poisoning scene since we twice see the murderer pouring poison into the ear of his victim. This is performed the first time in dumb show but on the second occasion the character is identified as one Lucianus, nephew to the King. This poisoning is performed because the play scene is also a duel scene—an attack by Hamlet on the King to catch his conscience and force him to unkennel his guilt. This attack is at least partly successful. It does force the King into the open and puts him, literally and metaphorically, on his guard. It also appears to have caught his conscience since Hamlet finds him on his knees at prayer and, because conscience is at work, rejects that opportunity for secret murder. If Hamlet here means what he says, and if the King had actually repented, then the opportunity for secret murder would have passed for ever. The attempt at repentance, however, merely starts the King upon his second secret murder, a murder which will eventually require the use of poison.

Hamlet had first attacked the King by using words as weapons under the cover of the antic disposition. He has now used the *Murder of Gonzago* under cover of the entertainment provided by the players. Claudius, in his attempts to penetrate the antic disposition, had used Polonius as a spy and Ophelia and Gertrude as bait for the trap. Now that Hamlet has put him on his guard he employs Rosencrantz and Guildenstern, formerly used as spies, as secret and perhaps unwitting murderers. When they, too, fail, Laertes is used as open duellist and conscious murderer and turns out to be a conscious murderer who chooses poison as his method.

The play scene, therefore, in *Hamlet* fulfils a dramatic function similar to Oedipus's speech to Jocasta. It harks back to make up and dramatizes what has gone before. In dumb show it dramatizes the original murder. In the Play, with its attack on the Queen and careful identification of the murderer, it predicts the poisoning of the King by his nephew. Claudius does, in the end, die by his own poison but the play is not an exact prediction of the manner of his death. Throughout *Hamlet* the audience are waiting for the Prince to fulfil prediction and obey the command of the Ghost. He does so, but obeys it in his own fashion, and not by committing the predicted secret revenge murder. The killing of Rosencrantz and Guildenstern is the closest that Hamlet comes in the play to deliberate secret murder. It can be justified or it can be condemned but, in the context of the play, it is the action of Hamlet's that most resembles secret murder by poison, the choice of Claudius, and that is farthest from trial by combat, the choice of King Hamlet. Yet, as Hamlet's words make clear, even it can be regarded as an incident in a deadly duel since the entire action of the play shows us a player poised between duel scenes and scenes of poison and invites our judgment. The actions of the chief player, Hamlet, bring about the predicted end of the play, the killing of Claudius, but in unexpected fashion. The determined end of the *Oedipus Tyrannus* is similarly brought about by the unexpected action of Oedipus in determinedly pressing forward to solve the problem which he had previously tried to escape and from which all others now draw back in horror. This double function of the play as summing up and prediction, the vision of the murder that is past and the vision of the murder that is yet to come, accounts for the double use of dumb show and play that troubled Henry James Pye as it was later to trouble Professor Dover Wilson.

The tension in *Oedipus Tyrannus* between prediction and free will is not solved intellectually, merely resolved dramatically. Similarly the tensions in *Hamlet* between the revenge murder called for by the Ghost, the secret poisonings so exactly practised by Claudius, and Hamlet's own vision of the struggle as similar to the task of the actor and the soldier engaged in a duty which is finally a duel, cannot be concluded by neat moral sententiae. The murderous and aggressive instincts of humanity remain one of the problems that no one can solve. Shakespeare does not offer us moral prescriptions but shows us Hamlet finely balanced between the open duel of the soldier and the secret murder of the poisoner and leaves us with the question, What, then, must we do?

Hamlet, like Oedipus, is called to perform a task. To set right a time which is out of joint. Like Oedipus he succeeds. Both Thebes and Denmark appear clear of pollution as these plays end. But, like Oedipus, he succeeds in such a fashion and about such a task that those who look pale and tremble at this chance, those of us who are but the audience to these acts, are left attempting to answer a number of difficult questions which appear to have no settled or received solutions but which each individual may yet be called upon to solve for himself as best he can. The audience has not remained mute. Instead it has indulged in a vigorous critical debate which, I believe, testifies to the importance of the questions asked and the skill and artistry of those who asked them. They hold a mirror up to nature and show us a reflexion that may be the head of the Gorgon and that may, also, bear an uncomfortable likeness to our own faces.

© NIGEL ALEXANDER 1967

1. Henry James, *The Art of the Novel*, ed. R. P. Blackmur (New York, 1934), p. 3.

2. J. L. Myres, *Homer and his critics* (1958), p. 9.

3. H. J. Pye, *Comments on the Commentators of Shakespear* (1807), p. ix.

4. *Ibid.* p. xiv.

5. H. J. Pye, *A Commentary Illustrating the Poetic of Aristotle* (1792), pp. 254 ff.

6. *The Art of the Novel*, p. 121.

7. Arthur Miller, Preface to *Collected Plays* (1958), p. 21.

8. Cedric H. Whitman, *Sophocles* (Cambridge, Mass., 1951), p. 141.

9. Bernard M. W. Knox, *Oedipus at Thebes* (New Haven, 1957), p. 47.

10. Anton Chekhov, letter to I. L. Shcheglov, 9 June 1888. *Letters on Literary Topics*, ed. Louis S. Freidland (New York, 1924), p. 8.

11. *The Art of the Novel*, p. 290.

12. H. J. Pye, *Comments on the Commentators of Shakespear*, p. 326.

13. Patrick Cruttwell, 'The Morality of Hamlet', in *Hamlet: Stratford-upon-Avon Studies* 5, ed. J. R. Brown and B. Harris (1963), p. 119.

14. L. C. Knights, *An Approach to Hamlet* (1960), p. 32.